Buying Property Abroad

About the author

Jeremy Davies is a freelance writer and journalist. He has written about personal finance and consumer issues for a range of national newspapers, magazines and online publications including The *Independent on Sunday, Moneywise* and *The Guardian's* website.

Acknowledgements

The author and publishers would like to thank the following for their help, advice and expertise. Simon Ball of Tuscany Now, Paolo Barbieri, Adrian Barrett, Tara Clark of Jobcentre Plus, Simon Conn and colleagues at Conti Financial Services, Steve Emmett of Brian French Associates, Fundacion de Propietarios Extranjeros, John Howell of John Howell & Co, Philip Jenkinson of Triplet & Associés, Stephane Lambert of Stara Planina, Sam Mooney of Languedoc France Property, Tracy and Massimo Orione, Lorenza Ponzoni, Eleanor Roberts of Chicfinance, Boyd Rogers of Red Field Property Care, Sam and Duncan Scott, Amar Sodhi of Avatar International, Linda Travella of Casa Travella, and David Wells of Abbey National France. Thanks also to the statistics people at the Department for Work and Pensions, OECD and EU; and to everyone who shared their experiences of buying property abroad, some of whom also appeared in case studies.

Buying Property Abroad

Jeremy Davies

CONSUMERS' ASSOCIATION

Which? Books are commissioned by
Consumers' Association and published by
Which? Ltd, 2 Marylebone Road, London NW1 4DF
Email: books@which.net

Distributed by The Penguin Group:
Penguin Books Ltd, 80 Strand, London WC2R 0RL

First edition March 2004
Copyright © 2004 Which? Ltd

British Library Cataloguing in Publication Data
A catalogue record for *Buying Property Abroad* is available from the British Library

ISBN 0 85202 970 5

For a full list of Which? books, please call 0800 252100, access our website at
www.which.net, or write to Which? Books, Freepost, PO Box 44, Hertford SG14 1SH.

Editorial and production: Alethea Doran, Ian Robinson
Index: Marie Lorimer
Original cover concept by Sarah Harmer
Cover photograph by KOS – Koserowsky/A1PIX

Typeset by Saxon Graphics Ltd, Derby
Printed and bound in Great Britain by Creative Print and Design, Wales

Contents

★ An asterisk next to the name of an organisation in the text indicates that the address or contact details can be found in this section

Introduction

Until recently, only the very wealthy could afford to buy houses abroad. But, with a buoyant UK housing market and the advent of low-cost air fares, more and more people on average incomes are now fulfilling their dream of a place in the sun. Government research in 2003 found that over 150,000 British householders own a second home abroad. Those whose stories have contributed to this book include a taxi driver with a house in the Loire Valley, an electrician with a flat in Madrid and a librarian about to take possession of a rambling farmhouse in southern Italy.

Television programmes, Sunday supplements and ex-pat diaries such as Peter Mayle's *A Year in Provence* and Annie Hawes' *Extra Virgin* infer that any of us, if we put our minds to it, could exchange our maisonettes for mansions overseas. A straw poll in any office or pub will probably reveal a surprising number who have already bought property in a foreign land, are actively planning to do so, or have it on their list of long-term goals.

With average house prices in some of the more popular British seaside resorts approaching £200,000, it is not surprising that those with a bit of spare cash are looking further afield than Bognor Regis for a holiday or retirement home. And with stock-market investments still in the doldrums and the long-term forecast for pensions looking distinctly gloomy, many are considering foreign-property investment as a way of providing for their futures – as well as offering an asset that they can enjoy in the present – with the added attraction of rental income. Whether it's a hilltop hideaway in Tuscany, a pied-a-terre in bustling Barcelona, an air-conditioned condo in Florida or a castle in Croatia, buying a property abroad can be an immensely exciting and rewarding experience. But the process is not without its pitfalls.

Other countries' legal systems can be complicated, and there is often a requirement to commit to purchases at an earlier stage than in the UK, meaning that potential purchasers can't just put in a tentative offer and not follow through. In some places there can be problems establishing a clean title to properties. In rural areas, rights of way, septic tanks, well access and the like can all prove problematic.

If you are buying an old property to 'do up', it may prove more dilapidated than it first appeared, or you could encounter problems with planning permission. When purchasing a new apartment in a complex, on the other hand, you might need to think carefully about the rules and regulations imposed by the residents' committee that manages the block. High property taxes, fees and deposits can also make purchases more expensive than headline prices might suggest. And, of course, in most countries, the whole purchase process is conducted in a foreign language. This creates huge potential for misunderstandings and plans going awry.

It is truly astonishing, therefore, how many people enter into foreign property purchases with an abandon they would never employ when buying a house in the UK. Some people really do go on holiday somewhere once, fall in love with the place, see a house they like and put in an offer there and then – only to discover later that they've committed themselves to buying an overpriced ruin. In other cases they consult lawyers after the event, having signed contracts that are not even translated into English, or 'buy' houses from fellow Britons who offer the opportunity to seal the deal without the hassle of local bureaucracy – and end up being duped out of tens of thousands and not owning a thing.

Buying Property Abroad aims to help potential purchasers avoid such traps. You may be doing initial research into what kind of property you want to buy and possible locations, or perhaps you have already seen somewhere you like. Either way, you are likely to need advice about how to handle the rest of the process.

Part I of the book looks at the many and varied ways in which you could join the growing phenomenon of British people buying homes overseas, examines the factors to consider when thinking about where to buy, and offers advice about the issues you need to weigh up. Part II looks at the most popular countries for British buyers. It offers brief descriptions of areas you might consider and what you might get for your money in each region, provides a step-by-step account of the buying process, and looks at some of the issues you might encounter as a temporary or permanent resident in your new home. A number of countries with emerging property markets of interest to British buyers are covered in brief.

It is still possible to find property abroad that seems unbelievably cheap compared to what you are used to at home – but the worst thing you can do is let 'bargain bucket' prices cloud your judgment. A house that costs £20,000 may cost you a lot more than that in heartache once you realise it needs £50,000 spending on it to make it habitable, there is an outstanding mortgage of £30,000 on it for which you have become liable, and that it takes you the best part of 12 hours to reach it.

There is no substitute for research when making sure you are looking for the kind of property that really suits your needs, or for expert advice to help you find the right place at the right price, and get through the legal minefield unscathed. Existing second-home owners and émigrés can also be an invaluable source of help, so search them out too, and listen to their stories. Be clear about what you want from a foreign property, realistic about what you can afford, and spend the time – and money – to employ good lawyers, architects, surveyors and the like; they may cost you more up-front but could save you a fortune later. This book will help you take the first steps, as you set about turning your dream into reality.

Part I

An overview

Chapter 1

The overseas property boom

Turn on a TV these days and you will never be more than a few minutes away from a programme about British people buying property abroad. In fact, the phenomenon has become such big news that towards the end of 2003 nearly three hours a week of TV screen time was being dedicated to the genre on the terrestrial channels alone. No fewer than 15 programmes had been produced or were being planned for terrestrial television in 2003 and 2004; peak-time audiences for the most popular programmes were over four million. Watching other people make decisions about buying property abroad has, it seems, become a national obsession.

How many of us are buying?

Are more people really buying abroad, or is it a mere whim of TV producers? How many of us actually make the dream into a reality? It is impossible to get hold of watertight statistics about the number of British people who own property abroad – there is no single agency to collect such figures, so the best one can hope for is educated guesses from a variety of sources.

The UK Foreign Office estimates that there are more than 15 million British people living overseas. But this figure includes everyone who leaves the UK for a period of more than three months, so students travelling in their gap year are counted, for example, as are people on extended holidays or working on short-term contracts in other countries. So it is highly unlikely that all 15 million live abroad in a permanent sense; and plenty of the ones that do will not have bought property there.

As for emigration figures, the European Union (EU) estimates that in 2002 there were more than 107,000 UK citizens living in Spain, and nearly 15,000 in Portugal. It says there were nearly 25,000 Britons living in Italy in 2001 although figures from the Department for Work and Pensions, show 29,000 pensioners there alone. The latest EU estimate for France is that there were around 75,000 living there in 1999 – although this number is likely to have increased dramatically since then, if the previous decade's growth of 49 per cent was anything to go by.

The Organisation for Economic Cooperation and Development (OECD) estimates are remarkably similar for Portugal and Italy, but less so for Spain: its figures for Spain, Portugal and Italy in 2001 are 80,000, 15,000 and 24,000 respectively. Figures for numbers of Britons living in France are not available. In 2001, more than 600,000 Britons were living in Canada and more than 200,000 in New Zealand; in 2000, 1.2 million lived in Australia and nearly 680,000 in the USA.

Figures from the UK Department for Work and Pensions (DWP) show how many UK citizens claim their state pension from abroad; the numbers are considerable (see table below).

Top 20 countries for UK pensioners (2003)

Country	Thousands of UK citizens claiming state pension from country, as at March 31, 2003
Australia	231.8
Canada	146.1
USA	118.0
Eire	92.1
Spain	54.4
New Zealand	39.1
South Africa	36.0
Italy	29.0
Germany	28.7
France	22.7
Jamaica	22.3
Cyprus	7.4
Netherlands	6.5
Pakistan	6.1
Portugal	4.8
Austria	4.7
India	4.4
Barbados	4.4
Belgium	4.3
Zimbabwe	4.0

Source: Department for Work and Pensions

All these figures suggest that more and more British people are indeed choosing a life outside the UK. According to EU estimates, for example, the UK population in Spain grew by 44 per cent in the three years to 2002, and in Portugal numbers went up by 20 per cent over the same period. Britons in Italy numbered between 23,000 and 25,000 for the whole of the last decade although these figures are probably under-estimates. Figures for France are less up to date, but in 1999 numbers were similar to those for Spain, and given their growth of 49 per cent between 1990 and 1999, one might confidently expect them to have continued spiralling upwards.

By OECD estimates, the British in Spain grew in number by a more conservative 17 per cent in the five years from 1996 to 2001; and by 25 per cent in Portugal during the same period. Numbers in Italy, Australia and Canada dropped slightly. Figures compiled by the Office for National Statistics, meanwhile, show that upwards of 150,000 British citizens a year migrated from the UK between 1996 and 2001 – the latest year for which figures are available. Of the 308,000 people of all nationalities who left the UK in 2001, 30 per cent were heading for the EU and 60 per cent intended to stay away for at least four years. Only a third of migrants were moving in order to work or study.

According to EU figures, the Costa del Sol is the fastest growth area in Europe in terms of population. While an estimated 2.5 million people lived on the coast in early 2003, this number is expected to rise to 6.5 million by 2011; an average increase of 444,000 people annually.

All those involved in overseas property – from estate agents to lawyers, from mortgage lenders to advertising executives selling space in overseas property magazines – agree that the market for first and second homes abroad has mushroomed since the turn of the twenty-first century. The numbers of Britons buying properties as second homes has been the subject of a government survey compiled by the Office of the Deputy Prime Minister. For 2002–03, it found that around 155,000 English households owned a second property outside the UK; in the same year 234,000 said they owned a second home in Britain, and of these 108,000 were holiday or retirement homes.

Where are we buying?

Although there are no definitive figures on favoured destinations, estate agents and mortgage lenders are agreed that the two most popular countries for British buyers are, by some margin, France and Spain. Within France, the most popular areas for UK property buyers are the south-east coast, especially the Côte d'Azur, and Paris. Other popular areas include Brittany, Normandy, the Dordogne region, Languedoc and the French Alps. In Spain, the southern and eastern coastal regions stretching from the Costa de la Luz in the far south-west to the Costa Brava in the north-east have been attracting British buyers for many years; more recently, some have begun to move inland too.

In the second rank are Portugal (with people mainly still buying in the Algarve, but with growing interest in Lisbon and its coast, and the more northerly Costa Verde), Italy (with Tuscany topping the list, followed by Umbria and, more recently, Le Marche) and the USA (Florida). Beneath them come a growing number of other countries with smaller, but expanding, numbers of British home-owners. These include Greece, Cyprus, Turkey, Malta, Slovenia, Croatia, South Africa and Dubai, to name but a few.

It is likely you will already have your own ideas about where you would like to own property, at least partially determined by your favourite holiday destinations (see table below). In the next two chapters we will look at different reasons why you might choose one location over another, and the issues you need to think about before purchasing.

British holidaymakers' favourite destinations

Country	Number of UK visitors in 2002
Spain	12,525,000
France	12,112,000
USA	3,602,000
Greece	2,958,000
Italy	2,650,000
Portugal	1,779,000
Cyprus	1,302,000
Turkey	991,000
Central/Eastern Europe	871,000
Canada	609,000
Malta	439,000
Former Yugoslavia	170,000

Source: Office for National Statistics

In Part II of this book, we will go on to explore in more detail the four most popular countries with British homeowners, in order of popularity. We will look at which are the most popular areas in each country to buy in, as well as suggesting some more unusual places to consider.

What are we buying?

If there is one thing that unites people who buy property abroad, it is their diversity. As the next chapter indicates, there are as many different reasons for buying property abroad as there are people who do it, and a huge range of properties that people with differing aims in buying abroad will find more or less attractive. So while the fact that increasing numbers of people are buying on the Côte d'Azur might suggest people are opting for purpose-built luxury, there are still plenty of buyers for whom a ruined Breton farmhouse requiring hundreds of thousands of euros' worth of restoration is the perfect choice.

France has been described as the 'thermometer' of overseas property-buying precisely because of this enormous diversity of supply and demand, which means the country acts as a good monitor of the market. At the time of writing, demand is very strong.

It is probably fair to say that purchases in Spain and Portugal are much more likely to be of the purpose-built villa or apartment variety, but even within this category there is a huge range of properties, appealing to hugely differing groups – from extremely exclusive golfing complexes in the Algarve to 'kiss me quick' high-rises in Benidorm. In Italy, run-down rustic properties in need of conversion – or their refurbished equivalents – are much more popular. Italian estate agents profess to be amazed at Britons' determination to buy the most remote hideaways, as far away from the nearest neighbour as possible.

Why is there an overseas property boom?

There are two main reasons for the upsurge of interest in overseas property ownership.

The UK housing market
The most likely explanation seems to be the knock-on effect of the property boom at home, in the context of a sustained period of low interest rates. As anyone who has bought or sold property in the UK

knows, house prices in many parts of Britain have risen rapidly in recent years. But because interest rates are low and stable, mortgage repayments are predictable and still relatively affordable. The UK base rate has been below 5 per cent since September 2001; between November of that year and February 2003 the rate stayed at 4 per cent for 16 months. It fell to a low of 3.5 per cent in July 2003.

So if you are already on the property ladder and employed, it is comparatively easy to extend your mortgage credit, should you wish to invest in more property. This can seem attractive with house prices rising steadily while stock-market investments and certain pension schemes are performing badly.

These factors have triggered the buy-to-let boom in the UK and, for those put off by spiralling domestic property prices, an increasing tendency to look abroad, where house prices are generally much lower and are rising, but nowhere near as fast. Lenders report that even first-time buyers who cannot afford to get on the property ladder at home are buying abroad.

UK house prices (as measured by the Nationwide index) grew by an average of more than 11 per cent a year between 1997 and 2001, and clocked up a headline annual increase of 31 per cent by October 2002. Prices have since slowed, but this does not detract from the fact that the UK has experienced, by some considerable margin, the biggest upward trend in house-price growth of all the countries in Europe over the last 30 years.

In contrast, Spain's annual rise of 12 per cent for 2002 – which made it the second most inflationary EU economy in terms of house prices – looks paltry; in France prices rose by around 4 per cent, while in Italy prices rose by an average of around 4 to 5 per cent a year between 1998 and 2002, but were still nearly a fifth below their early – 1990s peak. Property abroad has often been relatively good value, but in recent years much of what is on offer has become even more of a bargain.

Sterling may have been sliding against the euro (see table opposite), but a cursory glance through the plethora of overseas property websites should be enough to show even the most cautious of property hunters that prices are still considerably lower in parts of continental Europe.

Sterling/euro/dollar exchange rates

Month	Rate (number of € to £1)	(US$ to £1)
Jan 2004	1.4230	1.7618
Dec 2003	1.4252	1.6993
Nov 2003	1.4332	1.6893
Oct 2003	1.4270	1.6036
Sept 2003	1.4318	1.5924
Aug 2003	1.4042	1.6069
July 2003	1.4346	1.6773
June 2003	1.4052	1.6438
May 2003	1.4454	1.5818
Apr 2003	1.4763	1.5634
Mar 2003	1.4849	1.5949
Feb 2003	1.5074	1.6135
Jan 2003	1.5585	1.6009
Dec 2002	1.5697	1.5757
Nov 2002	1.5865	1.5487
Oct 2002	1.5852	1.5495
Sept 2002	1.5611	1.5311
Aug 2002	1.5839	1.5730
July 2002	1.5593	1.5667
June 2002	1.5741	1.4588
May 2002	1.6251	1.4426
Apr 2002	1.6117	1.4255

Source: HM Customs and Excise

A comparison of the average cost of homes in ten of the UK's most popular seaside resorts (see table below) with prices featured in the rest of this book indicates the widening price gap between home and abroad.

Average house prices in popular UK seaside resorts

Blackpool	£75,823
Brighton	£185,401
Clacton-on-Sea	£130,259
Great Yarmouth	£105,809
Lyme Regis	£199,228
Pwllheli	£147,251
Skegness	£99,491
Torquay	£128,426
Weston-super-Mare	£132,882
Whitby	£120,643

Source: Halifax

Low-cost air travel

It is hard to overestimate the impact of the budget airlines in freeing up the British to pursue what, ten or twenty years ago, would have remained an unfulfilled dream. Partly as a result of this development, Britons are taking more holidays than ever – the number of visits abroad by UK residents rose by 29 per cent between 1997 and 2002, and the number of nights spent abroad increased by 34 per cent over the same period.

The creation of new routes and the potential for substantially cheaper flights on these and more traditional routes, all year round, has opened up whole new worlds of opportunities for people looking for homes off the beaten track and yet within relatively easy travelling distance from our major cities; and for entrepreneurs looking to combine emigration with setting up new businesses in the tourist industry. On the south coast of France, for example, 'no frills' airlines now fly to no fewer than seven airports. In Spain, new routes to Jerez de la Frontera, Almería and Murcia have helped open up new areas to second-home ownership; in Italy, flights to Ancona have already brought the delights of Le Marche to a wider audience, and Pescara now looks set to do the same for the hitherto practically unheard-of region of Abruzzo and Molise.

The UK's property-buying exploits look set to ensure that, for increasing numbers of us, experiencing life in sunnier climes – or at least making investments there – is a dream we can now achieve.

Over the next three chapters we will reflect on how to make sure you pursue that dream in the most rational way possible, and then in the rest of the book we will explore the many and varied places in which you might want to consider buying, and the practicalities of doing so.

Chapter 2

Why buy abroad?

If you are reading this book, the chances are you have already given some thought to the idea of buying property abroad. But have you considered the idea deeply enough to be confident of the kind of property you want, where you want it to be and whether you can afford it?

CASE HISTORY: Dinah and Marcus

Londoners Dinah and Marcus Oliver bought and converted a run-down former agricultural building in the Lot Valley, south-west France, in 1998. They have three children, now aged 14, 10 and 8, and have so far used the house much less than they might have hoped.

'We came into some money and bought the place on a bit of an impulse, to be honest. We thought we'd be there all the time but we go there for a fortnight in the summer and, if we're lucky, another week or two a year perhaps. We let it out to friends and family too, which is fine, but it's not how we'd envisaged things, and I don't suppose it's earning us as much money as it could be either,' says Dinah. 'Marcus' work (as a freelance computer trainer) has ended up being less flexible than we'd thought, and it's quite a trek to go there for less than a full week. I think if it had been nearer, in Normandy or Brittany perhaps, we'd have gone over there more often.'

The Olivers are not alone – there are plenty of British property owners whose experience of owning a home abroad has turned out rather differently from what they had expected. For example, the process of converting a ruin into the home of your dreams might be more difficult and costly than you had imagined, or you might move abroad and find that you miss home and find living in a foreign country too lonely.

To avoid such problems, people who have made a success of buying abroad say it is important to be as clear as possible in advance about what you are doing and why. They say there are many different reasons for buying an overseas property. It is essential to be focused about what you want a property to achieve for you.

Avoid rushing into things, and make sure your choice of property springs from your head as well as your heart. Read up as much as you can on the area, visit as often as you can and talk to as many people who have already bought abroad – preferably in the same region or at least the same country – as is possible.

Most crucially, take advice from the professionals. Buying abroad, if done properly, is no more risky than buying in the UK – but it is just as complicated, involves just as serious a decision and is often achieved in another language. There are many issues to consider, which you may need to think about before you even start looking. For example: can you afford it, whose name should you put it in, and how many weeks might you be able to let it out for? Good advice costs money, but going it alone can cost you a great deal more in the long run.

Chapter 3 examines in more detail the factors to consider when choosing a property, but this chapter offers some initial ideas about the various types of overseas property you might want to own, and some words of wisdom from buyers who have already achieved their dreams.

Holiday homes

Whether in Torremolinos or Tuscany, many of us have spent long, sun-kissed evenings on the terrace of a favourite holiday restaurant and talked about how wonderful it would be to have somewhere abroad to call our own: a home from home to come back to time and again, where we could laze in the sun, recharge our batteries and enjoy the local culture.

What to look for
Holiday homes can range from the poky to the palatial, but the chances are you have some budgetary constraints and that apartments or small houses are the kinds of places you're looking for. Smaller conversion projects might be tempting, but you are unlikely to have the time or money to devote to a major restoration. If you have children and/or are thinking of renting your property out for part of

the year, go for somewhere with a pool if at all possible – even if it is near the sea. Accessibility will also be a major consideration, both for yourselves and anyone renting the property.

CASE HISTORY: Fiona and Graham

Fiona Cox says deciding to buy a house in Umbria while on holiday there is the most spontaneous thing she and her husband Graham have ever done.

'We know France much better and had toyed with the idea of buying a property there but never did anything about it. We'd only ever been to Italy on city breaks before, but we rented a lovely villa there during the summer and just fell in love with the area. We ended up spending the last three days of our holiday property hunting, and found a house that's just perfect. We kept telling ourselves not to be so stupid and think carefully about it, so when we came back home we worked out all the figures. It actually ended up making even more sense when we looked at it rationally, so we went for it.'

The couple, who have three young children, found the property, which needs an almost complete rebuild and is equidistant between the towns of Gubbio, Assisi and Perugia, through a local estate agent and were assisted in their search by a local *geometra* (see Chapter 7), who is now project-managing the restoration.

They made a written offer once they had returned to England and paid a deposit for the property around a month later. They bought the house outright but may raise finance against their British home to fund the renovation. Once the property is complete, Mrs Cox says the family will fit the property out as if it was their permanent home and offer it for holiday lettings for most of the year, apart from a few weeks when they will occupy it themselves.

Although she admits that she and her husband jumped into buying the house more quickly than she might recommend, she emphasises the importance of being sure about the place you are buying, as well as of doing months of research. 'We did it backwards I suppose – falling in love with an area and then doing the homework afterwards – but I'm still confident we're doing the right thing. You need to be sensible and think about all the implications, but you can do all the research in the world and still never find a perfect place.'

Co-ownership

If money is tight and you are looking to buy a holiday home to use for part of the year but no more, one option that may be worth considering is co-ownership – whereby you establish a consortium of owners, who each buy a share of the property.

Say you have three siblings, for example, and you all want to buy a holiday home together – you might each be able to raise £50,000 to put down, giving you access to a £200,000 property for the equivalent of three months a year each. Or this could be for 12 months, if it is big enough for you all to be there at the same time.

A variant on this theme is for one person to set up a co-ownership arrangement on a commercial basis. For example, you buy a property for £100,000 and sell six two-month shares in it for £30,000 each; that gives you a profit of £80,000. You could even keep one of the shares for yourself, leaving you a profit of £50,000 and eight weeks' worth of holiday home.

If you opt for any arrangement of this nature – even if it involves only friends or family – it is absolutely vital to set it up properly. You must take legal advice before you do anything. There are many issues to consider: who is responsible for maintenance and what happens if someone wants to pull out, to name but two.

Timeshare

Although most property experts advise against it, saying it is just an expensive way of paying for an annual holiday, another way of gaining access to a holiday home is timeshare. One company with 52 resorts around the world offers the following timeshare options for an outlay of around £10,000: a two-bed townhouse in a club overlooking a golf course in Mallorca; a two-bed townhouse overlooking Disneyland Paris' golf course; or a two-bed apartment in Marbella. In all cases, what you get is one week per year in the low season.

Timeshare in Europe has become a dirty word because of the mis-selling scandals of the 1980s, but since then legislation has been tightened up somewhat, and several major hospitality and travel companies such as Marriott, Airtours, Thomas Cook and Hilton Stakis have joined the market. Even so, you still need to beware of shady practices.

The first point to understand about timeshare is that it is not a way of owning property. What it does is give you access to a holiday home (or homes) for a relatively low cost – the average amount timeshare owners spend is estimated to be around £6,500. The downside is that, rather than buying a property outright, or even a share of it, timeshare gives you only the right to use a property for a proportion of the year, and the rest of the time, other timeshare owners get to use it. Timeshare agreements are generally for 50 or 80 years. It is not possible to take out a mortgage on a timeshare, because there is no property for the lender to repossess if you default on the loan – although timeshare companies will normally offer loans if you do not have cash at your disposal.

The legalities of timeshares vary according to where you are buying and, because timeshare developers tend to like to organise everything from the building of the resort to setting up finance options, it is vital to make sure you understand and are happy with every aspect of the deal before agreeing to anything. Otherwise, there is a danger of being swept along by a purchase process that can seem to develop its own momentum.

Remember, in a timeshare development every villa or apartment needs to be sold roughly 50 times – once for every week it can be used – in order to hit target. So it is hardly surprising that sales-people are keen to get things moving and complete the sale as quickly as possible. High-pressure sales techniques have damaged the image of the industry, but a mixture of legislation by the EU and individual member states has put some consumer safeguards in place, including a statutory cooling-off period to allow you to reflect on your initial decision.

If you are looking for a timeshare in Europe, you should check that the company you deal with is part of the Organisation for Timeshare in Europe (OTE)*, which represents around 170 out of an estimated 600-plus companies and has a voluntary ethical code to protect timeshare consumers' rights. The OTE does, however, allow members to take deposits before the cooling-off period is over, contrary to EU directives.

The managing of the timeshare resort can either be carried out by an owners' committee, a specialist management company or the developer itself; whichever it is, there will be annual fees for all owners covering expenses such as cleaning and maintenance, utility charges, insurance, taxes, the operation of common facilities (such as tennis courts or swimming pools), and (usually) a sinking fund to provide for major redecoration or refurbishment. This is an area of increasing concern and one you need to check carefully. Complaints about maintenance charges rising astronomically have increased in recent years. Developers may keep initial maintenance charges artificially low to lure buyers in, then increase them after a couple of years. There have also been allegations of owners' committees being 'rigged' so that developers' reps outnumber genuine owners' reps. You should make sure that the resort has a democratically run owners' club or organisation, or you could be at the mercy of the developer or management company when it comes to paying development costs.

Timeshare exchange is a common adjunct to timeshare. Through networks of resorts, exchange allows timeshare owners the ability to swap their timeshare for another – at a different time, location or both – with the confidence that they will receive another high-quality holiday in its place. If you are buying a timeshare in a resort with networking arrangements, you would generally join an exchange company automatically at the time of purchase; it then acts like a timeshare bank. If you choose not to use the week you have bought you can deposit it with the exchange company and subsequently withdraw equivalent weeks – at other times and/or other resorts – which have been deposited by other members.

Typically, you should have the right to sell or rent your time-share, and to include it in your estate. But you should not expect to make money on a resale, as owning a timeshare is more like owning membership to a club, rather than owning a piece of real estate. Equity does not really come into the equation. Examining the problems of resale in 2002 *Holiday Which?* concluded that: 'Con-merchants are out in force in the resale market. Agents cold-call potential sellers, promising a high sale price – and then disappear with the deposit. Always assume that any cold-caller is up to no good – especially if they say that they already have a buyer for your timeshare.'

In 1994 the EU introduced legislation to force all EU countries to adapt their national law by the end of April 1997, to establish common rules to protect consumers in all EU member states. However, be aware that the directive only covers transactions between commercial vendors and private buyers, so if you buy a timeshare through a private seller or a resale company, or buy a canal or narrowboat timeshare, you are not covered by the legis-lation. Companies selling timeshares of less than three years' duration are also excluded.

The four main points to the EU Directive are that:

- buyers must have a statutory minimum 'cooling off' period of ten days from signing the contract
- the taking of deposits before the end of the cooling-off period is prohibited
- contracts must be in the language of the member state in which the buyer lives
- purchasers must receive all descriptive information concerning the property and their rights.

It is essential to realise that the directive says nothing about the legal structures for timeshare – it simply protects you in the period up to and including the time of the purchase contract.

The timeshare concept was invented in the USA, and timeshares are fairly popular in Florida. There are two main types there – 'interval ownership' (where you actually own a proportion of the property) and 'right to use' (more akin to the European model). There is a ten-day cooling off period in the USA too, and prices are comparable to those in Europe.

Timeshare legislation says nothing about holiday clubs. These are a variant on timeshares that have appeared in recent years and some are sold by the more dubious entrepreneurs who have been scared off by the timeshare legislation. Holiday clubs generally offer deals lasting less than three years, thus avoiding the legislation. In 2002, UK trading standards departments received nearly 4,500 complaints about them. The Office of Fair Trading has investigated 100 holiday club cases. In 2002 *Holiday Which?* reported that: 'Despite timeshare legislation, con merchants continue to wheedle money out of their victims without any intention of delivering properties or holidays.' The magazine advises potential purchasers to steer clear of holiday club schemes until proper legislation is in place.

Homes for emigrating

Some people, for a whole host of reasons, see buying a property abroad as providing more than just a guaranteed number of holidays a year in familiar surroundings. Some have work that can be done from anywhere, or have a new job abroad, while others see scope for running an entirely new business from abroad.

If one of a couple is foreign, the pair may decide to move to his or her homeland, temporarily or permanently. In some cases, people simply fall in love with an area after spending a holiday there, and decide the time has come to leave behind their old life and start afresh. Parents may decide they would like their children to grow up in a sunnier climate and learn another language and culture while they are young enough to take it all in without too much effort.

Moving abroad, particularly when you are younger than retirement age, is a major decision and not to be taken lightly – especially if you have dependants. Deciding whether the move is right for them, and thinking about how you might earn a living in your new home, are likely to be foremost in your mind. Yet making the move can be really exciting and can work with careful planning.

What to look for

Regardless of your route into emigration, if you are moving to a new country you are likely to want somewhere capable of providing at least the same kind of space and living standards as you are used to at home. Houses outside the main tourist hotspots can provide excellent value and may give you access to a more 'authentic' lifestyle.

It can be worth considering buying a derelict property and restoring it to meet your particular needs. But avoid buying a property where you will feel uncomfortably isolated. If you are planning to support your new lifestyle through letting out rooms to tourists, you will need to be in a good, marketable location, preferably with a pool.

CASE HISTORY: Keith and Maria

Marketing consultant Keith Burns, his wife Maria and their two sons, Ben and Theo, moved to Brittany in 1995. Although the area has since become popular with UK buyers, at the time the family was the first to have set down roots in their village, which is near the town of Pontivy.

'We were lucky that Keith ran his own business and it was successful enough for him to be able to take a bit of a back seat and concentrate on setting us up here,' says Maria. 'He commuted back to London every couple of weeks. We bought two houses at right angles to each other; we live in one and rent the other out. Keith still does bits of consultancy work, I'm doing a bit of teaching locally, and the kids are at school – they're both completely fluent, and much better at it than their parents!

'Things have worked out really well for us, although if Keith hadn't been able to carry on bringing in a bit of money I think we'd have had to have bought somewhere a bit less out of the way, because the rentals side can be much harder work than one might imagine. I think you have to be adaptable people to move abroad, and quite resourceful – and there's no substitute for learning the language. It's important to really know an area before you decide to live there, too – we'd been on holiday round here for years. If you just stick a pin in a map and say "let's live there", it feels to me as if you must be running away from your previous life, in a way. This place was part of our life before we moved here – we just decided we wanted it to be a bigger part, I suppose.'

Homes for retirement

Some people's idea of a great retirement is pottering round the garden, looking after the grandchildren, and a few rounds of bridge; for others, moving abroad offers a healthier climate and relaxed pace of life that staying in the UK simply could not match.

Studies have shown that people's reasons for retiring to different areas vary considerably. A study on retirement migration to the Mediterranean found that 48 per cent of British expatriates cited climate as the main reason they had migrated to the Costa del Sol, for example. However, only 15 per cent of those who had retired to Tuscany put climate at the top of their list of reasons, with childhood or family links, business connections and admiration of Italy itself much more likely to bring about a move.

Making sure your pensions are sufficient to keep you in the foreign lifestyle to which you would like to be accustomed is an obvious first step when considering the feasibility of retiring abroad. Even if it does not feel like it at the time you retire, access to healthcare and other support networks should be a major factor.

Advice on pensions, benefits and the potentially enormous costs of healthcare abroad is given in Chapter 4.

What to look for

As with anyone buying an overseas property, your choice of retirement home will be determined largely by the strength of your finances. But regardless of how wealthy you are, you will probably be looking to scale down in your retirement years – both to keep your expenses as low as possible, and to minimise the effort you need to put in to keep the place shipshape. Depending on your health and lifestyle, properties close to amenities such as doctors' surgeries and pharmacies can be a sensible choice. If your language skills are poor, you may want to go for an area where plenty of English is spoken, or where you know there are good facilities to help you learn the local language.

CASE HISTORY: Jim

Jim Bunce, a retired hotel manager from Huddersfield, bought an apartment in a golfing complex near Javea, on the Costa Blanca, in the spring of 2003 and intends to retire there in 2004.

'The flat isn't finished yet but it should be ready in the spring and then I have to pay the last bit of the money. I'll be keeping this place on and renting it to one of my daughters, so I suppose if the worst came to the worst and I decided I couldn't hack it out there, I could come back. My wife and I went to Spain for years and always said we'd move there one day. She died a couple of years back but I'm going there if it's the last thing I do. I know people out there, and I love it. The property has its own shared pool and you get preferential rates for golf, which you can play through the winter. It feels like there's a real sense of community too. I can't wait.

'I don't think I'd be brave enough to move to the middle of nowhere – I'm a quiet sort of chap but I do need people around me and I need to know I can make myself understood. There are plenty of oldies around Javea so I reckon I'll be fine!'

Homes for investment

The recent performance of stock-market investments in the wake of the dotcom bubble and the 2001 attack on the World Trade Center have led many of us to question the logic of continuing to pin all our hopes on pensions and shares-based savings schemes to provide for us in our old age. Lower house prices, impressive capital growth and a strong rental market in parts of the continent mean that buying property abroad purely for investment purposes is an option many UK buyers – even first-time buyers – are now considering.

If you are looking for somewhere you can use yourself as well as an investment, apartments and villas in the main tourist regions are an obvious good bet, with golfing properties with pools performing particularly well for lettings because of their year-round appeal. Prices for the best properties will be at a premium though, so don't expect to do it on the cheap.

Flats in major cities and provincial capitals can be a good buy – in some cases for holiday lettings, in some for long-term tenancies and in some cases for both. If funds are limited, countries hoping to join the EU in 2004 and 2007 are hotly tipped by some sources to perform well in capital growth over the longer term. It is still possible to buy apartments in the centres of Prague and Budapest, for example, for next to nothing (see Chapter 9).

As in the UK, 'buying to let' successfully overseas is part art and part science. To make it into a successful business you need to buy the right kind of property, in the right area, at the right price, make it appealing and market it well. Do not expect to make a vast profit as some people in Britain have done over recent years. The property market in most parts of Europe is much less dynamic than ours, even though the trend is still upward. You will need to research carefully each element of the equation to be confident you are making the most of your capital investment – even more than you would if you were buying in the UK, where you will already have a good feel for what the market is like, at the very least in the area where you live.

You need to equip yourself with specific knowledge. For example, you may know that house prices in Spain have been shooting upwards in recent years, but do you know more particularly what has been happening to prices in Madrid? And within Madrid, which are the areas most likely to do well in terms of capital growth over the long term? Who might want to rent your property? And how might you maximise your chances of getting them to choose your property over your competitors'?

Remember that rental markets in Europe are very different from those in the UK – a much greater proportion of the French population rent property as compared to in the UK, for example, but tenants also tend to have much greater protection than they do here. Hence you should not assume you can rent somewhere out for six months and then evict your tenants, and you should make sure you set the rent at the appropriate level because otherwise you might be stuck with the same tenant on a low rent for a long time.

Whether you are considering investing in a property for holiday lettings or for more permanent tenants, think carefully about how you would manage the logistics of the arrangement. If you are based in the UK, who will keep an eye on the property, clean it, get it ready for the next tenants, and sort out maintenance problems and other matters?

Some of these issues would arise even if you were buying a holiday home that was just for your own use – but if you are renting your property out as a commercial venture they assume crucial importance. You must have all bases covered or you will start to lose business. To have your property professionally managed can prove extremely expensive, as shown in the following chapters. In the USA in particular, there are many rules and regulations about letting your property out. Whether you are permitted to do it in the first place, the safety measures that must be in place and how you must account for your earnings, for example – so you must think carefully about what you are getting yourself into.

If you are unsure about whether or not you can be sufficiently available to act as a decent landlord, an option worth considering is a 'leaseback' scheme, whereby you buy a property and lease it back to the developer, who then guarantees you a fixed income per year as well as free use of the flat for an agreed number of weeks. Leaseback schemes exist in various locations, including the Caribbean, and they vary considerably in terms of the small print.

The most solid of these schemes are in France, where the authorities are keen to address a shortage of high-quality tourist accommodation by attracting inward investment, and are happy to guarantee investors significant protection in what might otherwise be a potentially uncertain marketplace. French leasebacks are mainly in Paris and on the Côte d'Azur and the properties tend to be new-build or renovated apartments which are let as part of what is effectively a four- or five-star 'aparthotel'.

Deals typically involve a tie-in of nine years, during which time investors are guaranteed a rental income of 4 to 6 per cent, per year, depending on how many weeks' use they themselves want from the flat. This money is paid regardless of whether the flat stands empty 365 days a year.

Always make sure your lawyer scrutinises such contracts, because they can involve restrictions – for example, you may not be able to sell the property until after a set period. As with any other purchase involving apartments in a shared building, there will be service and maintenance charges to pay.

What to look for

If you are buying somewhere purely as an investment, try to forget your own personal preferences – this is not somewhere for you to live in, it is somewhere to make you money! You may find that buying a flat in a foreign city to rent out to permanent tenants makes more sense than buying a holiday home, where frequent changeovers mean the running costs can go sky-high. But if you do want a place that doubles up as a holiday home for you, try to get the right balance between giving yourself enough time to enjoy holidays there, and maximising your income by letting for as big a chunk of the year as possible. If you know the area well and are confident enough of your marketing skills, you may make a good return by buying somewhere a bit unusual and slightly off the beaten track, and renting it to a particular market. If you do not, you are probably best to keep to the more tried-and-tested areas, and may even want to buy a property with an established lettings record.

Homes for all reasons

As is so often the case in life, many of us end up buying somewhere for a variety of reasons, rather than for a specific purpose. Ideally we might want to move abroad permanently but feel that it is impossible at present, perhaps because of work or family commitments. As a result we might decide the next best thing is to buy a holiday home and make as much use of it as possible, but choose one that could also serve as a place for retirement.

Sometimes a property might meet several requirements at once, acting as holiday home, retirement home and investment simultaneously – but just as often it will not. If what would suit you best for

---

CASE HISTORY: Miles and Philippa

Miles and Philippa Porter sold one of their two London flats in the summer of 2002, and traded it in for two Spanish properties – an £80,000 flat in the historic centre of Barcelona and a *masia* (traditional Catalan farmhouse), costing a similar amount, further inland.

When they moved from the UK, the couple initially rented a flat in Barcelona while they searched for properties; they bought the *masia* first and spent around £100,000 refurbishing it; they now live in it for most of the year. In summer 2003, they bought the flat in Barcelona, which they are currently renovating to let out to tourists. They hope to use it themselves for a few weekends a year if they have vacancies and 'when we fancy a shot of urban excitement', as Miles puts it.

'We bought the flat because we think Barcelona's a great city and it's on the up. Considering how major a city it is, the prices are affordable and the great thing is, it gets tourists all year round. Obviously we're lucky because we were able to cash in the London flat and buy it outright, but we still intend to run it as a proper business. We are considering using an agency to do the cleaning and stuff, but we'll do the marketing ourselves and because we're close by we can be on hand to sort out any maintenance problems.'

---

now is to have somewhere to go to a few weeks a year, you might be better buying a sure-fire letting property in an area you would not necessarily want to retire in, that fulfils your holiday needs over the next few years and gives you a solid income. Later on you could sell that property and buy somewhere more to your taste for retirement, or you could keep the property for income and buy your retirement home out of the proceeds of selling a home in the UK.

What to look for

It can be very difficult to find a property that fulfils the functions of holiday home, investment vehicle and retirement retreat. For example, unless you can tolerate a huge influx of tourists every summer, you would be unlikely to want to retire in the kind of area that does best out of tourist lettings and, especially if you have a large family, the chances are that what you want out of a holiday home is something rather larger than you might want in your twilight years. All-round properties do exist – it is just a question of searching and being prepared to be flexible. But the best advice is probably to focus on enjoying and/or making money out of an overseas property during your 30s to 50s and then, if necessary, selling it on once you have decided where you want to spend your retirement.

CASE HISTORY: Frank and Jo

In his 50s, Frank White and his partner Jo bought a house in the hills of the Algarve in the autumn of 2002 – they are currently using it as a holiday home but also hope to semi-retire and move into it permanently in about three years' time. The couple had been on holiday to the area several times and decided to buy a holiday home for themselves and to generate a letting income, which could at a later stage help fund a retirement home.

They were in the process of looking for a new-build holiday apartment but on a viewing trip the estate agent showed them two ruined farm buildings which a builder was in the process of knocking together, doing up and selling. They fell in love with the place instantly.

'We had to borrow more to afford it, but it's worth it because the house fulfils our eventual dream of somewhere to emigrate to. It's just so frustrating now because we want to be there all the time but can't be for a few more years.' says Frank, who hopes to run a small antiques business from Portugal to supplement his pension.

Chapter 3

Where to buy

Making the decision to buy a property abroad can be as personal or impersonal as you like. Some people decide purely on the basis of mathematical calculations of capital investment performance and rental yields; others have long-standing reasons for moving somewhere, or seem to jump into a purchase through an almost spiritual attachment to a country, region or place. The chances are that, whatever your reasons for buying abroad, you will want to consider some or all of the factors detailed in this chapter.

Part II of this book (Chapters 5 to 9) provides brief summaries of some of the main areas where British people are already buying property, and a few that estate agents reckon to have solid potential. It offers a short description of each region, and shows some examples of properties recently offered for sale, to give an idea of what you can get for your money.

Climate

For many British people, weather is the biggest factor that drives them to search for a property abroad, but it is all too easy to assume that anywhere south of Dover has idyllic climatic conditions when in fact, even in the Mediterranean, temperatures and rainfall can vary enormously.

If you are considering somewhere as a place to buy, make sure you do some research about its climate all year round – not just for a few weeks in August. After all, in recent years British summers have been far from unpleasant, so you may prefer to stay at home during the peak season and make some letting income – and then visit when the weather is still good but the crowds have gone home.

France

Generally speaking, the south has a milder winter than further north, which is not dissimilar in climate to the south coast of England. The southern winter is often pleasantly warm, but cold spells can occur for instance when the mistral (a cold blustery wind) blows down the Rhône Valley to the French Riviera. In Nice, average daily maximum temperatures reach 13°C (56°F), some five hours of sunshine can be expected, and there are about 22 dry days a month on average. Corsica's temperatures will be two or three degrees higher, but it is also wetter, with only 18 or 19 dry days on average.

A steady warming-up process takes place during the spring months, although the mistral can still sometimes make its presence felt. Average daily maximum temperatures rise to about 20°C (68°F) by May, with daily sunshine hours dropping to about nine or ten, and there are approximately 23 dry days.

The Mediterranean coastline has plenty of sunshine during the summer months, and refreshing sea breezes make sunbathing very pleasant indeed. Average daily maximum temperatures reach a warm 27°C (81°F) in August, and an average of 12 hours of sunshine per day is the norm; 25 to 30 dry days per month can be expected during the summer season.

The south of France retains warm conditions through September and October (daily average highs still in the mid-20s Celsius), although heavy rain and flooding can sometimes occur and by November that figure has fallen to 17°C (63°F). About 22 dry days can be expected on average, but daily sunshine hours will have fallen to five by November.

Mainland Spain

Southern Spain has a warm, dry winter, although the ski slopes high up in Andalucia are only a short drive away and at high altitudes it can be bitterly cold. Daily average maximum temperatures vary from 9°C (49°F) inland at Madrid to 17°C (63°F) along the Mediterranean coast. Average dry days number about 23 to 24, and typically six hours of sunshine can be expected. Winters in Gibraltar are considerably wetter than much of southern Spain due to exposure from Atlantic storms. However, the winters do tend to be rather warmer than the mainland.

By late spring, Spain is experiencing settled warm weather, but beware of some rather cool nights. Daily average maximum temperatures will have risen to about 21°C (70°F) in Madrid, and two or three degrees higher on the coast. Average dry days remain at about 23 to 24 but daily average sunshine hours have increased to about 11 per day. Average maximum temperatures in Gibraltar are broadly similar to the Spanish mainland, but there are more dry days (about 27) on average.

In the summer, the Spanish coastline enjoys sea breezes, keeping the temperatures bearable. Daytime maximum average temperatures reach 30 to 31°C (86 to 88°F), a good 11 to 12 hours of sunshine can be expected on average each day, and there are about 28 dry days on average. Gibraltar enjoys a typical Mediterranean climate with a very dry summer, some months having no rain at all. The daily average maximum temperatures are slightly lower than those of southern Spain, peaking at about 29°C (83°F).

The early part of autumn serves as an extension of summer, with daytime highs still well up at about 28°C (82°F) on the coast, and the sea is still very warm. By November, the daytime highs have fallen back to about 20°C (68°F). Daily sunshine is around five to six hours, coupled with about 24 dry days. Autumn temperatures in Gibraltar are lower than those on the mainland, topping at about 24 to 25°C (76 to 78°F).

The Balearic Islands

Winter daytime average maximum temperatures peak at about 15°C (59°F), with about five hours of sunshine per day and some 22 dry days each month on average.

They begin to warm respectably during the spring months, peaking at about 22°C (72°F) in May. By then, there are about 10 hours of sunshine on average per day, and also 25 dry days.

The peak summer season sees average daily maximum temperatures up to a very warm 29°C (85°F) with an average of 11 hours of sunshine. The summer months are essentially dry, with up to 30 dry days.

Autumnal sea temperatures are still comfortably high for swimming, and so with daily average maximum temperatures remaining at about 27°C (81°F) in September and early October, the area is an ideal spot for a late holiday. However, these temperatures will have fallen back to 18°C (66°F) by November. The months have now become rather wetter, with about 22 dry days. Sunshine hours fall to about five by November.

The Canary Islands

In winter, the Canary Islands are amongst the favourite places for sun seekers, with average maximum temperatures a pleasant 21°C (70°F) throughout, coupled with about six hours of sunshine. Typically, there are 21 dry days each month during the winter season. Individually, the islands vary enormously: the easterly islands of Fuerteventura and Lanzarote are hot and dry; the tiny westerly ones are much wetter, lusher and cooler. The mountainous central islands of Tenerife and Gran Canaria have mixed climates: sunny and arid in the south, much cloudier and greener in the north.

With their ocean climate, the Canaries are only slightly warmer in spring than in winter. But the daily average maximum temperature rises to 24°C (75°F) by May; this is also a drier season than winter, with about 26 to 29 dry days on average. Seven to nine hours of sunshine can be expected on average each day.

During the summer months, the Canaries are generally hot, dry and very sunny. Daytime average temperatures reach 29°C (85°F) throughout the season. There is an average of 30 dry days and 11 hours of sunshine.

The autumn brings a slow decrease of average maximum temperatures, down to around 24°C (75°F). By November, the islands are rather wetter, with 21 dry days on average, and there is also a reduction in the number of average sunshine hours to about six per day.

Portugal

During winter, Portugal experiences a similar temperature pattern to the Spanish coast, i.e. average daytime highs of about 16°C (61°F). But the Portuguese resorts are much wetter, with only about 14 dry days on average. Five to six hours of sunshine can be expected per day on average.

A gradual warming-up process takes place during the spring months, daytime average maximum temperatures reaching up to 22°C (72°F) by May. The Atlantic-facing coast remains wetter than the Mediterranean-facing Spanish coast, with about 18 dry days per month. It can experience heavy storms. Sunshine hours number about ten on average.

During the summer months, Portugal receives refreshing sea breezes, making for very pleasant conditions. Daytime maximum temperatures reach 25°C (78°F), and 11 or 12 hours of sunshine can be expected. There are as many as 29 dry days on average.

As in other regions, September and the first part of October form an extension of summer. Daytime average maximum temperatures can still be as high as 26°C (79°F), but will have fallen back to about 17°C (63°F) by November. Daily sunshine hours fall back from about nine hours in September to about five or six hours in November. The end of the autumn has reverted to being a wet period, with about 12 to 17 dry days on average per month.

Mainland Italy

In winter, northern Italy is prone to frost and fog, while the south, although warmer, tends to be wetter. Average daytime maximum temperatures range from 7°C (45°F) in Venice in December to 13°C (56°F) in Naples and Rome. The average number of wet days ranges from about 25 in parts of the north to 18 near the coast. About three to four hours of sunshine are expected each day.

In the spring, the sirocco, a hot wind from Africa, can bring quite high temperatures to parts of Italy, but thunderstorms are frequent in the Italian Alps. Average daily maximum temperatures range from about 15°C (59°F) in March to 23°C (74°F) in May. Some 23 to 25 dry days are expected on average each month, and there are seven to ten hours of sunshine on average.

In summer, the area around the Alps experiences numerous thunderstorms, and inland parts of southern Italy suffer extremely hot nights. Average daytime maximum temperatures reach about 30°C (86°F) throughout the summer, and southern areas are mostly dry, with 29 to 30 dry days expected. Between ten and eleven hours of sunshine per day are typical.

As in the spring, the sirocco wind may well bring very high temperatures to parts of Italy during the autumn, accompanied by high humidity. Daily average maximum temperatures are still pleasantly high in September, at typically 26°C (79°F), but fall back to about 15°C (59°F) by November. The number of dry days varies from 24 or 25 in September to about 19 in November. Sunshine falls steadily from eight hours a day in September to three or four in November.

Sicily, Sardinia and Malta

In the winter months, these islands are generally milder than further north. Average daily maximum temperatures are about 15 to

16°C (59 to 61°F), with between four and six hours of sunshine each day. Sicilian and Sardinian dry days average about 23, while Malta is about four to five days wetter.

Springtime sees the temperatures warming up nicely, attaining an average daily maximum of about 23°C (74°F) by May. Daily sunshine hours will have increased to some ten hours by the end of the spring, and on average there are between 25 and 29 dry days each month.

June, July and August are the major holiday months for the area, with long spells of fine, sunny weather. Average daily maximum temperatures reach 30 to 31°C (86 to 88°F) in August on Sicily and Sardinia, but refreshing sea breezes tend to keep Malta 2 to 3°C lower. The summer months tend to be dry, with only one or two wet days expected on average. Daily average sunshine levels out at about 11 hours.

September and even October can remain very warm, but there soon follows a marked drop in temperature, with daily average highs falling to about 19°C (66°F) by November, when there are an average of 22 dry days, coupled with about six hours of sunshine.

Greece

December is the warmest winter month in the Eastern Mediterranean, with the Greek mainland experiencing values of 16°C (61°F). Corfu can expect four to five hours of sunshine, but both the mainland and the islands get 14 to 18 dry days per month.

In Greece and the islands, spring temperatures reach an average maximum of 25°C (78°F) in May, sometimes enhanced by the presence of the sirocco wind from Africa. The summer months can be extremely hot and the summer months are almost totally dry. Ten or more hours of sunshine are expected on average.

The high temperatures can continue well into the autumn and the sirocco may affect the Greek Islands at this time of year, holding average highs at about 29°C (85°F), falling to 19°C (66°F) by November. Greece and the Greek Islands become progressively wetter through the season, with 15 to 17 days by November, when only four to five sunshine hours can be expected. Ferry services are frequently cancelled in winter.

Turkey

The Turkish winter is not particularly warm, with daily average maximum temperatures reaching about 10°C (50°F). Just two or hours of sunshine can be expected on average per day. It is a wet season with only about 12 or 13 dry days per month.

The beginning of spring continues with similar average conditions, but a steady warming-up occurs. By May, daily average maximum temperatures have reached 21°C (70°F), daily sunshine has increased to a more respectable nine hours, and the average number of dry days has risen to about 23.

The summer brings quite hot weather to Turkey, with daily average maximum temperatures climbing to about 28°C (82°F) by August. It is a reasonably dry season, with up to 27 dry days each month; 11 or 12 hours of sunshine can be expected on average.

Autumn sees a rather rapid decline in average maximum temperatures. Values of 15°C (59°F) will be recorded by November. Daily sunshine average values decrease steadily throughout the season, down to just four hours per day on average at the end of November.

Florida, USA

Between December and February, Florida is dry and sunny, with afternoon temperatures at about 25°C (77°F). On average, 24 days of the month are dry with about seven hours of sunshine. The nights are usually cool.

In the months March to May, the average temperature rises to about 28°C (82°F), with about nine hours of sunshine per day. About 22 days of each month are dry.

The summer months from June to August are hot, with average daily maximum temperatures soaring to 31°C (88°F). A lot of rain falls from frequent showers and thunderstorms, and the number of dry days in the month falls on average to about 15, although the sunshine hours stay on average at about nine hours per day. Late summer is the hurricane season in the Gulf of Mexico and the Caribbean, although several years may pass between Florida being seriously affected.

Temperatures remain high from September to November, averaging almost 30°C (86°F) at first. September is the wettest month, with some 11 days being dry on average, but this improves to about

21 days in November. About seven hours of sunshine per day can be expected.

Environment

No matter where you are thinking of buying, think carefully about its physical surroundings – not just in terms of how beautiful it is, but the extent to which it meets your particular needs. If you are buying a holiday home purely for yourself, reflect on the kind of environment that is your ideal – for example, hills and forests or sun and sand?

If you have children, is there enough to keep them occupied? You may be buying in southern Europe, but this does not necessarily preclude you from looking for somewhere with access to good skiing – parts of France, Italy and Spain all have mountainous areas within easy reach if you choose wisely, for example. If you are likely to want the property to generate letting income, consider how attractive the location is to other people as well as to yourselves. You may find a particular town in mid-France an ideal place for a holiday home because you have family there, but other people might find the place unremarkable.

Living somewhere permanently, or even temporarily, is very different from staying there for a week or two in the summer, so if the property is going to serve as a full-time home for any length of time, check out all the local amenities. How close is the nearest supermarket, for example? What about the nearest doctor's surgery, pharmacy, school, garage, computer supplies shop, or whatever else is important to keep your life running as normal?

Remember that the various countries of Europe have very different balances between urban and rural life. According to the United Nations, France can claim just two cities out of the top 100 most populated cities in Europe (Paris at number 8, and Marseille at 46) and the next biggest, Lyon, is way down the list at 130. Spain, by contrast, has six (Madrid at 5, Barcelona at 17, Valencia at 53, Seville at 58, Zaragoza at 71 and Malaga at 84); as does Italy (Rome at 6, Milan at 20, Naples at 32, Turin at 39, Palermo at 59 and Genoa at 62). These cities are bigger than all those in the UK except London (which came in at number 2, after Moscow). City life is much more a part of south European cultures than one might expect. So if you need a regular fix of cosmopolitan flair, consider trying Catalonia (for Barcelona) or even Normandy (where the weather is rather more British in character but at least you are within striking distance of Paris), rather than the rural depths of the Massif Central.

At the same time, be aware that the cities of France, Spain and Italy empty themselves of locals during the month of August and especially around the middle of the month – as everybody ventures to their favoured holiday locations. If you happen to want to buy in one of those locations, be prepared for the crowds every summer, or arrange to be somewhere else and make money from rental.

Accessibility

It may sound blindingly obvious, but it's important for your property to be accessible. Being able to get to it easily will be vital whatever your reasons for buying, but especially so if you're looking to generate income from letting the property out. The travel industry works on the assumption that, as a rule of thumb, a quarter of potential visitors will be put off if they have to travel for more than an hour from the airport at the end of their journey. If the travelling time rises to 90 minutes, half will be deterred from coming. Clearly there will be exceptions to this rule – we would all consider a longer drive if we thought there was something really unusual at the end of it – but if your property is fundamentally nothing special, think long and hard about how distance might affect its earning potential.

Of course it may well be that the only way you can afford the kind of property you want is to look deeper into the wilds of the countryside; or that the particular house you've chosen is high up a mountain, and that is the way you like it; in which case, make sure you are happy that the inconvenience is, for you, a price worth paying.

On a more general note, remember that however attractively priced budget airlines can be, and however much they have opened up new areas for holidaymakers and potential homebuyers, they are not all suddenly flying supersonic. If you add together check-in and check-out times, journey times (see table below) and travel at either end, what seems like a short journey can pretty soon start to feel like an odyssey notwithstanding any delays that might occur along the way.

Some flight times from London Heathrow

City	Flight time from LHR
Paris	1hr 15mins
Barcelona	2hrs
Rome	2hrs 30mins
Malaga	2hrs 45mins
Malta (Valletta)	3hrs 20mins
Tenerife	4hrs 20mins
Cyprus (Larnaca)	4hrs 30mins
Turkey (Izmir)	6–8hrs (indirect)
Bulgaria (Varna)	7hrs 45mins (indirect)
Florida (Orlando)	12hrs 30mins

Consider how much time you would really spend in your dream overseas home, and whether you would repeatedly make trips that length to get there. Remember also that airlines, ferry companies, train operators and road builders have their own priorities, and these may not always coincide with yours. Ryanair's scrap with the EU over Brussels Charleroi airport could have enormous implications for French routes, for example; the airline's chief executive has also made clear already that the company will not be keeping less profitable routes open just for the sake of second-home owners who have bought places on the strength of their proximity to airports.

It may be impossible to insure yourself against every eventuality, but it is definitely worth thinking about worst-case scenarios as you stack up the pros and cons of buying in a particular location: how would you get there if the newly introduced air route disappeared?

Affordability

An obvious financial issue to think about when deciding whether to buy an overseas property – and which one – is how much you can afford. This means doing more than looking round a few property websites, seeing what the headline prices are and then working out how much a UK lender would give you on a buy-to-let mortgage.

For a start, buy-to-let mortgages simply do not exist in the main countries UK second-home seekers want to buy houses in. Second, even if they did, do not make the assumption that you could get as good a level of return on a foreign property as one might, for example, from renting out a property on six-month tenancies in a university town in the UK.

Letting the property out to tourists may well be part of how you make it affordable, but that is a decision you will need to work out for yourself, after a lot of homework into which areas have the best prices, what kinds of properties attract what level of rent, what properties are most in demand, what occupancy levels you might expect, how you would manage the property for letting and the costs of that, and so on. To get a rough idea of rents achievable in France, for example, see the table below.

Unfurnished rents in regions of France (2002)

Region	Apartments – average rent (€ per sq m)	Houses – average rent (€ per sq m)
Paris	16.9	N/a
Île de France	13.0	12.1
Centre	8.0	6.7
West	8.3	6.9
North and East	7.9	7.2
Rhône-Alpes	8.4	8.3
South-east	9.4	9.0
South-west	8.2	7.1

Source: FNIAM

For their part, lenders will not lend on the basis of 'buy to let', so it is important to have plenty of money – rather than just borrowing power – behind you if you are serious about buying a second home. As an approximate figure, one seasoned observer suggests you should ideally have a lump sum of at least £30,000 behind you to start investing in foreign property. Abbey National France generally works with a maximum loan-to-value ratio of 85 per cent, which means you would have to find an initial deposit of 15 per cent plus the additional costs and taxes involved in buying, which can be as much as 12 per cent on top. On a property costing £100,000, that means finding at least £27,000 in hard cash.

If you have substantial equity – as plenty of people who have sold properties in London and the south-east of England in the last few years do – make sure you are then clear about the implications of taking on another property for your monthly disposable income.

To calculate what European lenders think of as monthly afford-ability, you should look at your net income (after tax) and divide it by three. Out of this figure, you need to be able to afford all your fixed monthly outgoings: other mortgages, loans and any maintenance payments. You can also include any credit-card repayments in there too, although lenders generally do not include these in their calculations. Lenders in France and other European countries would consider lending up to the amount of the remainder.

Especially if you are buying somewhere that needs a considerable amount of renovation, be careful not to underestimate the cost of the building work. In many parts of the continent – Tuscany being a classic example – there are strict rules about building techniques and materials, which mean you cannot economise, even if you wanted to.

Building work is not cheap, and it can be particularly hard to keep a lid on costs if you are hundreds of miles away. Many experts recommend entrusting the project management to an experienced local architect or similar professional; this may be expensive, but could save you even more in the long run. Always get quotes from several people wherever possible, and check professionals' credentials carefully. In later chapters we examine some typical costs for renovation projects; the table below shows the rate at which building costs across Europe have been increasing in recent years.

How building costs have changed in the last ten years

Country	percentage increase 2000–2002	percentage increase 1992–2002
EU average	6	24
Spain	4	25
France	8	21 (1993–2002)
Italy	6	20
Portugal	5	25
UK	12	40
Hungary	15	figure not available

Source: Eurostat

A crucial point to remember – and one where countless British buyers have come unstuck in the past – is to factor variations in exchange rates into your calculations. These can have a huge effect on how much the property ends up costing you, both in terms of the size of the initial price agreed and deposit paid and – if you are taking out a euro mortgage – the ensuing monthly repayments.

Say you bought a property for €100,000 at a point when you could get €1.5 to the pound. That translates to a cost of just under £67,000, which you might find affordable. It is more than possible that by the time you complete contracts, the exchange rate will have dropped to 1.3 – which means the property will end up costing closer to £77,000: an increase of £10,000. Changes in currency rates can be particularly significant if you are buying off-plan, because the property might easily not be finished until 18 months after you agree a price.

There are several ways to minimise the effects of such fluctuations. One, if rates are on a downward trend and you have the money at your fingertips, is to buy the currency now and allow it to accrue interest until such time as you need to pay it to the seller.

Another method – more suitable if you are borrowing money or cannot afford to have the full amount tied up for the entire period of waiting – is to arrange what is called a 'forward contract' for foreign currency, via one of the specialist foreign exchange brokers. This way, you can fix an exchange rate for delivery on an agreed date in the future – you can draw money down whenever you want it during the period of the contract, or extend the deal if the construction of the property is delayed, for example. You will normally need to pay 10 per cent of the agreed amount up front, with the remainder payable at the end of the contract. Whichever approach you take will involve a risk, so as with any other kind of investment decision, do plenty of research and take a range of soundings.

Rental incomes

As explained in Chapter 2 and above, making money from renting out overseas property can be fraught with difficulties. The location of your property, the facilities it offers, how well it is presented and how widely it is advertised can all play a part in determining whether or not you get tenants, and how much they are prepared to pay.

The table opposite shows how average rents differ between a range of European countries, illustrating that the cost of renting is enormously cheaper in Portugal and some of the countries hoping to join the EU than it is in the UK or France, for example. Buying property to let out to permanent tenants in most of these countries, while having the advantage of providing a regular income, might not produce a substantial profit.

Rent levels across Europe

Country	Relative price level index (2001)
EU average	100
Greece	77
Spain	75
France	107
Italy	71
Portugal	31
UK	121
Cyprus	91
Czech Republic	20
Poland	26
Slovenia	40
Turkey	22

Source: Eurostat

Holiday lettings

The table below shows a selection of market rents in some typical tourist hotspots. It gives an indication of the levels of income you might expect particular types of property to generate; and illustrates how big the variations in income can be, depending on the location, quality and facilities you can offer visitors.

Examples of tourist rents

Location	Details of property	Low-season rent per week	High-season rent per week
France – Côte d'Azur (Vence)	• Converted former Roman watchtower in the Alpes Maritimes • 15 minutes from Nice • Own pool • Five bedrooms (sleeps 10)	€2,500	€3,850
France – Normandy (Vimoutiers)	• Small, oak-beamed cottage • Two bedrooms (sleeps 4) • Large, shared garden	€195	€290
Spain – Costa del Sol (Marbella)	• Penthouse apartment in a golf complex, overlooking the 18th fairway • Two bedrooms, each with a private terrace (sleeps 4) • Shared pool with sea views	€1,000	€1,200
Spain – Costa Blanca (Torrevieja)	• Ground-floor apartment in *urbanizacion* on outskirts of town	€200	€410

continued overleaf

Examples of tourist rents *(continued)*

Location	Details of property	Low-season rent per week	High-season rent per week
	• Two bedrooms (sleeps 4) • Shared pool		
Italy – Tuscany (Chianti)	• Large, characterful house halfway between Siena and Florence • Set in its own olive grove, with its own pool • Four bedrooms plus ample living space (sleeps 10)	€2,200	€2,800
Italy – Abruzzo (Pescasseroli)	• Medieval house in tiny village in the heart of the Abruzzo National Park • Two hours from Rome, 100km to the sea • Two bedrooms (sleeps 4)	€350	€600
Portugal – Algarve (Quinta da Lago)	• Four-bedroomed air-conditioned villa (sleeps 8) • Private pool and maid service • Borders sixth fairway of golf course	€1,400	€4,000
Portugal – Lisbon Coast (Ericeira)	• Ground floor of rustic cottage, plus annex • 3km from village centre/beach • Two bedrooms (sleeps 4)	€200	€370
USA – Florida central (Davenport)	• Brand-new four-bedroomed, three-bathroomed house (sleeps 8) • In gated community • Private pool • 15 minutes to Disney World	$1,500	$2,000
USA – Florida north west (Destin)	• Two-bedroomed condo (sleeps 4) • In gated development with balcony • Shared pools and use of private beach	$300	$800

Cost of living

The cost of living varies enormously depending on where in the world you live; so if you are thinking about moving abroad permanently, these differences may have a significant impact on how much money you need to have coming in and therefore what type of property you can afford. Few people would choose to retire to Oslo or Zurich, currently ranked as Europe's most expensive cities, for example, unless they were extremely wealthy. Lisbon, the EU's cheapest city, might prove a much more sensible bet.

The table below gives an indication of what a basket of goods and services costing $100 in the USA might cost elsewhere in the world. The figures, compiled by a global web resource for expatriates, are based on everything from the price of bread to the cost of healthcare; they take no account of average earnings or the cost of accommodation, so as to give a simple snapshot of the cost of everyday living

The relative cost of living in different countries: figures are on an index where USA=100

Country	Cost of living (relative to USA)
Australia	114
Austria	130
Belgium	127
Brazil	110
Canada	105
China	127
Colombia	83
Czech Rep	89
Denmark	133
Egypt	109
France	131
Germany	122
Greece	109
Hungary	80
India	93
Ireland	123
Italy	128
Mexico	112
Netherlands	118
New Zealand	101
Poland	100
South Africa	87
Spain	123
Switzerland	167
Thailand	105
UAE (United Arab Emirates)	124
UK	140
USA	100

Source: Expat Forum

(although some figures may represent expatriate lifestyles, when it is often possible to live a good deal more cheaply by 'going local'). Bear in mind that these figures do nothing to illustrate differences in cost of living within countries; life in northern Italy is considerably more expensive than in the south, for example, and cities anywhere tend to be more costly than rural areas.

Healthcare costs

No matter where you're moving to, and at whatever age, healthcare can be a particular source of expense. If you are at, or approaching, retirement age and/or have had any kind of health problems, it could make the difference between whether or not you can afford to live overseas.

The quality of healthcare in most European countries compares well to that provided by the NHS, but it can prove more expensive. The E111 form (or E121 form if you are a pensioner) allows you the same treatment for free that a native person in your new home country would get. However, you may still find yourself facing considerable extra costs. In France, for example, the state only pays for around 70 per cent of health costs and the additional 30 per cent may have to be met by you.

Many expatriates in various countries opt for health insurance, with the most expensive, comprehensive policies costing up to £3,000 a year for a retired couple in Europe. Healthcare is notoriously expensive in the USA, where treatment standards can be outstanding, but only for those who can afford it. A family of four or an older couple retiring to the USA might need to pay up to £10,000 a year for a fairly comprehensive policy.

If you are travelling back and forth rather than staying abroad permanently, make sure that, as an absolute minimum, you are covered by adequate travel insurance – if you are travelling to the USA, ensure its upper medical expenses claim limit is at least $500,000 or preferably more than $1 million. Bear in mind that dental costs can also be higher than in the UK; insurance can be added to some international health plans.

Chapter 4

General advice

The preceding chapters have focused on the ins and outs of buying property abroad, examining why you might want to go down that route, where you might want to buy and how to achieve your dream. Put down on paper, the whole process can seem complicated. But in real life, with the right attitude, a sensible mix of qualified professionals around you, and access to sufficient funds, there is no reason why things should not run as smoothly as they would if you were buying a property in the UK.

Once you have bought a property, even if it is purely for investment purposes, you have taken on a commitment for as long as that property is in your ownership. There are many on-going matters you need consider. If you are letting the property, you must learn to excel as a long-distance landlord or, if you are using one, as manager of your managing agent. The chances are that the same will be true if you have bought a holiday home, unless you are wealthy enough to leave it empty for long periods while you are not able to visit.

If you are restoring or extending a property, either as a holiday home or a more permanent base, you must quickly develop managerial and financial expertise, and probably your linguistic abilities, in order to deal effectively with your appointed contractors, or at the very least, the person you have appointed as project manager.

This chapter provides information on the resources you are likely to need when buying property abroad, and advice on issues to consider if you plan to live overseas long-term. For specific details on individual countries, see the chapters in Part II.

Useful contacts

Lawyers
The Law Society of England and Wales* operates a searchable database of solicitors operating in this country. It includes those

who qualified here and also 'registered European lawyers' (EU lawyers working in this country and registered with the Law Society) and 'registered foreign lawyers' (registered as qualified to go into partnership with English/Welsh or EU lawyers).

The database allows you to search by location and specialism, and if you type in the relevant country it will list UK law firms that have offices there. If you want to find solicitors practising wholly outside England and Wales, these are listed in the Law Society's printed *Directory of Solicitors and Barristers.*

To find foreign lawyers in other countries, ask around for recommendations or try one of the international legal directories. The Foreign Office (see 'Government bodies' on pages 56–8) maintains a list of English-speaking lawyers, translators and doctors in countries where the UK has diplomatic representation.

Notaries

In France, Spain and other European countries the notary (*notaire* or *notario*) is the public official who checks title deeds, draws up sale contracts and records the formal deed of sale. However, it is not the notary's job to advise or protect the interests of either the buyer or the vendor, which is why you still need to appoint a lawyer. If you need to find a notary or check out a notary's credentials, contact the notaries' representative body in the country in question. The Conférence des Notariats de l'Union Européenne★, which represents around 35,000 notaries, covers ten European countries: Austria, Belgium, France, Germany, Greece, Italy, Luxembourg, Netherlands, Portugal and Spain. Its website, which is mainly in French, has links to the notaries' professional organisations in each individual country.

Estate agents

You are likely to find an estate agent through personal recommendation or by travelling around the area you are interested in. If in doubt, or to check up on an estate agent, you may wish to contact the Confédération Européenne d'Immobilier (CEI)★. It represents more than 25,000 estate agents across Europe, and aims to stand for the estate agency profession; its members subscribe to a code of conduct. The CEI covers 13 countries: Austria, France, Germany, Greece, Hungary, Ireland, Italy, Netherlands, Portugal, Romania,

Slovak Republic, Spain and the UK, and its website contains links to the relevant national estate agency bodies in each country.

In the UK, the Federation of Overseas Property Developers, Agents and Consultants (FOPDAC)★ represents estate agents, property developers and specialist consultants (including lawyers and mortgage brokers) who are active in the international property markets and who aim 'to conduct their activities in a manner which seeks to protect the interests of those who have decided to purchase, or sell, a property overseas. Membership of the Federation is restricted to companies or individuals whose probity is beyond reasonable question'. The body has been in existence since 1973. Its website includes a full list of FOPDAC members and relevant contact details.

If you are thinking of buying a timeshare, make sure the companies you deal with are members of the Organisation for Timeshare in Europe (OTE)★, whose members operate to a voluntary code of conduct. Its website includes a full list of OTE members and links to their websites. For information on individual companies contact the Timeshare Consumers' Association★, which keeps a tab on rogue operators.

Useful contacts in Florida include the Florida Association of Realtors★ and the Florida Association of Mortgage Brokers (FAMB)★.

Architects and surveyors

For major building works requiring an architect, you are likely to want to employ someone local, but you may wish to talk to the UK-based Royal Institute of British Architects (RIBA)★ too – both to get an idea of how best to make use of the services of an architect, and to get help finding one. The organisation has an online database of over 4,000 registered practices, and this does feature practices based in other countries as well as in the UK.

The Architects' Council of Europe★ represents around 350,000 architects across the European Economic Area and EU accession states. The website also includes links to architects' national representative bodies in each country, which should be able to offer guidance on finding a reputable architect. These include:

- France: Conseil National de l'Ordre des Architectes (CNOA)★
- Italy: Consiglio Nazionale degli Architetti★

- Portugal: Ordem Dos Arquitectos★
- Spain: Consejo Superior de los Colegios de Arquitectos de España (CSCAE)★.

The Royal Institution of Chartered Surveyors (RICS)★ has branches throughout Europe (Austria, Belgium, Cyprus, Czech Republic, Denmark, France, Germany, Greece, Hungary, Italy, Malta, Netherlands, Poland, Portugal, Russian Federation, Spain, Switzerland); and the rest of the world (including South Africa, the United Arab Emirates and the USA). The RICS website has links to contact details for each individual country's branch.

Embassies/consulates/chambers of commerce

For general information about countries, embassies and consulates may offer advice and provide information on subjects, such as visas, relevant to people considering moving abroad. They can also help put you in touch with relevant government departments and be of assistance once you are installed in your new home. Chambers of commerce can be important resources if you are looking for particular kinds of companies or tradespeople when abroad, and if you are thinking of setting up in business yourself. Details of consulates in different countries are provided in the 'Addresses and websites' section at the end of this book.

Government bodies

The Foreign and Commonwealth Office★ publishes a list of UK embassy and consulate contacts in foreign countries, as well as producing country-specific advice for people considering travelling or moving abroad.

If you are planning to move abroad, you may find the British Consulate useful in certain circumstances; its role is to 'do everything they properly can to help British people in difficulty abroad'. It can:

- issue emergency passports, and in some places full passports
- contact relatives and friends and ask them to help you with money or tickets
- tell you how to transfer money
- in an emergency, cash you a sterling cheque worth up to £100 in local currency, if supported by a valid banker's card

- help you get in touch with local lawyers, interpreters and doctors
- arrange for next-of-kin to be told of an accident or a death and advise on procedures
- visit you if you have been arrested or put in prison, and arrange for messages to be sent to relatives and friends
- put you in touch with organisations that help trace missing persons
- speak to the local authorities on your behalf
- only as a last resort, in exceptional circumstances, and as long as you meet certain strict rules, give you a loan to get you back to the UK, but only if there is no-one else who can help you.

UK law says consulates must charge fees for some services – the table of fees, last updated in October 2003, is available on the Foreign and Commonwealth Office website.

The Inland Revenue* produces tax advice for people considering a move abroad, or buying a property that might produce income liable for taxation. The Centre for Non-Residents (CNR):

- handles operational and technical work (including compliance) relating to non-resident individuals, non-resident trusts and certain non-resident companies
- operates and provides advice on all aspects of the Non-Resident Landlords Scheme
- handles claims and applications for relief by all categories of non-residents under double-taxation treaties
- considers individual entitlement to UK personal allowances
- provides guidance on the residence and domicile status of individuals
- provides guidance about UK National Insurance liabilities while you are abroad
- provides guidance about EC Regulations and bilateral convention rules on Social Security
- handles operational and technical work (including compliance) relating to transfers of assets abroad.

As a starting point, the leaflets to read are:

- *IR20 – Residents and non-residents. Liability to tax in the UK*
- *IR138 – Living or retiring abroad? A guide to UK tax on your UK*

income and pension
- *IR139 – Income from abroad? Guide to UK tax on overseas income*
- *IR140 – Non-resident landlords, their agents and tenants.*

The Department for Work and Pensions (DWP)★ provides information about entitlement to state benefits while overseas, and the Pension Service (part of the DWP) provides more detailed information about retiring abroad. For further information and to find local contact details to discuss matters further, follow the links on the DWP website.

The Department of Health (DoH)★ produces guidance on accessing health services abroad. For trips of less than three months' duration within the EU, an E111 form or (if you are retired) an E121 form will give you the same rights to treatment as a national of that country. This does not mean treatment is free, though – for example in France only around 70 per cent of health costs are reimbursed by the state. Further information on healthcare provision in the countries most popular with UK property buyers is provided in chapters 5 to 8; for comprehensive details, contact the countries in question using the contact details provided on the DoH website.

Living abroad

Integration with the community

If you are planning to live full-time in your new property, your future life will depend to a great extent on your willingness or otherwise to integrate with the local population. Studies of the phenomenon of UK residents moving abroad have found that language is the single biggest indicator of the extent to which such people integrate with local communities.

In a study of Britons who retired to the Costa del Sol, Tuscany, the Algarve and Malta, for example, researchers from the University of Sussex found widely differing patterns of linguistic involvement amongst British retirees in the four regions. Those who had retired to Tuscany displayed by far the greatest (self-defined) fluency, with almost 75 per cent of those questioned describing themselves as 'very fluent' or 'quite fluent', as compared to percentages in the 20s and 30s for the other locations.

There is more to integration, or lack of it, than linguistic skills, however. In a recent project on British people living in the Île de France, a researcher from the University of Sheffield identified no fewer than six categories of study participants, whose educational, professional and social backgrounds all contributed to fairly distinct ways of experiencing life in and around Paris. These groups ranged from 'established British families', 'young British families', 'professionals' and 'graduates' to 'bohemians' and 'mixed-relationship migrants'; the latter group, by virtue of mixed marriages, being 'by far the most integrated and assimilated of all expatriates'.

This appears to indicate that cultural and social background will determine the level of success when opting to live in property abroad. Much has been written about the insular nature of the British community on the Costa del Sol – the stereotype being that the region is full of working-class families who have sold up and moved to Spain for sun, sand and cheap cigarettes, and have hardly assimilated with local culture.

One sociologist from the University of Aberdeen who has studied expatriate communities recognises the insularity of UK residents who live on the Spanish Costas, but argues that this is not entirely of their own making: 'British permanent migrants are not expected to integrate, are not enabled to learn the language, are not included in the local structures of control, and are not included through either work or family ... however, the migrants themselves construct and maintain a marginal community, and even an economy, which serves to marginalise them further.'

Whether UK residents who buy property abroad should be making more of an effort to integrate in the country's cultural and political life is a matter for debate. For some, isolation is the objective. But for many, part of the mental preparation is to think ahead about how to develop and sustain social networks, whether as a permanent expatriate or a regular visitor.

Work and schooling are major integration channels for expatriates. This can make integration for part-timers, retired people and 'empty nesters' a particular challenge. Networking with other expatriates can, however, often occur through clubs and communities, sometimes centred round a particular interest such as golf, art or music.

Whatever your personality, try to be confident that the property you buy, the place it is in and the people amongst whom you will be living all 'fit' your character. A different climate, new landscape and new language might be ideal, but if you are unhappy or depressed to begin with, do not expect a move abroad to solve every problem – in some cases it could make them worse. One English building consultant who manages property restorations in France for British clients says that, having observed many people preparing to emigrate, his biggest worry is that the vast majority of them are doing it for all the wrong reasons: 'I would say 90 per cent of the people I've come across have got something wrong in their life,' he says. 'They've left their job, got divorced or whatever, and by moving abroad they're trying to get their lives together. Many of them are looking for something unattainable, and they're throwing away a lot by coming to a place that fundamentally they know nothing about. You can live wherever you want, but you cannot run away from yourself.'

Transferring work skills abroad

If you are below retirement age and plan to move abroad, the chances are you will need to earn some money once you get there. Depending on the kind of work you do, one potential barrier to earning a living in your new home is whether or not you can get your qualifications recognised. Comparability of professional diplomas, whether for regulated or unregulated professions, can be a problem.

Within the European Economic Area (EEA), your diploma, certificate or qualifications should, in theory, be recognised as they stand. Freedom of movement applies in Austria, Belgium, Denmark, Finland, France, Germany, Greece, Iceland, Ireland, Italy, Luxembourg, the Netherlands, Norway, Portugal, Spain, Sweden and the UK. However, recognition is not granted automatically; applications are considered individually.

The General System for Mutual Recognition of Professional Qualifications is operated by means of two European Directives, which between them cover all regulated professions and occupations. Anyone who is recognised as fully qualified to practise a regulated profession in one EEA country is allowed to practise that profession in another. Regulated professions are those that are legally restricted by the state or by professional bodies to people with certain qualifications; examples include medicine, law, accountancy and teaching. 'Fully qualified' means having gained a professional qualification after at least three years of higher-level post-secondary education.

For unregulated professions, recognition of qualifications is up to the competent authority in the host country. You can prepare in advance by obtaining a recognised translation and certified copies of your diploma (with original stamp and signature) and any other documents that support your case.

Within the EEA, the general rule is that nationals of other EEA countries are subject to the same conditions as nationals of the host country. However, if a profession is regulated in the host country but not where the qualification was awarded, the host authorities may require evidence of two years' professional experience.

Applications for recognition must be sent to the relevant institution, which is usually the ministry of education. You will probably be expected to provide your birth certificate, evidence of degrees, diplomas and professional qualifications, a certificate of good health and evidence of sufficient financial standing. The relevant authority has four months in which to process your application and make a decision. You have the right to appeal.

For seven professions – medicine, nursing, dentistry, midwifery, veterinary surgery, pharmacy and architecture – there are directives that ensure a direct comparison between qualifications and no restrictions on practising in any other EEA country. The only additional requirement that can be imposed is a language course.

If you are planning to travel to or from a country outside the EEA, the status of your qualifications and professional standing will be up to the authorities of the two countries concerned. For advice, contact the ministries of education and relevant professional bodies in both countries.

You can obtain a direct comparison between your academic qualifications and those recognised in your host country from the branch in that country of the National Academic Recognition Information Centre (NARIC)★. This is an international network and is available in many locations throughout the world, including EU member states. To compare vocational qualifications, contact the European Centre for the Development of Vocational Training (CEDEFOP)★.

Regardless of what qualifications you hold, language can be the biggest stumbling block to gainful employment. Bear in mind also that conversing in the workplace involves sophisticated levels of vocabulary and grammar. In the absence of high-level language skills, many UK expatriates earn money from the properties they own – perhaps by running a guest house or letting out part of the property to tourists or permanent tenants. Others earn some money by teaching English, or run businesses aimed at other expatriates; this has particularly been the case in southern Spain.

If you do want to set up a business, make sure you do not fall foul of local bureaucracy in the process. Paperwork overseas is often more strict than we are used to in the UK. In most of southern Europe all small businesses must be registered with the local chamber of commerce, for example, and there can be fees due up front (see later chapters for more details).

European Employment Services Network

As a member of the EU/EEA, the Employment Service in the UK has details of vacancies throughout the EU supplied to it through the European Employment Services Network (EURES)*. This is a partnership between all of the employment services in the EU/EEA, to support free movement of workers.

The EURES system facilitates the circulation of vacancies and enables access of up-to-date information on living and working conditions in each EU/EEA member state via a computer network. There are about 500 specially trained staff throughout the EU/EEA who administer the EURES system. They are called Euroadvisers and they specialise in the practical issues surrounding employment in the member states. Euroadvisers can be contacted via local Employment Service Jobcentres.

Vacancies on the EURES system, and details of local contacts for each country, can be found on the EURES website. The search criteria can be refined to specific professions and regions within countries.

Drawing pensions abroad

If you spend part of the year anywhere overseas but remain a UK resident, you will get your state pension paid in full. In most cases, if you retire abroad you will be entitled to some form of UK state pension and can continue to claim this even if you settle overseas permanently. Around one million people currently claim the state pension abroad.

But caution is needed. To receive pension rises you must live in the European Economic Area or one of the other 20 or so countries with which the UK has a social security deal. Elsewhere the pension may be frozen. So, someone retiring to Canada or Australia, for instance, would start off receiving the same amount as they would have done if they had stayed in the UK, but the pension would not increase with rising living costs and so its value would, over time, diminish.

Personal and company pensions will generally continue to be paid in full and overseas pensioners are, on the whole, entitled to any rises. But check in advance, because some company schemes, for example, will pay a pension only to a UK bank. Bear in mind the costs of transferring the money between currencies, and the fact that the value of your pension is subject to the vagaries of the exchange rate.

If you are going overseas before drawing a private or company pension, you may want to look into getting the whole fund transferred to a pension scheme in your new home country. International transfers are a complex area, though – and need Inland Revenue approval. Take independent advice.

Government advice for anyone retiring abroad

The following is the UK government's official advice to anyone considering retiring overseas.

As an EEA national, you have the right to live in any EEA country. If you are thinking of retiring to a non-EEA country, speak to the British Consul abroad and the foreign consulate in the UK.

Work out what your retirement income will be; this will help you work out how best to provide for your future as well as making decisions about your current life. Remember to allow for exchange-rate fluctuations and inflation.

Before you go

- **Request an UK State pension forecast** A retirement pension forecast tells you, in today's money values, the amount of state pension you have earned already and the amount you can expect to receive at state pension age. Obtain form BR19 from your local social security office or contact the Retirement Pension Forecasting and Advice Unit (RPFA)★. If you wish to obtain a pension forecast from abroad you should contact the Inland Revenue★ and ask for form CA3638. You will still receive your state pension on retirement (provided you have reached state pension age) if you live overseas, but it may not be increased annually if you are going to live outside the EEA or if you reside within the EEA but are not covered by EC social security regulations.

- **Find out about your tax liability abroad** Whatever your age (for further information on this, see relevant sections in the following chapters), remember that if you retire abroad you will still have to pay UK tax on income you receive from the UK, over and above your age-related personal allowance. If you go to live in a country that has a double taxation agreement with the UK, you may be able to pay less tax. See the Inland Revenue leaflet *Income tax and pensioners* (IR121) for further information.

- **Think about offshore banking** Once you are no longer resident in the UK, different taxation rules apply depending on your country of residence. You may want to seek independent tax advice and consider the benefits of offshore banking before you retire abroad. An offshore bank account can play an important role in helping to minimise your tax liabilities. Additional benefits may include asset protection, estate planning, confidentiality, security and the ability to deal with English-speaking professionals who understand culture sensitivities and the unique needs of expatriates.

- **Think about welfare rights** If you are going to another country in the EEA, or to a country that has a social security agreement with the UK, you may be able to claim a benefit that you would not normally get abroad. Or you may be able to claim a benefit of that country. The benefits you receive in the UK may also be affected by your move abroad. Each benefit has different rules and some UK benefits cannot be exported, for example housing benefit. For further information see the Department for Work and Pensions leaflet *Going Abroad and Social Security Benefits* (GL29).

- **For countries within the EEA** see leaflet *Your social security insurance, benefits and health care rights in the European Community,* *and in Iceland, Liechtenstein and Norway* (SA29). The rules that co-ordinate member states' social security schemes also cover Switzerland.

- **If you are going outside of the EEA**, bear in mind that the UK has reciprocal social security agreements with a long list of other countries. The reference numbers of the leaflets explaining what these agreements mean for you are in brackets after the country names, and can be obtained from the DWP*: Barbados (SA43), Bermuda (SA23), Canada (SA20), Cyprus (SA12), Guernsey (SA4), Israel (SA14), Jamaica (SA27), Jersey (SA4), Malta (SA11), Mauritius (SA38), New Zealand (SA8), Philippines (SA42), Switzerland (SA6), Turkey (SA22), USA (SA33) and Yugoslavia (SA17) (this applies to the Republics of the former Yugoslavia).

- **Find out about health costs abroad** If you go to a country in the EEA and you are entitled to UK state retirement pension, incapacity benefit at the long-term rate, widows' benefits or bereavement benefit, you need form E121. When you ask the DWP about getting your pension paid to you in another EEA country, it will automatically check to see if you can get the E121 as well. If so, you will receive the same free or reduced-cost medical treatment as a qualified pensioner of the country you are in, under its state healthcare scheme. You are also strongly advised to get health insurance to cover private medical and dental treatment, and medical repatriation to the UK.

- **Let people know your change of address** Let your social security office, the Inland Revenue National Insurance Contributions Office – International Services, and the DWP know when you are going to leave and give them your address abroad. Let them know if you later change your address. If you come back to the UK, let them know that too. Then if anything needs to be done about your contributions or benefit rights, it can be done straight away.

When you arrive

- **Register with the local authorities** This will give you access to the local welfare services after a short period of time. If you are moving to another EEA country you must apply for a residence permit within three months of arrival.

- **Register with the British Consulate** This will help the Consul keep in touch with you if you get into difficulties, or in the case of an emergency abroad. In countries with large expatriate communities the Consulate may also have a fact sheet to help retired UK expatriates settle in.
- **Ensure your passport is valid** Fill in the next-of-kin details on the back page. If your passport is about to expire apply to the British Consulate to have it renewed. For EEA countries your residence permit also serves as an identity document, so you do not need to carry your passport around with you all the time.
- **Open a foreign bank account** Within the EEA you can apply for a non-resident bank account on arrival. Once your residence permit has been granted – usually after three to six months – you can open a normal bank account. In many countries, your retirement pension can be paid directly into your bank account there.
- **Learn the local language** Try to fit in with the local community. Hospital and local welfare services staff will not usually speak English. You will find day-to-day life much easier if you can make yourself understood.
- **Make a will** If you die intestate abroad this can cause great difficulties for your heirs. Seek professional legal advice. You may require separate wills for assets and property held in the UK and other countries. Your local British Consul can provide a list of English-speaking lawyers who can assist you. (See pages 145–9 for further details on the particular importance of this in Spain and Portugal.)
- **Check local traffic regulations** Driving is permitted on a valid UK licence in EEA countries. You will need to be fully insured. You may be required to exchange your UK licence for an EEA national licence once you have gained resident status. Licences are valid for 5 years from 45 to 70 years old and two years thereafter. For other countries you will also need to take an International Driving Permit (IDP), which must be obtained before you leave the UK.
- **Find out about British associations, clubs, publications and charity organisations** for the expatriate English-speaking community. Lists of these can be obtained from your local British Consul.

- **Keep your vote** To vote in UK elections your name must appear on the electoral register. Once registered as an overseas elector, you will be able to vote in Parliamentary elections and European Parliamentary elections in the UK, but not in local government elections or the elections for the Scottish Parliament, the Welsh Assembly and the Northern Ireland Assembly). You can register to vote as an overseas elector for up to 15 years after you were last registered in the UK. To register contact the electoral registration officer at the local council where you were last registered as an elector when living in the UK. For further information see the Electoral Commission★ website.

Schools

Later chapters include brief descriptions of the education systems in the countries most popular with UK holiday home buyers – should you decide to make your family's relationship with the country more permanent. If you would prefer your child or children to be educated in English, there are a range of English-language schools across Europe. To find out more contact The European Council of International schools★.

Part II

Countries

Part II

Chapter 5

France

You can travel around France for decades and never really feel that you know it, so spacious and diverse is its geography and so regionally distinct are its people. Many British visitors, even on the strength of limited exposure to parts of France, fall uncompromisingly in love with the place.

Where to buy

Half a million Britons already own homes in France, and pockets of the north and south-west now have significant expatriate communities. From châteaux to derelict barns, there are properties to suit every pocket, in locations ranging from magnificent cities to splendid rural isolation. From relatively wet and windswept Brittany in the north, to sun-drenched Provence and snow-capped Savoy, France really does have something to offer everyone. It is ultimately a question of finding an area that appeals to your taste and lifestyle – and then the homework really starts.

Brittany

The defiantly Celtic region of Brittany is more like a country within a country than simply a French *département*. Formerly an independent duchy, Brittany was incorporated into France in 1532, but roughly 1 per cent of Brittany's 28 million inhabitants still speak Breton, a separate language with strong links to Welsh and Cornish; in parts of the region, the black-and-white-striped Breton flag flies and signposts are bilingual.

Brittany is famed more for its wild, rugged coastline than for its weather, which betters that of the south coast of England, but only just. The northern and western stretches alternate between steep

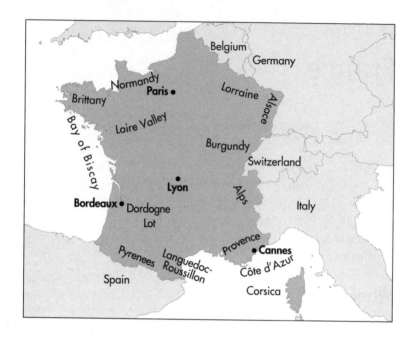

cliffs and sandy coves, with evocatively named stretches including the emerald, pink granite and heather coasts. Like its British counterpart, Cornwall, cider, seafood, smugglers and Arthurian legend all form part of Brittany's rich heritage.

Some of the highest property prices in Brittany are in the main towns and resorts, including St Malo, whose dramatic ramparts mark it out as the most fascinating and historic trading port in the region; Quimper, which has a fine Gothic cathedral and is the centre of the Breton faience pottery industry; half-timbered Dinan; and Dinard.

Further inland, in what the Bretons call the *argoat,* are villages interspersed with wood, heathland and river estuaries, and a plethora of cottages and farms ripe for renovation. Northern Finistère (the north-western part of the region) and inland areas of Morbihan (inland of Lorient and the prehistoric menhirs at Carnac) are good bets if you want to find a shell to restore.

What you can get for your money

Price	Location	Description	State of repair
€30,000	Josselin (Morbihan)	• Two-roomed country house built in 1750 • Internal space of 114sq m and 180sq m of land	Total renovation needed
€57,000	Plougourvest (Finistère)	• Detached stone mill, mainly 19th century, on four floors • Attached outbuilding • Total 280sq m plus 7,000sq m of land	Roof replaced but otherwise complete renovation needed
€66,000	Languidic (Morbihan)	• Three-bedroomed semi-detached house with convertible loft • Outbuildings and garage • 4,000sq m of land	Partially renovated
€162,000	Plumelliau (Morbihan)	• Substantial three-bedroomed, house • Two bathrooms • Two large outbuildings plus garage • 4,000sq m of land	Main house already restored
€181,000	Taule nr Morlaix (Finistère)	• Semi-detached four-bedroomed stone house • Outbuildings • 1,100sq m of land	Main house renovated; outbuildings could be converted into gîtes

Normandy

Like Brittany, its western neighbour, Normandy offers a mixture of maritime, urban and rural pleasures, but all in all it is a rather more sophisticated package. Cultural treasures litter the region – from Mont-St-Michel, the stunning Gothic icon that rises 80 metres from the waves at the end of a causeway, to Monet's garden at Giverny, Richard the Lionheart's castle at Les Andelys, the windswept Second World War beaches, the Bayeux Tapestry and Rouen's magnificent twelfth-century Cathedral de Notre-Dame.

There are beautiful coastal towns, from the harbour of Honfleur to the Norman Riviera at Deauville and Trouville; and, further inland, the rolling, agricultural hinterland (known as the Bocage) that feeds the region's addiction to cream, butter and cheese, and produces an abundance of fruit, some of which becomes Calvados, the delicious local apple brandy.

Many of the more fashionable, somewhat overdeveloped, coastal resorts have seen property prices rise steeply in recent years, thanks to Parisian weekenders. There are, however, still bargains to be had in the more pastoral regions, where small market towns and hamlets of half-timbered houses vie with stone-and-slate cottages and farm buildings for bargain hunters' attention.

What you can get for your money

Price	Location	Description	State of repair
€23,000	Sourdeval	• Detached stone house on two floors • 1,500sq m of land	Complete renovation needed, including connection of water and electricity
€30,000	Grandcamp-Maisy	• One-bedroomed flat in a typical fisherman's house • 20m from the sea	Completely renovated
€57,000	La Ferte Mace	• Ancient farmhouse • Outbuildings and courtyard • 2,600sq m of land	Needs complete renovation
€108,000	Flers	• Six-bedroomed farmhouse built around 1800 • 240sq m (including 38sq m living room) • Outbuildings and 4,200sq m of land	Needs partial renovation
€192,000	Launay	• Three-bedroomed, half-timbered detached house built 1850, in a small hamlet • Over 120sq m, with 33sq m living/dining room, and 27sq m conservatory • 2,774sq m enclosed wooded garden	Completely renovated

Languedoc-Roussillon

With budget airlines now flying to Nîmes, Montpellier, Carcassonne and Perpignan, not to mention Toulouse (which is outside the region but easily accessible), there are few areas of France so geared up for an influx of British property buyers as Languedoc-Roussillon. The combined territories of Languedoc and Roussillon include five *départements*: Aude, Gard, Hérault,

Pyrénées-Oriental and Lozère – the first four of which enjoy the sunny climates and Mediterranean coastlines that make for prime second-home territory.

The name *languedoc* comes from *langue d'oc* – a reference to the ancient language, also known as Occitan, that once spread into Spain and north-west Italy, and is still spoken and taught in parts of southern France. Occitan culture helps give this corner of the republic a somewhat Catalan air – and it is indeed much closer to Barcelona than to Paris. Historically the area was considered a backwater for centuries after incorporation into France, which occurred in the wake of the Albigensian Crusades, waged against the Cathars – a back-to-basics Catholic sect declared heretics by Pope Innocent III in the early thirteenth century.

More recently, wine growing and the development of grand, modern and forward-looking cities such as Montpellier, Toulouse and Perpignan have helped regenerate the region, as has the growth of purpose-built holiday resorts such as La Grande Motte, Cap d'Agde, Port Leucate and Port Bacarès.

What you can get for your money

Price	Location	Description	State of repair
€60,000	Aude	• Small two-bedroomed village house with attic • No land	Minor repairs needed; attic could be converted
€70,000	Perpignan	• Third floor, one-bedroomed apartment in city centre • Covered balcony • Allocated parking	No work necessary
€100,000	Le Barcarès	• Three-bedroomed house in the style of a round fishing hut • On a complex including pool, gym, restaurant etc. • Letting agency on site if required	Newly built
€890,000	La Grande Motte	• Architect designed four-bedroomed house over three floors (260sq m) • Four bathrooms • Overlooks 18th hole of a golf course • Pool • Includes two one-bedroomed apartments • 700sq m of land	Newly built

But you need not restrict yourself to modern resort villas. There are plenty of beautiful towns and villages, as well as the usual isolated farmhouses and cottages, to be found in the region, and sophisticated apartments in the cities.

Provence/Côte d'Azur

The Provence region, with its mountains, sandy beaches and warm climate, is one of the most popular areas in the whole country – second only to Paris. Resorts such as St-Tropez and Ste-Maxime attract royalty and celebrities, and it is not hard to see why – the region enjoys 300 days of sunshine per year and has a spectacular coastline with white sandy beaches, craggy cliffs, tranquil bays and numerous exotic islands. The interior is filled with vine-covered fields, hilltop villages and olive groves.

Historically, the region has been a major crossroads for different civilisations, and has a wealth of fantastic towns to show for it, including Avignon, Arles, Orange and Aix-en-Provence – considered by many French people to be the jewel in their country's crown. And then there are the cities: Marseille, France's second city – a down-at-heel, cosmopolitan hotchpotch of a port; and Nice, the infuriating and exuberant capital of the Riviera.

If money is no object and Cannes or the Cap d'Antibes are your idea of a good time, there is no shortage of million-pound pads to be found on the Côte d'Azur, along with bijou apartments in upmarket villa complexes. The area is so rammed with tourists during the summer that anyone with more than a garden shed to rent out is guaranteed bookings.

For the less well-heeled and those looking for a bit of peace of quiet, the landscapes of Provence and the Côte d'Azur are actually extremely varied, from rocky inlets with parasol pines and turquoise water, to the Camargue plains, Vaucluse's vineyards and the thyme-and-lavender-scented plateaux of Haute-Provence.

Wherever you go prices are high, relative to neighbouring regions, but Marseille and Nice offer excellent bases for the more urban émigré or landlord. If you head away from the coast and go far enough off the beaten track there are still affordable homes to be had, for example in the medieval hill villages of the Haut Var.

What you can get for your money

Price	Location	Description	State of repair
€74,000	Sillans la Cascade (Haut Var)	• Village house on four levels • 100sq m plus cellar	Needs total renovation
€100,000	La Garde Freinet	• One-bedroomed mezzanine apartment • Private gardens including pool and tennis courts • 15km from the sea	Very good
€123,000	Nice	• Fourth-floor 45sq m studio flat in the city centre • Balcony • Three-year tenancy agreement in place	Very good
€318,000	Near Draguignan, Haut Var	• Four-bedroomed village house built in 1750 • 240sq m of living space and 80sq m cellar • 16sq m of terraces • Panoramic views	Very good
€885,000	Ste-Maxime	• Three-storey, three-bedroomed villa with views • Pool • Electronic gate, alarm, air-conditioning, fireplace etc.	Excellent

Dordogne/Lot

What the British call the Dordogne, the French call Périgord, and the serious property hunter should be aware that the Dordogne is, in fact, just the most famous of several rivers around whose banks nestle a green and wooded paradise of farmland, rolling hills and sleepy, often unspoilt, towns and villages.

The Vézère, Dordogne, Lot and Aveyron rivers, all of which drain into the mighty Garonne, create a beautiful and largely homogenous landscape that stretches from Limoges in the north to Toulouse in the south. The region is one of the gastronomic centres of France, celebrated among other things for its foie gras, duck, truffles and mushrooms, for the vineyards of Médoc, and for great local wines from Bergerac, Monbazillac and Cahors.

It is also brimming with history: the French and English fought over the region for 300 years in the Middle Ages, so the region is dotted with castles, bastide towns (walled and gated fortified settlements) and fortified churches. The valleys are also known as the 'birthplace of art', thanks to numerous breathtaking cave paintings, the most famous of which can be found at Lascaux. Sarlat and Rocamadour are among the region's towns and villages that are now firmly printed on every tourist map. But there are many lesser-known places just as likely to produce a gem of a barn, cottage or village house – with bargains more likely in the rather less explored Lot valley, and southward towards the Aveyron.

What you can get for your money

Price	Location	Description	State of repair
€67,000	Souillac	• Semi-detached, three-storey house • Ground-floor shop • Three one-bedroom apartments upstairs	Needs renovation
€84,000	Le Pizou	• Three-bedroomed house built in 1930 • 120sq m • Wooded garden and 2,000sq m of land	Needs renovation
€99,000	Rocamadour	• Detached barn on two levels, floor measurement 25m by 7.5m, plus 3,000sq m of land	Complete internal renovation needed
€150,000	Montpou	• Three-bedroomed house on two floors (110sq m) • Two bathrooms • 10m by 5m pool • 7,300sq m garden	Fully converted
€228,000	Verteillac	• Five-bedroomed house (130sq m) • Two adjoining barns • 0.2-hectare garden and 2500sq m of land	Partially restored

The Alps

The French Alps offer scenery as dramatic as can be found anywhere in Europe, and as a result are a big draw for tourists – whether they are skiers in the winter or hill walkers in the summer. The region between Sisteron in the south and Lake Geneva in the north features no fewer than four national or regional parks – Ecrins, Queyras, Vanoise and Vercors – with the pleasant modern city of Grenoble nestling between the unspoilt Chartreuse and Vercors massifs.

To the north and east, the Savoie and Haute-Savoie *départements* showcase France's world-famous skiing resorts, including Val d'Isère, Tignes, Chamonix, Courchevel, Méribel and Megève. For non-skiers too, there are plenty of beautiful towns and villages on and between the mountains – such as Annecy, Samoëns, Briançon and lofty St-Véran, which at more than 2,000 metres above sea level lays claim to being the highest village in Europe.

Property prices are at the high end of the scale, unsurprisingly given the touristic appeal of the region – but if all you need is to stash your ski gear and smarten yourself up before après-ski, it is still possible to find a place without breaking the bank.

What you can get for your money

Price	Location	Description	State of repair
€55,000	La Plagne	• 30sq m one-bedroomed apartment • Balcony, ski store and cellar	Good
€220,000	Chamonix	• 43sq m apartment • In a chalet surrounded by gardens and woods, with views of Mont Blanc • Garage, cellar, large balcony	Good
€310,000	Lac du Bourget	• Large four double-bedroomed house • Garage, cellar and workshop • One hour from Geneva	Good
€410,000	Haute-Savoie	• Early 20th-century stone chalet hotel • 19 bedrooms plus public rooms and three cellars • Adjoining two-bedroomed chalet • All rooms with balconies	Main house could be converted into apartments

Getting to France

By air

bmi flies from Aberdeen to Toulouse; Belfast City to Nice and Paris Charles de Gaulle (CDG); Cardiff to Paris CDG; Edinburgh to Nice, Paris CDG and Toulouse; Glasgow to Nice, Paris CDG and Toulouse; Leeds Bradford to Nice and Paris CDG; London Heathrow to Nice and Paris CDG; Manchester to Nice, Paris CDG and Toulouse; and Teesside to Nice and Paris CDG.

bmibaby flies from East Midlands to Nice, Paris CDG and Toulouse.

British Airways flies from Belfast City to Paris CDG; Birmingham to Bordeaux, Lyon, Nice, Paris CDG and Toulouse; Bristol to Paris CDG; Edinburgh to Lyon and Paris CDG; Glasgow to Paris CDG; London City to Paris CDG; London Gatwick to Bordeaux, Marseille, Montpellier, Nantes, Nice, Paris CDG, Toulon and Toulouse; London Heathrow to Lyon, Nice and Paris CDG; and Manchester to Lyon, Nice and Paris CDG.

easyJet flies from Bristol to Nice; Liverpool to Nice and Paris CDG; London Gatwick to Marseille, Nice and Toulouse; London Luton to Nice and Paris CDG; London Stansted to Lyon and Nice; and Newcastle to Paris CDG. It also flies from Paris Orly to Marseille, Nice and Toulouse.

Ryanair flies from Glasgow to Paris Beauvais; and London Stansted to Bergerac, Biarritz, Brest, Carcassone, Clermont-Ferrand, Dinard,

The buying process

Whatever kind of property you are looking for in France, be it a Parisian garret, a Breton farmhouse or a seaside bolt-hole on the Côte d'Azur, your first challenge will be to find a place you like, at a price you can afford.

The second will be to make sure the legalities are dealt with in a way that best suits your circumstances. British people may have been buying second homes in France for decades now, but plenty have encountered difficulties in the process, by assuming that because France is our nearest neighbour, the legal process is similar. The truth is, the rules on everything from marriage to inheritance are different across the Channel, and these – as well as differences

La Rochelle, Limoges, Montpellier, Nîmes, Pau, Perpignan, Poitiers, Reims, Rodez, St Etienne, Strasbourg and Tours.

By sea
Brittany Ferries sails from Portsmouth to Caen and St Malo; Plymouth to Roscoff; and Poole to Cherbourg.
Condor Ferries sails from Poole and Weymouth to St Malo via Jersey and Guernsey.
Hoverspeed sails from Folkestone to Boulogne; Newhaven to Dieppe; and Dover to Calais.
P&O sails from Dover to Calais; and from Portsmouth to Cherbourg and Le Havre.
Sea France sails from Dover to Calais.

By train or road
Eurostar trains run from London Waterloo (and Ashford) to Paris, with some stopping at Calais and Lille; there is also a separate service to Lille, Disneyland Paris and, from December to April, Moutiers-Salins and Bourg St Maurice in the French Alps.
Eurolines runs coaches from most major UK cities to various destinations in France.
Eurotunnel car shuttle runs daily train services through the tunnel, which runs from near Folkestone to near Calais.

in approach to buying and selling real estate – can have a major impact on how to go about any house purchase.

Understanding 'small print' can be hard enough in English. Before you go any significant distance down the road towards buying a home in France, it is well worth engaging the services of a bilingual French lawyer, or at the very least an English lawyer with considerable experience of British people buying French property.

Make sure you understand all the financial implications of the decision you are about to make. And keep at the forefront of your mind the fact that once you make a formal offer to buy, you are committed to the purchase (in contrast to the system in England and Wales). It is vital to make sure that before you sign anything, you are happy with the contract, and that it protects your interests as far as possible. At a later point, you will finalise the transfer of the property – but this is straightforward relative to the rest of the buying process.

Finding a property

Most British people buying a property in France will do so through an estate agent (*agent immobilier*). French estate agents, unlike those in England, are supposed to be professionally qualified and hold a licence to practise (*carte professionnelle*). In most cases they will also have indemnity insurance and a bond (*pièce de garantie*) guaranteeing that if they run off with your deposit, you will get your money back.

In practice, however, there are plenty of perfectly good estate agents operating in France who do not have a licence – some of them catering specifically for British clients – but to be sure that your agent will comply with appropriate codes of conduct, and has adequate insurance in place, look out for those with a *carte professionnelle*.

Bona fide agents must display their *carte* in their offices, and must give details of it and any insurance and bonds on all correspondence and contracts. If you have any doubts about an agent, ask to see proof of its licence and any insurance it has. If an agent does not have a bond, this does not mean it is to be avoided at all costs. Obtaining a bond costs money and involves compliance with complicated accountancy rules, so some agents choose not to go down that route. On a practical level, dealing with a non-bonded agent means you should not give them the payment for any deposit you put down on a property – this should be paid to the notary dealing with the transaction instead. Unlike estate agents, all notaries are bonded.

If you want to protect yourself further, look out for estate agents who are members of one of the French estate agents' professional bodies – the Fédération Nationale des Agents Immobiliers et Mandataires (FNAIM)★ and the Syndicat Nationales des Professionnels Immobilier (SNPI)★.

They may be more tightly regulated, but do not expect as comprehensive a service from *agents immobilier* as one might from a good estate agent in Britain – especially in rural areas. There are unlikely to be acres of shop fronts filled with beautifully described homes, and you may even find it difficult to get hold of printed particulars, plans and/or photographs for properties, which can make it hard to get a good 'feel' for the market in the area you are interested in. Many estate agents are sole traders or work in small firms; there are very few local or national groupings of agents as in the UK.

To sell a property on behalf of a vendor, the agent must have written authority to do so. The main types of authority are the ordinary authority (*mandat simple*) and the exclusive authority (*mandat exclusif*). With the *mandat simple*, the agent has authority to sell the property, but this may have been given to other agents too and the vendor also retains the right to sell the property himself or herself. With the *mandat exclusif*, the agent is the only one allowed to sell the property, and the vendor may or may not also be able to sell directly, depending on the wording of the *mandat*. Both types of authority are time limited, and must also specify the estate agent's fees and who is liable to pay them.

It is important to get details about the type of *mandat* from the outset, because although in France, as in England, it is normally the seller who pays the estate agent's commission, this is not always the case. In some places it is the buyer who pays; in others, you might be expected to contribute half. If you are relatively wealthy, this may seem like a minor detail – but bear in mind that estate agents in France charge much higher levels of commission than in the UK. Around 4 to 5 per cent is fairly typical, and in some cases it can be as high as 10 to 12 per cent. As a general rule, the cheaper the property, the higher will be the commission as a percentage of the overall cost; commission on properties in more popular, touristy areas is often charged at a premium too.

Given the prices estate agents charge, it is perhaps unsurprising that many French people sell their homes without using one at all – preferring to sell via a notary (*notaire*), or by putting up their own 'A vendre' sign, or through press advertisements. Around a fifth of French property is estimated to be sold through notaries acting as selling agents. This is particularly common in more remote areas, despite the fact that notaries are, in theory, independent agents of the state and therefore impartial to the success or failure of transactions.

In this scenario, which can seem particularly worrying for the foreign buyer, the notary acts for the seller and charges you, the buyer, a fee for setting up the sale – or charges the seller, who inflates the price of the property accordingly. He or she could theoretically do all the legal paperwork for both parties. Tread very carefully!

If you were to go down this route, it would be vital as an absolute minimum safeguard to appoint a second notary to look after your interests. This is common practice in France and it is a sign of how high notaries' fees are that it is typical for the two notaries to simply split the fee on such occasions, so it adds nothing to the bill. Many British buyers, even if they are buying through an estate agent, prefer to appoint their own notary or, if funds allow, a French qualified solicitor or British solicitor with experience of French property transactions.

Another way of finding property in France is to go through a UK agent, of whom there are many specialising in French property. The vast majority will not be licensed French estate agents, but they often deal with several French agents and are skilled in picking out properties that might particularly appeal to a British audience. Especially if they have a website, these agents can be really helpful in allowing you to cast your net wide and search for a bigger variety of properties, without having to make too many speculative fact-finding trips.

Such agents should split the commission of the French agents whose properties they are advertising, so using them may, in theory, cost you nothing extra. Having said that, some agents offer a service whereby they undertake to find a selection of properties for you and arrange viewings. Simply being able to deal with an English-speaking agent might also be important to you – in either case you may be happy to pay an extra commission.

Always check the agent's charges so you are aware of exactly what you are paying for. Be particularly careful if an agent offers you a global price to cover the price of the property, tax, notaries' fees and commission, for example, because they may have slipped in an extra, hidden fee somewhere.

It is difficult to check UK estate agents' credentials definitively, but as a starting point it is worth asking for details of how much experience they have had in the French market. Ask to speak to previous clients, and check if they are members of the Federation of Overseas Property Developers, Agents and Consultants (FOPDAC)*, a body whose members abide by a voluntary code of conduct.

Agreeing to buy

In Britain, as many vendors and buyers know to their cost, it is possible to make an offer on a house and never get anywhere near exchange of contracts. Weeks or even months can pass, during which surveys are carried out, mortgages arranged and searches done, and only once all the details are ironed out does anyone formally commit to their respective sides of the bargain. In France, contracts are signed at a much earlier stage in proceedings – before searches and mortgage applications are completed, for example – and it is crucial to know what you are getting yourself into before you put pen to paper.

There are several kinds of preliminary contract in France. The most common is the *compromis de vente*, also known as the *promesse synallagmatique de vente*, and what you must appreciate is that there is nothing preliminary about it. The *compromis* is an agreement that commits both parties to the transaction. At its simplest, a *compromis* lays down that the seller must sell the stated property at the stated price, on a fixed date, to the buyer; and that the buyer must buy it. If for some reason you fail to complete the transaction the buyer can take you to court and force you to do so.

On the surface it may seem that the *compromis* is weighted in favour of the seller, but, as the buyer, you have the scope to build 'get-out' clauses (*conditions suspensives*) into the contract. This is the most crucial element to buying any property in France. What you must do before you sign is ensure that there are sufficient get-out clauses included in the contract to protect you from anything that might put you off completing the deal – whether it be problems with the property itself, or with your ability to complete the transaction. Because you are signing it in advance of having done the searches, completed a mortgage application and sorted out whether or not there are outstanding loans secured against the property, for example, the *compromis* should anticipate any problems with these areas and leave you free to walk away.

There are numerous standard clauses that appear in a *compromis* as a matter of routine. The *conditions* that you wish to add are down to you and the seller to agree (see box overleaf). In theory it is possible to include any number of *conditions*, perhaps relating to gaining planning permission for work you want to do, or to the results of a structural survey – but remember that all *conditions* have to be agreed by the seller if the sale is to go ahead, so they must not appear too onerous from his or her perspective. A seller would be unlikely to agree to a clause about you needing to sell your house in England in order to raise the finance for the purchase, for example, because at the very least it might lead to a delay in the signing of the *acte de vente* (deed of sale – see page 95).

What goes into a *compromis de vente*

Standard clauses
- The names of the parties to the transaction
- Full description of the property and land registry details
- Statement that full details of the title will be included in the final deed of sale (*acte de vente*)
- A date for the signing of the *acte* – usually 60 days after the signing of the *compromis*
- Statement about when the buyer will take possession of the property
- The price
- Receipt for the deposit
- Statement that the property is sold subject to any rights that exist over it, but that the seller him- or herself has not created any
- Statement that the property is sold with vacant possession
- The name of the notary who will prepare the *acte*
- Provision for who will pay the costs of the purchase
- Details of any estate agent involved and who is paying the commission
- Details of what will happen if the contract is broken
- Addresses of the parties.

Example of issues to address through conditions suspensives
- Not being able to secure adequate mortgage finance
- Problems obtaining a *certificat d'urbanisme*, which certifies the planning status of the property
- The possibility of the French Rural Development Agency (Federation Nationale des Societes d'Amenagement Foncier et d'Etablissement Rural, also known as SAFER) exercising its right of pre-emption over the sale
- Land registry searches showing mortgages against the property that the sale price would not fully cover
- Problems relating to rights of way.

Negotiating over *conditions suspensives* can be a time-consuming business and generally takes place in a pressurising context. The seller wants to tie you in to buying the property with as few conditions as possible; you need to be sure the property is absolutely right, and affordable, for you – but at the same time you want the peace of mind of knowing that the seller is not going to sell to anyone else. It is important, then, to stay calm and sanguine throughout, and only commit yourself to a purchase you are sure about – even if that means doing preliminary checks that risk scuppering the whole deal.

Remember too that it is vital to get the wording of *conditions suspensives* right. For example, unless you are buying in cash you should insert a clause saying the purchase will go ahead only if you can raise mortgage finance. But if the clause said only that, and you then found it difficult to find a satisfactory mortgage offer and tried to pull out of the deal, the seller could insist that the sale go ahead, arguing that there are plenty of loans available, even if they are at a punitive interest rate. If instead your clause says the purchase is subject to you securing a loan from a particular lender, at a certain rate, you assure yourself of a reasonable escape route.

As an initial outlay, you will normally be required to pay a deposit (*les arrhes*) of around 5 to 10 per cent of the purchase price on signing the *compromis*, which you forfeit if you fail to complete the transaction. If, on the other hand, the seller fails to complete, he or she must pay you twice this amount.

Other issues you will have to think about include how you want to own the property, whether as a sole owner, joint owners or through a private company; and how to structure the purchase from the point of view of inheritance tax, which – if you are married – means deciding which *régime matrimoniale* to use when you declare your *état civil* in the final deed (see also pages 103–4).

In some areas, an alternative form of preliminary contract, called a *promesse de vente,* is used. Here, the seller offers to sell the stated property at a stated price to a stated person within a stated period – normally up to six months. The buyer, in accepting the *promesse,* normally pays a deposit (*indemnité d'immobilisation*) of around 5 to 10 per cent of the purchase price, in return for which the seller keeps the property off the market for the agreed period. The *promesse de vente,* like a *compromis,* should include get-out clauses setting out the circumstances in which you, as the buyer, can pull out and recover your deposit. If the seller pulls out you are entitled to claim compensation, although doing so can be a lengthy and complicated process.

There are two main differences between the *promesse* and the *compromis*. The first is that if you have signed a *promesse* you, as the buyer, have made no commitment to buy, other than the possible forfeit of your deposit, so the seller cannot force you to complete. The second is that the *promesse* need not be signed in front of a notary but must be recorded at the local tax office (*cadastre*).

Just in case you get cold feet after signing a *compromis*, it is, thanks to a recent change in the law, possible to pull out up to seven days later. But beware, especially if you are in the UK, because the precise nature of French bureaucracy combined with the vagaries of two postal systems can mean this cooling-off period gets eaten up before all the necessary paperwork can be sorted out.

Surveys

When you first inspect the property, look carefully for any visible defects (*vices apparentes*), because by law the vendor is not obliged to disclose anything that you could have discovered yourself. Hidden defects (*vices caches*) must be disclosed by law – but bear in mind that a canny seller will have done his or her best to disguise them and hope for the best. Always ask if he or she has had any structural work done to the property and why, and request copies of the planning permissions, guarantees and/or invoices.

The only way to be anywhere near sure the property is in sound condition is to have a survey done. There is no tradition of pre-purchase house surveys among the French, and although legally there is nothing to stop you inserting a *condition suspensive* stating that the sale is conditional on a satisfactory survey, the seller is unlikely to agree to this unless there is something very visibly wrong with the property. You may have more chance of agreeing on a clause covering a specific defect – stating that the seller needs to sort out a particular patch of damp, for example – but this relies on the problem being identifiable with the naked eye.

If you do commission a survey, the seller will almost certainly insist on keeping the property on the market until you are ready to sign contracts. So it is down to your personal judgment whether or not to pay for a survey, and which kind to go for. On the one hand, an in-depth survey could reveal problems so serious that you might think twice about the whole idea (termites are a problem in many parts of France, especially in the south, for example, and can destroy a building from the inside out); on the other hand, they can be expensive and could jeopardise the sale.

It might be tempting to think the cost of a survey could be defrayed by subsequent negotiations over defects it has revealed, but this relies on persuading the seller that problems with his or her house exist and are serious enough to warrant a drop in price. If that fails it is down to you to decide how much you want the property and whether, post-survey, it remains the house of your dreams.

If you want to arrange for a survey, you have various options. There is no exact equivalent of a UK surveyor in France, but the professional you would be most likely to employ would be an *expert immobilier*. He or she can produce two types of report – the *expertise*, which is not dissimilar to the British 'homebuyer's report'; and the *bilan de santé*, which is more like a full structural survey. Expect to pay up to €700 for an *expertise* and up to €2,000 or, for larger properties, 1 per cent of the purchase price (plus TVA, the French equivalent of VAT) for a *bilan de santé*. Detailed inspections, for example to examine for insect infestation, will cost extra – although they can save you a lot of money in the long run.

Some *experts*, especially those in areas more popular with British buyers, now produce reports in English similar to those one would expect at home. Otherwise you are likely to incur translation costs. You may be lucky and have an *expert immobilier* recommended to you by a friend; common sense dictates that it might not be best to use one suggested by your estate agent. Otherwise, you can find an *expert* from Yellow Pages or get a list from the Chambre des Experts Immobiliers (FNAIM)★ in Paris, which lists members by *département*.

Enterprising UK surveying firms have begun to operate in France too. If you go down this route, check that they are experienced with French construction techniques, have professional indemnity insurance to cover work in France, and are members of the Royal Institution of Chartered Surveyors (RICS)★, the Association of Building Engineers★, or the Architecture and Surveying Institute★. You may wish to engage an architect to conduct a survey instead, although unsurprisingly this is likely to focus mainly on issues of design and construction – you can obtain a list of architects from the Royal Institute of British Architects.

Unfinished and 'leaseback' properties

Especially if you are looking to buy on the south-eastern seaboard, you may be attracted by a new development, in which case you will be buying a property that does not yet exist, or has been only partially completed.

France's government-sponsored 'leaseback' scheme (see also Chapter 2) may make such properties particularly attractive. Under the scheme, you can buy a property in a government-approved tourist complex – usually an apartment, house in a development on a golf course or such like – and enter into a contract with a leaseback company, whereby you grant a lease of your property to them for a minimum of nine years.

The company then rents the property to tourists and undertakes to pay you a fixed, index-linked annual rent – normally between 5 and 6 per cent of the price of the property – regardless of how successful it is at letting the property out. The company is also responsible for all the outgoings, such as utility bills, repairs and so on.

In addition to your fixed earnings from the property, you are normally allowed to use the property yourself, free of charge, for around four weeks a year. You can usually buy the property free of VAT – which means it can be possible to borrow up to 95 per cent of the price you pay, rather than the usual 75 to 80 per cent.

At the end of the nine years the property is entirely yours, although you may wish to continue renting it out through the same agency, which is normally on site and has hopefully built up considerable repeat trade.

If you are buying an unfinished property the sale is described as a *vente en l'état futur d'achèvement*. Rather than a *compromis*, you would sign a *contrat de réservation* as the preliminary contract. There are strict rules about how such contracts must be drafted. On the financial side, you pay an initial sum that represents the property's value at the point of signing the reservation, with further, staged payments as the building goes up (for example 35 per cent at foundation stage, 75 per cent once the building is watertight and 95 per cent on completion of the building; with 5 per cent retained to cover small outstanding jobs noticed up to a month after completion).

Finalising the transaction

Making sure the *compromis* covers you against all eventualities may seem like a stressful exercise, but even after you have signed on the dotted line there is still much to be done to progress your purchase towards completion. First, you will need to sort out your mortgage, which can be a complex business in itself (see pages 98–100). Second, you will need to arrange for searches to be carried out. It is important to note that the standard searches in France relate specifically to your property, however, so they will not give you any insight into other factors that may affect your enjoyment of your home, such as whether or not a motorway is about to be built just outside your front gate.

As a minimum, make sure to arrange searches that focus on:

- The title deed of the property (*titre*), which must be registered at the Land and Charges Registry (*conservation des hypothèques*). This search will prove whether the seller owns the property and has a right to sell it; it will also provide information about mortgages secured against the property, and about other claims on it, such as rights of way.
- The registered plan of the property (*plan cadastral*). In France, every property is divided into units known as *lots* or *parcelles*, each of which has a cadastral number (*référence cadastrale*), and should appear on the *plan cadastral*. The plan will not necessarily be accurate in terms of land measurements or site boundaries, however.
- Planning issues. The *certificat d'urbanisme* (see box overleaf) or *note de renseignement d'urbanisme* is the most important document here – it provides details of the planning rules applicable to a particular property. This search must come back *positif* if you wish to apply to do any restoration or other work on the building. The *certificat* is valid for one year, although this can be extended by a further 12 months. As in the UK, any major changes to French property must be preceded by planning permission (*permis de construire*) (see pages 97–8).

Certificat d'urbanisme

The *certificat d'urbanisme* is a certificate of town planning or urban development in France. It states the rights attached to a specific property and the buildings on it with regards to their function and purpose, future development and zoning of the property and the associated taxation on all land and buildings in the area. A *relevé* or *matrice cadastraux*, available from the *mairie*, states the current use of the land and the use to which it may be put. But for further information you should request a *certificat d'urbanisme*, which should be free.

There are two types of *certificat d'urbanisme*: the certificate of information (*certificat de simple information*) provides information on the existing rights for development of the property but does not tell you if it may be developed beyond what is already allowed; the operational certificate (*certificat opérationnel*) provides information on whether a specific development may be undertaken on the land.

It is strongly advisable to ask for a *certificat d'urbanisme* before buying property or land in France. It provides information on the development potential of the property and the limitations and obligations attached to that property of any existing rights to build. This can affect your intended plans for the property, as well as its future value. It does not give you authorisation to build, but is needed if you plan to make any changes to a property and/or apply for a building permit. It states the existing rights to develop the land, the taxation mode, the zone (urban, agricultural or other), the existent or envisaged water, electricity, cleansing and servicing of the ground and other factors.

If you request a *certificat* with the intention of renovating existing structures or building new structures you must state clearly the intended purpose of the buildings as well as the probable surface area of all planned buildings. Your operational certificate will declare if the ground can be used for the operation described (and in the event of negative answer, it will say why the project cannot be undertaken). If you are buying a property for renovation and development, especially in more rural areas of the country, you are strongly advised to include a 'condition of sale' clause in the *compromis de vente* which is dependent on the results of your operational *certificat d'urbanisme*.

Your architect or surveyor should be able to prepare your *certificat* application; the *mairie* must deliver your *certificat* within two months of your application. Once you have your *certificat*, you have two months to contest or change any of the details contained in the document. Read it carefully when you receive it to check for errors. After the two months have passed you will be unable to make any changes, and will need to re-start the process with a new application.

The *certificat* is valid for one year, and within this year you may present an application for a *permis de construire* (building permit). This must be presented in accordance with the requirements/permissions of the *certificat* – so, for example, if the *certificat* you obtained at the time of purchase noted that the property was for use as a private home and you then submitted plans to develop a gîte complex, your plans would be thrown out.

If the total surface area of all the floors of your proposed project exceeds 170 square metres, the *permis de construire* must be prepared and presented by a registered French architect. For smaller works and those exempt from needing a *permis de construire*, you can present an application for a *declaration de travaux*. Examples of exempt structures include 'buildings of low importance' that fall within specific height and area limitations including open swimming pools, frames and green-houses within a size limit, and structures under 20 square metres. The *mairie* can provide you with further information.

If you need to, you can apply for an extension of the *certificat d'urbanisme*, called a *prolongation de validité*. It can be extended for one year from the date of the officially stamped letter from the *mairie* which comes with the *certificat*. Request an extension of the certificate for one year, no later than two months before the expiry date of the old certificate. This demand must be done by letter, in duplicate, addressed to the mayor accompanied by the original *certificat* and sent by *lettre recommandé* (registered post) with *accusé de réception* (a receipt confirming delivery).

- Local authority plans. The *service d'urbanisme* at the town hall (*mairie*) should allow you to see and/or take a copy of the *plan d'occupation des sols*. This will indicate how your land and neighbouring land is 'zoned', i.e. whether it is in a national park, urban development area or whatever, which governs whether there are any restrictions on you building on your land, or on neighbours building on theirs. It will also reveal any plans in the area for new motorways, roads, railways and the like.

- Pre-emptive rights (*droits de pré-emption*). There are circumstances in which other parties might have a pre-emptive right over the property. For example farmers who have use of land, and their successors, may be entitled to an agricultural tenancy (*bail rural*), which gives them first rights to buy the freehold; neighbouring farmers may also have such rights. (Your seller may have already asked them and they may have refused the offer, but their tenancy may continue nonetheless. You may decide this is no problem, but bear in mind that future buyers may take a different view.) Other authorities may have pre-emptive rights, for example if the property is needed for a road-widening scheme, and the *Société d'Amenagement Foncier et d'Etablissment Rural (SAFER)* may have a pre-emptive right over transactions involving agricultural land exceeding 2,500 square metres.

Your *compromis de vente* and its *conditions suspensives* should cover you if the results of these searches are unfavourable and/or if remedial action is required. For example, if any problems arise from the search of the *plan cadastral*, you may need to engage the services of a land surveyor (*géomètre*) – the only person legally qualified to establish whether the land being offered for sale belongs solely to your seller. A *géomètre* can prepare a definitive plan (*plan de bornage* or *d'arpentage*) to correctly site the property's boundaries, confirm whether buildings, fences and the like actually lie on your land, and sort out party wall issues.

If you are buying a property that is part of a *copropriété* – an apartment in a block, or a house that is part of a development built around a golf course, perhaps – make sure you understand all the rules, fees and accounts that relate to the shared parts of the building. These are summarised in the *règlements de copropriété*.

Once all the details of the transaction are sorted out to everyone's satisfaction – a process that can take several months – the final stage of the buying process is to sign the deed of sale (*acte de vente*). The *acte* must be signed in front of a notary, either by you and the seller in person or by someone who holds power of attorney for you. It contains much of the information that appeared in the *compromis de vente*, along with other elements such as tax calculations (see box overleaf).

What goes into an *acte de vente*

- Name and address of notary.
- Identification of the parties (including their *états civils* – see page 104), and details of anyone with power of attorney.
- Full description of the property (including details from the *cadastre*) and any restrictions affecting it.
- Statement about the current claim to ownership of the property, whether or not it is free of tenants, and liability for bills up to the date of completion.
- Price and methods of payment.
- Statement about the taxes payable for the sale, including capital gains tax from the vendor and other duties.
- Confirmation that the sale has taken place.
- Details about town planning and reference to the *certificat d'urbanisme*.
- Confirmation that anyone with pre-emption rights (as named) has renounced them.
- History of how the vendor came to own the property.
- Date on which the buyer becomes owner, and confirmation of vacant possession.
- Charges against the property, with the sellers' warranties and guarantees.
- Details of French mortgage finance used to buy the property (no details will be given if you are buying through a UK re-mortgage).
- Statement of sincerity (*affirmation de sincérité*), that all statements in the *acte* are true, the price has been fully stated and the notary has warned the parties of the sanctions that may flow from false declaration.

Once the money has been transferred and the *acte* has been signed, the notary will pay your taxes to the state, you will settle his or her fees and then, from the money due to the vendor, pay the estate agent and any debts on the property. You must then present your title and mortgage for registration at the land registry – you have two months to do this, but the sooner the better because the theoretical danger remains that someone else could register a debt or judgment against the property before you have registered it as yours – which would mean they had first call on the property.

Some time after completion, the notary should send you the paperwork relating to the purchase, together with his or her final bill, an explanation of how the money has been spent and possibly a small refund against his original estimate.

Fees and taxes on French property purchases

Stamp duty

This is payable on properties more than five years old, and is charged at 4.8 per cent of the declared value, of which 3.6 per cent goes to the *département* and 1.2 per cent to the *commune*. Properties less than five years old are exempt from stamp duty, but you must pay value added tax (TVA), which is currently running at 19.6 per cent.

Notary fees

These are fixed by law and non-negotiable. There is a sliding scale whereby the first €3,049 is charged at 5 per cent of the declared price; the part of the price between €3,049 and €6,098 is charged at 3.3 per cent; the part of the price between €6,098 and €16,769 is charged at 1.65 per cent, and the rest is charged at 0.825 per cent. Notaries' fees will be subject to TVA.

Other fees

If you are taking out a mortgage secured on the French property, you will generally have to pay an arrangement fee of 1 per cent of the amount borrowed, a valuation fee of up to £200, and a 1 to 2 per cent registration fee to register a first charge against the property; the notary will also charge you an extra fee for administering this. Most of these charges will also be subject to TVA.

Restoring old property

If you are buying a property to restore, you may wish to employ an *expert immobilier* to give you a full assessment of the building as it stands, and how much it might cost to put right.

For a large project, you would probably need to employ an architect to draw up plans and oversee the work; otherwise, ask a few experienced qualified builders (*maîtres d'oeuvres*) or relevant tradespeople to suggest what might be achievable with the property and what costs might be involved. To find tradespeople, the best approach is either personal recommendations or to ask around locally – perhaps starting with the mayor or local chambers of commerce. The local equivalent of the *Yellow Pages* is also good source.

All licensed builders and tradespeople in France must have a *Siret* number, issued by the relevant chamber of commerce – which signifies registration for TVA (the French equivalent of VAT). A builder who is properly qualified and registered should also have *Decenel* insurance – a type of bond which gives you a guarantee of workmanship for up to ten years, depending on the kind of work involved. Builders should also have *responsabilité civile* – third-party insurance which covers them if they accidentally damage property in the course of renovating it.

Your architect, *géomètre* (surveyor) or *maître d'oeuvre* may commission tradespeople on your behalf or if your French is up to it you may decide to go it alone. Either way, try to get estimates (*devis*) from several people, with as much detail as possible, showing schedules of prices and the TVA marked against each item of work. Once you have agreed a schedule, sign a copy for the contractor and keep a copy for yourself; this can act as a contract.

You should take out insurance known as *dommage et ouvrage assurance* to cover you if anyone working on your property has an accident.

Keep all your receipts for building work (materials and labour) because these can be set against the perceived 'gain' in property value and deducted from French capital gains tax if you sell it at a later date; they also act as proof that you have paid TVA.

The other issue to deal with in any restoration project is planning permission. For building work covering a net area of less than 170 square metres your notary can obtain planning permission at the time of purchase. If you are planning to change the use of the building or its external appearance, a notary or *géomètre* must apply for outline permission in the form of a *certificat d'urbanisme positif* on your behalf.

For larger projects, you will need full architect drawings and plans, which must be signed, dated, copied and presented in a particular way, taken to the *mairie* (town hall) and a written receipt issued. Your application will be displayed at the *mairie* and within 15 days you will receive a date by which you can assume you have tacit approval – normally around two months from the time of initial application.

During this period the mayor and town or village council will consider the application, but however positive a sense you get of their opinion on the application, beware of starting work before the final date passes, because all applications go to the departmental planning office (*direction départmentale de l'équipement*) and projects approved by the local council can be overruled.

If your property is a protected building, is located in a protected area or potentially affects a historic building, you may have to gain clearance from the Architecte des Bâtiments de France – the equivalent of English Heritage.

Financial matters

There is little doubt that cheaper property is available in France than in the UK, but it is important to look beyond the headline price when deciding whether you can afford to make the commitment of owning a second home, let alone whether you want to live in it permanently.

Be sure you have thought about the best way to finance your purchase; and consider the longer-term financial implications of tying up a proportion of your money in a property abroad. Take independent financial advice – if necessary from several sources – before signing on any dotted lines.

Mortgages

Just like buying property anywhere else in continental Europe, your main choice when buying in France is whether to take out a euro-mortgage or re-mortgage your UK home and raise finance that way.

Whichever approach you take, you are likely to need a substantial amount of capital to kick-start your purchase.

French lenders will generally lend up to 75 per cent of the value of the property, although some will go up as far as 80 per cent. It is possible to get 100 per cent loans, but this depends very much on circumstances and on being introduced to the lender through a broker or in some cases, estate agent – who will be paid commission for having introduced you. There is usually a lower limit of around £20,000 on the amount lenders will lend.

The vast majority of French mortgages are lent on a repayment basis, although some specialist providers may agree an interest-only deal; most are for 15 years, but occasionally 25-year loans will be considered – so long as they are fully paid off by the age of 70, or sometimes 65.

Bear in mind that the French attitude to mortgages is very different from the British – renting is still the norm in France, and French people who do buy tend to borrow as little, and for as short a time, as possible. In the UK, taking out a home loan over a longer period can secure you a better rate. In France the opposite is normally the case. Whereas in the UK mortgage providers decide how much to lend on the basis of your income and their own multiplier, French lenders will assess you according to your ability to service the loan.

Lending practices do vary, but, as a general rule, lenders look at your net income (your earnings after tax and national insurance have been deducted), divide it by three and say that this amount should cover all your existing monthly outgoings plus the proposed repayments on the new mortgage. Under French consumer protection law, lenders are not allowed to let you be in debt for more than a third of your income. Existing outgoings include mortgages, loans and any maintenance payments – although credit-card repayments do not count. If you are applying for a joint loan, both incomes will be taken into account.

So if your joint net monthly income is £3,000 and you have a mortgage on your UK property that costs £500 a month, and a car loan that costs £200 a month, the lender would look at the first £1,000, take off £700, and consider offering you a loan with repayments of up to £300 per month.

Generally speaking, lenders will not consider rental income for mortgage purposes, unless you are renting out a property to permanent tenants rather than for holiday lettings. However secure it may seem, rental income from leaseback schemes will also not be taken into account.

Most French mortgages are fixed rate, and rates are generally lower than in the UK, although it is important to bear in mind that payments will fluctuate with the sterling/euro exchange rate. Variable rates are possible, and you may also come across a variant called a constant rate mortgage, whereby your repayments are fixed, but the term of the loan varies according to interest rates. If you are offered one of these, make sure you know what you are letting yourself in for.

Negotiating a re-mortgage on your UK property may be a cheaper option in terms of set-up costs, especially if you stay with the same lender. You will not need any extra life insurance; and, particularly if you are on a fixed-rate deal, the cost of the loan will be much more predictable, rather than fluctuating with the exchange rate.

The big disadvantage, though, of this arrangement, is that if everything goes pear-shaped, your main home is at risk – so borrowing through a re-mortgage is probably a sensible approach only if you are borrowing relatively small sums.

Taxes on property

French tax regimes differ from the British in many respects, so to understand all tax aspects of your foreign property, make sure you take expert tax-planning advice before you make the decision to buy.

Property taxes (taxe foncière and taxe d'habitation)

These are local taxes; the first is payable by the owner of the property and the second by the person who lives in it. The *taxe foncière*, a land tax, is payable whether or not there is anyone living in the property. It is based on the property's theoretical rentable value (*valeur locative*), with the level of tax applied to this varying from one *département* to the next. Where renovation work has been carried out recently, the *taxe foncière* can be waived for two years.

The *taxe d'habitation* is an occupancy tax levied on all property residents, regardless of whether they are owners or tenants. It is normally paid by the person resident on 1 January. You may be able to persuade your local tax office (*direction des impôts*) to grant an exemption if the property is being completely renovated and is uninhabitable. Anyone retired or who has elderly dependants can negotiate a reduction from the local *mairie* (town hall).

The price of these taxes combined is generally lower than what one would pay in council tax for an equivalent property in the UK. Bear in mind though that you may also have to pay a separate tax for rubbish collection (*ordures*), and if you have bought in a condominium you will be liable for a service charge.

Income tax (impôt sur le revenu)

If you own a second home in France, even as a non-resident, you will be subject to tax in France if you let your property out. It is worth taking advice from a French accountant or tax specialist to make sure you follow all the rules and choose the most tax-efficient way of dealing with this income.

You must report rental income profits on an income tax return – called a *Déclaration des Revenus (Cerfa 2042)* – and submit it to the *Centre des Impôts des Non-Résidents* in Paris before 30 April each year (the French tax year-end is 31 December). The method used to determine your taxable income from rentals varies according to the level of annual turnover. If it does not exceed around £50,000, you will pay tax on 30 per cent of turnover, with the remaining 70 per cent treated as expenses. If you earn more than that, there are two different ways of working out the tax – the 'simplified real' or 'normal real' regimes; the simplified regime is, as the name suggests, much simpler and means you can avoid preparing detailed accounts.

If you let out land or an unfurnished property, you will be liable for *revenus fonciers*. For this form of income tax, you can offset expenses relating to the management of the property against the income it generates, and the remainder will be taxable. The kinds of expenses that can be offset include repairs, maintenance, insurance and mortgage interest. If the income the property generates is fairly low – around £3,000 or less per year – you can opt to declare the full income and have a general allowance for expenses of 33 per cent offset against it; if you take this approach, you are then not expected to keep detailed records about your expenses. Again, take advice to be sure of minimising your tax liabilities.

Wealth tax (impôt de solidarité sur la fortune)

If you are buying a very high-value property, you may be liable for wealth tax, which is charged on all assets in France including land, buildings, cars, furniture and other valuable assets. Many items are exempt from the tax, however, and the tax is, in any case, zero-rated if your assets add up to less than €720,000. Bear in mind too that the value of your home can be discounted by a fifth for the purposes of wealth tax calculations.

Capital gains tax (plus value)

If you sell a French property that is your second home, you will be liable for capital gains tax over there. This is taxed at 33 per cent of the net gain – that is, the profit you have made on the property after expenses such as the costs of the acquisition and sale and the cost of repairs and improvements (normally calculated by tripling the value of full written receipts for materials bought in France and including your French address). After the first two years, the taxable gain is reduced by 5 per cent for each year. The tax is taken at source when the sale goes through.

Plus value is not charged if the property is your main home, although to prove that this is the case, you will need to have a *carte de séjour* (residence permit), and to have filed at least one tax return and be able to prove you are living in the house.

Gift tax (droits de donations)

As in the UK, tax is payable if you make a gift of assets including property – although there are exemptions, which can be used as part of inheritance tax planning. Gifts to spouses, children, grand-children and people with disabilities are partially exempt from gift tax. Always take advice because, for example, if you bought a house in the name of your children this might create a gift tax liability.

Inheritance tax (droits de succession)

Even if you are resident in the UK, your French property will be taxable in terms of inheritance tax. As explained above, making gifts before you die can, as in the UK, reduce your inheritance tax liabil-ities. In France, inheritance taxes are paid by the recipient of the inheritance, and are charged at different rates according to the size of the inheritance and how the recipient is related to the donor – so parents, children and spouses pay the lowest rates, with siblings, more distant relatives and other people paying much higher tax. On a property worth €100,000, for example, a child or spouse might expect to pay 0 per cent on the first €7,500, 10 per cent on the next

€7,500, 10 per cent on the next €15,000 and 20 per cent on the rest; someone unrelated, by contrast, would pay a flat rate of 60 per cent.

Passing on property to your heirs

The inheritance regime in France is very different from that of the UK, so it is vital to take advice from an expert in French law before buying property. How you apportion ownership of your new home could have serious tax implications.

You may be buying the property on your own, in which case it will be in your name, unless you set up a company to buy it (see below). If you are buying with a partner, there are two options – separate ownership (*en indivision*) or as a sort of joint tenancy (*en tontine*). With the former option, if you die your half will be disposed of according to fixed rules of inheritance (see box below). If you buy

---

Inheritance tax

The inheritance tax rules in France are extremely complex and, especially if you have children from more than one relationship, you will need expert advice to understand how they might affect you. Assets disposed of under French inheritance law are split into a freely disposable part (*quotité disponible*) and a protected part (*réserve héreditaire*). The reserved part must be given to the following people:

- If you have one child of any age, your own or adopted, but not including step-children; or if your child, now deceased, left children – they take 50 per cent of your total estate
- If you have two children (as above) or a mixture of living and deceased children who left children – they take 66 per cent
- Three or more children (as above) take 70 per cent
- If you have no children but you have a living parent or grandparent on one side, they take 20 per cent of the total estate (although this can be reduced to a life interest if you have a surviving spouse and your will specifies this)
- If you have no children but a living parent or grandparent on both sides, 20 per cent of the total estate must go to each branch of the family (or as a life interest as above).

---

en tontine, your half will pass to the other joint owner automatically on your death. A person who owns *en indivision* can also insist on the property being sold, even against the wishes of the other owner.

So where would this leave your surviving spouse? When French people marry they specify a *régime matrimonial* under which their relationship will work. There are two options – common ownership of assets (*communauté de biens*) and separate ownership of assets (*séparation de biens*). As the name suggests, under common ownership all assets acquired after the marriage – even if they are written down as being in one or other party's name – belong to both. Under separate ownership, each spouse can own assets in his or her own name and the other has no automatic claim over them.

It is up to you to decide how you want to deal with your French property, but you will need to state a matrimonial option (you are asked to declare one or the other in the *état civil*, which goes into the *acte de vente*) and stick to it.

If you opt for *séparation de biens* (the normal approach, as this is closer to UK marriage) and the property is owned *en indivision*, your part of the property will be disposed of as above. If you go for *communauté de biens* and make a *clause d'attribution* that on your death the property passes to the other partner, he or she will become the owner, without needing to pay inheritance tax (but only if you have no children by a previous relationship). The tax bill on the second owner's death will be much higher than it might otherwise have been, however.

Buying *en tontine* can help you get round inheritance tax rules, and so can setting up a *société civile immobilière* (SCI) – a type of company through which you can buy property and leave it to whoever you like. SCIs can also be useful for non-married couples. Again, take expert advice, if necessary from several sources, on which approach would work best for your particular circumstances.

Renting your property out

Many people who buy in France choose to let their property out at some point, and rental income can be a vital way of covering some of the expenses involved in owning a second home – although, especially if you are taking out a mortgage, you would be well advised not to rely on it to make the whole project affordable.

It is important to be clear about what your purpose is in buying a property, before you even start looking for one. If what you want is purely an investment vehicle, you may find you are better off buying a property with good rental potential, that you yourself would not be interested in as a holiday home.

Rental potential varies enormously from region to region and property to property, with climate, geography, architecture, cultural and sporting facilities, size and standard of accommodation, accessibility and price all playing their part in determining how much income you might be able to generate.

Wherever you buy, do not expect your property to be let all year round. Parts of France have more all-year-round appeal than others, so the tourist season is longer in Paris than in most parts of inland France, for example, and, in terms of climate, the Côte d'Azur and surrounding areas have more sunshine hours per year than the rest of France. But even a well-equipped apartment in Paris or Nice is unlikely to attract visitors for many more than 20 weeks of the year, unless it is particularly beautiful, you market it well and have lots of friends prepared to pay you the going rate to stay in it. In many areas, especially if you are new to the lettings game, filling your property for ten weeks a year might be a challenge at first – although of course this does have the advantage of giving you plenty of time to enjoy it yourself.

Letting agencies stress that, in most parts of France, properties with swimming pools and at the very least a large garden will draw in the most bookings. Pools also allow you to charge considerably higher rates than would otherwise be the case.

The example in the box overleaf illustrates how much one gîte-owning couple, based in the north of the Dordogne, generated in rental income in 2002. In their case this represented a return of nearly 10 per cent on their investment, although this is a relatively high figure compared to many rental properties.

If you are letting a property in France from a base in the UK, the costs of employing someone else to manage it on your behalf can soon mount up. One experienced house-letter in the Corbières region estimates that for a three-bedroomed house typical charges would be €135 per changeover for laundry and cleaning, plus €50 a month for key holding and caretaking, and €20 to €30 an hour for dealing with specific issues, such as unblocking toilets or meeting tradespeople. For an idea of possible costs involved in running your property as a business, see page 189, which relates to Italy but is a useful starting point for working out expenses across Europe.

CASE HISTORY: Sara and David Ambrose

Sara and David Ambrose own a farmhouse and two three-bedroomed barns in the Dordogne. These have separate gardens and a shared swimming pool. They live in the farmhouse and let the two barns all year round. Their rates for each barn in 2002 were £800 per week for the high season (July and August), £600 for the mid-season (June and September) and £325 for the low season.

Taken as a whole, Sara and David filled the properties for eight weeks at high-season rates, four weeks at mid-season rates and the equivalent of five weeks at low-season rates (although during the low season, they accepted shorter lettings so to generate this amount took longer than five weeks).

Their income was therefore £12,800 (eight weeks at £800 per barn per week) plus £4,800 (four weeks at £600 per barn) plus £3,250 (five weeks at £325 per barn), which adds up to £20,850 for the year (£10,425 for each barn).

This reflects a good return on their initial investment. However, they have no other jobs to occupy their time, they own the properties outright and they live on site. This allows them to keep on top of any problems with the properties and avoid having to pay someone else to manage them on their behalf.

This is without considering the costs of marketing the property in the first place. Bear in mind that letting agencies may charge as much as 20 per cent of your letting income plus TVA. Remember also that throwing money into advertising will not necessarily pay dividends; any directory or website worth its salt can attract a surfeit of business for July and August, but will it really translate into bookings outside the peak season?

Living in France

Whether you plan to make regular weekend visits to your holiday home in Normandy, or to move your entire family to Languedoc, there are many practical and financial issues to think about before purchasing.

Work

As a resident of the EU there is, officially at least, nothing to stop you getting a job in France. If you intend to stay in France for more than three months you will need to get a residence permit (*carte de séjour*), which relies on being able to show that you have a job or other source of income, and a place to live. *Cartes de séjour* are available from *mairie* (town hall) in small towns, or from the *gendarmerie* or *préfecture* in larger towns and cities. Some employers may ask for a *carte de séjour* before they will take you on; it is possible to obtain a temporary one.

If you are retiring to France you will still need a *carte*, and will be expected to produce evidence that you have sufficient revenue and medical insurance to mean you will not be a drain on the state.

There are various ways of finding a job in France, but it is worth bearing in mind that unemployment is relatively high, and you will need excellent French to get by in the workplace. One way of researching possible work avenues before you go is to use the European Employment Services Network (EURES)* (see page 62).

Government employment offices (*agence national pour l'emploi*) offer similar services to UK job centres. There are also private recruitment agencies and a host of job websites. In major cities there can be scope to teach English, especially in the business sector; although normally you will need to have a recognised TEFL (teaching of English as a foreign language) qualification.

Classified job advertisements appear in many French newspapers, including the weeklies *L'Express* and *Carrières et Emplois*; the latter carries the week's job adverts from *France Soir* and *Le Figaro*.

It is worth networking and taking advice from native French wherever possible, if only to get a better idea of some of the cultural differences relating to job seeking. For example, CVs in France tend to be shorter, with educational qualifications holding more sway later into one's career than is the case in the UK. Covering letters are very formal, tend to be hand-written and you should normally include a photo. The French also expect to follow-up job applications, sometimes with several phone calls, to check on the progress of the recruitment.

If you want to set up as self-employed in France, you will need to register your business at the *chambre de commerce* (for businesses), *chambre des métiers* (for artisans) or *chambre d'agriculture* (for farmers, horticulturists etc). If in doubt, talk to your *mairie*. If you need to raise finance to help you set up, be prepared to have a fair bit of capital yourself – you are unlikely to secure borrowing unless you can match it yourself, and repayment periods are short.

Tax

If you are planning to live and work in France, you must be prepared to deal with a rather different income tax regime. If you are married, income tax is generally assessed on the basis of your household's income.

Without going into the complexities of it, the taxman looks at your joint salaries and makes adjustments according to how many children or other dependants you have – the idea being to avoid large families with working children paying too much tax. Once these adjustments are made, the tax is calculated in bandings as in the UK, but tax is charged at a higher rate and on lower incomes, so for example the tranche from around €14,000 to €24,000 is charged at 31 per cent; net income above around €46,000 is charged at nearly 53 per cent.

Even if you are paying tax at source as an employee, it is vital to consult a French tax expert to be confident that you are paying the right level of tax and not inadvertently dodging tax – for which, as in the UK, the penalties in France are severe. (For information on taxes relating to property, see pages 100–03.)

Banking

If you are moving to France, or even if you will be based in the UK but own a second home in France, you will almost certainly want to open a French current account (*compte de cheques*), if only to pay utility bills by direct debit (*virements*). One French bank, Crédit Agricole, runs a telephone and internet banking service called Britline, aimed at British customers; alternatively you may want to open an account at a French bank branch near your property.

There are two main differences between French and British current accounts – the most important being the non-existence of overdraft facilities. First, if you write a cheque above and beyond whatever cleared funds are in your account, the account will be closed and your name will be passed to the Bank of France, meaning you will not be able to open another one for the next five years. Second, cheque guarantee cards do not exist in France – so you need to be particularly careful not to lose your chequebook.

Insurance

In France you are required by law to have home and car insurance; even if you are renting for a period while you look for a property to buy, you are liable for damage to the landlord's property, including common spaces.

The typical home insurance policy (*contrat multirisque habitation*) insures you against theft, fire, storms, floods, burst pipes, explosions, lightning and natural disasters; it may also give you and your family third-party coverage (*responsabilité civile familiale*) in case any of you cause damage to others and are sued. Be careful if you are insuring a holiday home, because some insurers will not provide cover beyond a specified period of absence; some also insist on insuring your main home before they will offer cover for a second one.

There are three levels of car insurance in France – third party (*au tiers*); third party fire and theft (*au tiers illimité* or *au tiers complet*) and comprehensive (*tous risques*). You can also pay extra for *protection du conducteur* cover, which pays out to compensate you if, as a driver, you are unable to work following injury. The amount you pay will, as in the UK, depend on your accident and claims record (*bonus-malus*); you may need to get documentary proof from your UK insurer for your no-claims bonus to be transferable to France.

Pensions and retirement

Probably the biggest legal difference between the UK and France that may affect people of retirement age is the inheritance regime (see pages 103–4). It is vital for anyone considering retiring to France to think carefully about inheritance tax planning in advance.

Under UK law there is the concept of 'domicile', which basically means that if your roots are in the UK (for example, if your parents were from the UK, even if your birthplace was elsewhere), no matter where you choose to live you are liable for UK death duties. At the same time, if you live in France or own property in France you will be liable for French inheritance tax.

Under a double taxation agreement between the two countries, you should not have to pay taxes to more than one jurisdiction, but it is certainly worth exploring ways of minimising your eventual tax liability in advance of emigrating – if only because inheritance tax in the UK is fairly high, relative to that in France. Bear in mind, however, the implications of France's strict inheritance laws – especially if there are stepchildren in the equation.

Other issues you may need to think about in order to make your finances as efficient as possible include the use of trusts, to shelter assets from tax; and/or life insurance policies which will pay out if you die and pay off any death duties.

In terms of receiving your pension once it has matured, some pension schemes allow the money to be paid into any bank, anywhere; others insist on it being paid into a UK bank account. You may want to arrange for the bank to transfer this money to you several times a year. It is also possible to make an annual arrangement with currency dealers whereby the money is sent at an exchange rate that applies for the whole year and therefore gives you certainty of income. Alternatively you may wish to just draw the money out of an ATM using your UK card whenever you need it.

If you have a government pension – from the civil service or police, for example – it will be taxed in the UK; otherwise pensions can be paid gross and then taxed in France.

As with all financial issues related to buying property and/or moving abroad, take independent financial advice before making any firm decisions.

Health

As an EU resident you are entitled to make use of the French health service through an E111 for up to three months or, if you are living in France, your *carte de séjour*. This qualifies you for a *carte vitale* – a microchip card which contains all your health service details including your social security number and social security contribution data.

Under the French system, if you are working and therefore contributing to the social security system (like our National Insurance) you pay for health service fees and are then reimbursed, via the *carte vitale*, direct into your bank account. Reimbursement levels vary according to the treatment in question – for example, you will get back 75 per cent of the cost of visits to a government-approved GP (*médecin conventionné secteur*); 80 per cent for hospital visits; 75 per cent for dentists; 70 per cent for opticians; and 65 per cent for most medicines.

If you retire to France you will be entitled to state medical assistance on the basis of your contributions to the UK National Insurance scheme. You will need an E121 form to confirm your status as a pensioner. Information on social security and health cover for self-employed UK residents in France is available from the Benefits Agency: ask for leaflet SA29. Further information on cover for self-employed people can be obtained from the Caisse d'Assurance Maladie des Professions Libérales d'Ile de France★.

Many people in France take out private medical insurance (*mutuelle* policies) to cover the shortfall between medical fees and reimbursements.

Schools

The French education system is very highly regarded on the world stage; but any British parents considering a move there should be aware that teaching is more traditional than back home, with a greater emphasis on learning by rote and less on developing children as independent learners.

There is an impressive level of nursery provision through the *écoles maternelles*, which cater for children aged three to six; pre-nurseries known as *jardins d'enfants* are also available. *Écoles primaires* take children from six up to the age of eleven, and teach them French, history, geography, civic studies, maths, science, PE, art/crafts and music. From the age of nine, children learn a language – normally English. At 11, they go to a *collège d'enseignement secondaire*, starting off with a general curriculum and beginning to specialise from 14. They take exams at 15, with the more academic pupils then going on to a *lycée*, which prepares them for the *baccalauréat* at age 18; for the less academic, more technical and vocational courses are available, and results of annual exams create traffic between the two streams.

There is a thriving private sector in French education, mainly catering for parents who want a more religious-based education for their children; and there is a plethora of English-speaking and international schools in France, especially in Paris, the other major cities and around the Côte d'Azur (further information about these is available from the British Council). Private education is generally much cheaper in France than in the UK, because the state subsidises all schools that follow the national curriculum.

Cars

If you are thinking of bringing your car over to live with you in France, you should contact French Customs (*Direction des Douanes*). They will be able to tell you how long you can drive a British-registered vehicle in France; and what to do to get it registered in France. Occasionally minor modifications might be necessary to change the car to meet French specifications. There is a local customs office in every main town in France. Information is also available on the Internet. For long-term residency it is easier and safer to switch to a left-hand drive vehicle.

Utilities

Electricity is cheaper in France than in the UK and is run, along with gas services, by Électricité de France-Gaz de France (EDF-GDF). The most common electricity tariff is called *heures creuses, heures pleines*, whereby you get eight hours of cheap-rate electricity per day. If a property you are considering buying has no mains electricity, get EDF-GDF to give you an estimate of how much it would cost, as this can prove very expensive – especially if your property is remote.

Mains gas is available in towns and cities throughout France, but in the countryside you are more likely to have to buy it in bottles at the supermarket, or have it delivered to a domestic tank. When choosing a house, bear in mind that your consumption costs are likely to be around three times higher in an old house as compared to a brand new house that meets the latest insulation standards.

Wood-burning stoves are common in the French countryside, and you can buy wood cut into lengths ideal for a woodburner, or for an open fireplace. The French tend to order wood by the *brassée* (four cubic metres' worth), so bear in mind the storage implications of this.

Water is supplied by a range of private companies, is metered, and can be expensive. Attitudes to water consumption in France are different from those in the UK – for example, people are long-accustomed to drinking bottled water, showers are far more common than baths and most new toilets have a half-flush option.

Chapter 6

Spain and Portugal

Since the package tours of the 1960s opened Spain up to northern Europe, British property hunters have traditionally focused on the more obvious stretches of the Iberian Peninsula to find retirement and holiday homes. There is still plenty of real estate to be had in such places, the difference being that now there are growing numbers of quieter, less imposing developments springing up in between large-scale resorts such as Torremolinos and Benidorm.

In Portugal, the Algarve has long been popular with British people keen to live a life of quiet luxury, often in retirement. More controlled development continues there, and the north of the country has also been opening up more to home-buyers in recent years.

Where to buy

Iberia is geographically, linguistically, climatically and culturally diverse in ways matched by few regions in Europe; in the south it has a long holiday season and generally speaking, property is still good value. Whichever area you prefer, and whatever your purpose in buying, there is no shortage of choice.

Enterprising estate agents in both Spain and Portugal are heading a bit further inland to appeal to a newer audience of house buyers, keen to sample more of an 'authentic' lifestyle. Meanwhile cheap flights and the 'city break' boom are attracting a younger audience of home-buyers to think about investing in cities as well as the rural idyll.

Barcelona

The capital of the culturally independent, politically semi-autonomous region of Catalonia, Barcelona vies with Madrid for

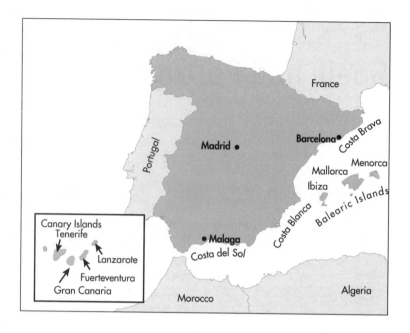

the title of Spain's most exciting city. A cosmopolitan metropolis on the Mediterranean coast, it has much to recommend.

From the narrow streets of the Barri Gòthic and El Born, to the wider avenues of Las Ramblas and the Eixemple, Barcelona has a rewarding historic centre. Within a short metro ride, beyond the harbour, the crowded tenements of the Barceloneta spill out onto Barcelona's most central beach, which continues past the Olympic Village that did so much to rejuvenate the city in 1992, and on towards the Costa Brava.

With the possible exception of Gaudí's extraordinary Modernist architectural efforts, this is a compact and elegant rather than a breathtaking urban landscape; but Barcelona is nevertheless a thriving cultural hub, simultaneously traditional and Modernist and with a charm and energy that few cities in the world can match.

Flats in the centre are, predictably, fairly expensive by Spanish standards, but if you are willing to sacrifice space for location, there are still bargains to be had, and a year-round 'city break' market if you are looking to cover some of the costs with rental income.

What you can get for your money

Price	Location	Description	State of repair
€115,000	Cuitat Vella	• Apartment in 100-year-old block • 35sq m of living space	Completely renovated
€192,000	Eixample	• Attic flat in 100-year-old block • 45sq m of living space • Two bedrooms • 15sq m terrace	Recently refurbished
€495,000	El Born	• Spacious 120sq m converted apartment, with views over church • Two bedrooms • Two terraces	Newly converted
€690,000	Castellvi de Rossanes	• Modern, colonial-style house outside Barcelona with views to Monserrat • 340sq m of living space • Five bedrooms • Four bathrooms • Terraces and 1,000sq m of grounds	Recently built

Madrid

Spain's capital since the mid-sixteenth century, Madrid is a rather less intimate city than Barcelona, but no less enticing for that. At 646 metres above sea level, this is the highest capital in Europe – which helps give Madrid a singular climate which some describe as being, at any given point, either way too hot or way too cold.

Packed to the rafters with cultural and historic delights – the city has more than 200 churches, for example – the artistic highlight is almost certainly the Prado, one of the most important museums in the world. Architectural treats abound, including the Palacio Real, the Plaza Mayor and even the main railway station, the Estacion de Atocha. But it is the people themselves who bring this most vibrant of cities alive, whether by contributing towards the pulsating nightlife or by making use of the impressive range of public spaces in the city – a stroll in the beautiful Parque del Buen Retiro is de rigueur on a Sunday afternoon.

Decent-sized flats in the city centre are, predictably, fairly expensive and may need some renovating; more modern houses with gardens can be found to the west of the city but although they offer much more space, these are often expensive too.

What you can get for your money

Price	Location	Description	State of repair
€126,000	Centrico	• 45sq m studio flat • Lift and concierge in building	Satisfactory
€184,000	Latina	• 55sq m three-roomed flat plus bathroom • In a 1950s building	Satisfactory
€330,000	Barajes	• 110sq m apartment overlooking park • Four bedrooms • Two bathrooms • Garden and terrace • Lift	Needs minor updating
€516,000	Retiro	• Seven-room apartment plus two bathrooms • Garage • 160sq m of living space	Recently converted

Costa del Sol, Costa de la Luz and Costa del Almería

The classic images of Spain – flamenco dancers, Moorish architecture, Don Juan, Carmen – nearly all originate from Andalucía. This dry, mountainous region stretches from Portugal in the west to the border with Murcia in the east, and takes in no fewer than eight of Spain's provincial capitals (Almería, Córdoba, Cádiz, Granada, Huelva, Jaén, Malaga and Seville).

Andalucía is one of the warmest regions in Europe, with hot, dry summers and mild winters – so it is hardly surprising that it now plays host to more than 400,000 foreign residents, lured there since the 1950s and 1960s when Costa del Sol resorts such as Torremolinos first edged their way to the top of Britain's holiday hit parade. More recently, the Costa de la Luz, around Huelva and Cádiz, and the Costa de Almería, have begun to feature on the package-tour trail; and *urbanizaciones* (holiday estates), town-centre apartments and golf resorts of variable architectural merit now cram much of the coastline.

Meanwhile, home-seekers looking for unspoilt Spain have gone inland to discover previously little-known whitewashed villages in rugged landscapes yet within easy travelling distance from the region's two main airports, at Malaga and Almería – in areas such as Axarquia and the Alpujarras, for example.

There are still plenty of rustic properties awaiting conversion to be found off the beaten track, while on the coast are great numbers of purpose-built holiday properties.

What you can get for your money

Price	Location	Description	State of repair
€50,000	Cutar (Axarquia, eastern Costa del Sol)	• Whitewashed village house on three levels • 100sq m of living space	Needs total restoration including new roof
€81,000	Roquetas de Mar (Costa de Almería)	• One-bedroomed apartment • 56sq m of living space • 10sq m terrace • Shared pool and parking • 50m from beach	Satisfactory
€102,000	Estepona (Costa del Sol)	• One-bedroomed apartment in *urbanizacion* • 52sq m of living space • Large terrace • Communal pool • Furnished • Includes car	Satisfactory
From €140,000	Almerimar (Costa de Almería)	• New development of two- or three-bedroomed apartments • 5 mins from golf course • Lake with private beach • Facilities include two pools and tennis courts • 75m from sea	Not yet completed
€198,000	Manilva (western Costa del Sol)	• Three-bedroomed townhouse • Two bathrooms • Two terraces, garden and garage • 130sq m living area plus 25sq m of terraces	Needs minor work
€526,000	Aquadulce (Costa de Almería)	• Four-bedroomed, air-conditioned villa overlooking golf course • Four bathrooms • Own pool • Three terraces and garden • Large garage • Attached but separate one-bedroomed guest flat	Recently built

Costa Calida, Costa Blanca and Costa del Azahar

Second only to the Costa del Sol, the Costa Blanca has been extremely popular with the British since the 1960s, and there are substantial expatriate communities throughout the region, which includes the touristy Benidorm and the prettier, rather more discreet villa complexes of Denia, Javea, Calpe and Altea to the north.

What you can get for your money

Price	Location	Description	State of repair
€48,000	Cartagena (Costa Calida)	• Two-bedroomed village house • Several km from town of Cartanega	Needs total refurbishment
€87,000	Torrevieja (Costa Blanca)	• First-floor apartment in an urban block • Two bedrooms • Shared pool • Furnished	Satisfactory
€138,000	Ribarroja, near Valencia	• Rural house • Currently split into two apartments (one with two bedrooms; the other with three bedrooms) • Large pool • Gardens	Minor work needed; could be made into single house by replacing external stairs
€195,000	Javea (Costa Blanca)	• Three-bedroomed apartment • 100sq m of living space • On second floor with open views over the centre of the port • Terrace • Air-conditioning in lounge and main bedroom	Totally refurbished
€217,000	Lliria (inland, north-west of Valencia)	• Substantial three- to four-bedroomed 1970s house • Two bathrooms • Two terraces and garden on 1,000sq m plot • Swimming pool	Minor work needed

Property prices are lower here than in the Andalucian Costas, and even more so on the Costa Calida, which runs to the south of Alicante and is now served by budget routes into Murcia airport – although there is little to recommend this Costa apart from the climate and the sporting opportunities proffered by the growing number of golf-linked *urbanizaciones* around La Manga.

North of the Costa Blanca runs the Costa del Azahar, relatively unknown outside Spain and which takes in the coastline of the

Valencia and Castellon provinces. It includes a number of small-scale family resorts, including Benicarló and Peñíscola, which are very busy in August but quieter for the rest of the year. The biggest resort on this Costa, Benicassim, meanwhile, has emulated Ibiza by marketing itself as a hotspot for beach ravers.

Costa Dorada and Costa Brava

The Costa Dorada stretches down from Barcelona in the north towards the Costa del Azahar in the south. Its most famous resort until fairly recently, Salou is a smaller version of Benidorm and Torremolinos, and still has plenty of affordable property on offer. The more upmarket resort of Sitges, just south of Barcelona, has become a much more popular prospect for property hunters. It is a well-known and long-established gay centre.

What you can get for your money

Price	Location	Description	State of repair
€195,000	Begur (Costa Brava)	• Restored three-bedroomed fisherman's house • Terrace and garden • In old part of town, with sea and mountain views	Good
€250,000	Tortosa (inland from Costa Dorada)	• Palazzo-style villa in town • Five bedrooms • Three bathrooms • 400sq m of living space on an 800sq m plot	Needs minor restoration
€295,000	Sant Feliu (Costa Brava)	• Apartment with terrace and views • Three bedrooms • Two bathrooms	Recently built
€450,000	Playa d'Aro (Costa Brava)	• Four-bedroomed villa with two bathrooms and fantastic views • Total built area 200sq m • Pool, terraces, garden, parking on 1,200sq m plot	Excellent

Prices in Sitges and along much of the Costa Brava to the north of the Catalan capital have risen considerably in recent years, as week-enders from Barcelona and foreigners continue to buy up coastal properties within what is becoming a well-established commuter belt.

Girona airport offers budget links to the north of the region, where there is some potential for restoring ruined *masies* (huge farm chalets that can be found on hillsides throughout Catalonia) – especially because of the added advantage of proximity to the skiing regions of the Pyrenees – but as a whole, the beauty and geography of the region, rather than low prices, will always be the Costa Brava's strongest selling point.

Less-explored areas of mainland Spain

Although north Europeans have been visiting, and in parts colonising, Spain en masse for decades now, they tend to concentrate on finding themselves a 'place in the sun'. So while the more adventurous might look a few kilometres inland rather than in the more obvious resorts, most still focus on the southern and eastern coasts of the Iberian peninsula. All of which leaves huge, relatively underpopulated, parts of the country largely unexplored by British tourists.

Spain's north coast has been a popular destination for Spanish holidaymakers for many years for example, as they flee the very summer temperatures which draws so many northerners further south. More recently Bilbao's Guggenheim Museum has brought the Basque Country to a wider tourist audience, along with occasional TV and newspaper articles about the charms of Galicia's fjords (*rias*) and the pilgrimage trail to Santiago de Compostela.

What you can get for your money

Price	Map Location	Description	State of repair
€30,000	Cistierna (León)	• Six-bedroomed house with one bathroom • 200sq m • Remote rural location	Needs major restoration
€30,000	Lugo (Galicia)	• 120sq m house • 500sq m land	For total refurbishment
€54,000	Caceres (Extremadura)	• 60sq m apartment in small town • Three rooms plus bathroom • Terrace	Good
€162,000	Vallejo de Mena (Burgos)	• Farmhouse • Outbuildings • 2,000sq m of land • Close to Bilbao airport and Santander ferry port	With major work could make two separate three-four-bedroomed properties

Further south, the country is much more mountainous and there are plenty of spectacular, culturally idiosyncratic regions to discover, such as the two Castiles (Castilla-León and Castilla-La Mancha) and the Extremadura, as well as the softer landscapes of the Rioja wine region.

Outside the cities and the Costas, property prices are considerably lower. There is much to be said for those adventurous enough and who speak reasonably good Spanish to hire a car and see what they can find. Certainly there are many small, historic towns relatively untouched by the twenty-first century.

Balearic Islands

What you can get for your money

Price	Location	Description	State of repair
€60,000	Santa Ponsa (Mallorca)	• 35sq m studio • Balcony • Shared pool • Near golf courses • 30 mins to Palma Airport	Satisfactory
€133,000	Mahón (Minorca)	• Two-bedroomed apartment on third floor • 74sq m of living space • Small balcony • Parking	Good
€316,000	Port de Pollenca (Mallorca)	• Recently refurbished four-bedroomed townhouse • Two bathrooms • 198sq m of living space	Good
€1,600,000	Ibiza Town	• Spacious air-conditioned villa • Five bedrooms • Four bathrooms • Security gates, swimming pool, gardens and views • 15 mins into Ibiza Town, 15 mins to beach	Excellent

Apart from a few notable exceptions, such as San Antonio in Ibiza and Magaluf in Mallorca, the local communities of the Balearic Islands have retained their own character remarkably well in the face of package tourism on a major scale since the 1970s.

The capitals of each of the three main islands – Palma (Mallorca), Mahón (Menorca) and Ibiza Town (Ibiza) – are bustling towns in their own right, however dependent the local economies are on the tourist trade. Elsewhere, *urbanizaciones*, some with sporting facilities attached, have appeared – generally fairly sympathetic to the local landscape, and offering plenty of space and beach access. There are also plenty of quiet, characterful villages away from the main sprawl; on Mallorca are Port de Pollenca and poet Robert Graves' favoured retreat at Deya, for example.

Despite being a firm favourite with UK visitors for many years now, the Balearics have been much more popular with Germans for property investment, but the season, especially in Mallorca, can be surprisingly long so buying a holiday home here can, if the price is right, still be a shrewd move.

Canary Islands

What you can get for your money

Price	Location	Description	State of repair
€87,000	Chio (Tenerife)	• Three-bedroomed rustic house • 70sq m of living space, with planning permission for house of twice that size • Sea and mountain views	Derelict
€130,000	Puerto de Mogán (Gran Canaria)	• Air-conditioned apartment • One bedroom • Garden • Views over the harbour • Part-furnished	Immaculate
€153,000	Adeje (Tenerife)	• Three-bedroomed apartment • Two bathrooms • 95sq m of living space • Balcony with sea views • Garage	Good
€428,000	Corralejo (Fuerteventura)	• Two-bedroomed villa near beach • Three bathrooms • 160sq m of living space on 900sq m land • Own swimming pool	Excellent

The Canary Islands' natural resources – an outstanding year-round climate that is often referred to as an 'eternal spring', combined with superb beaches and extraordinary volcanic landscapes – make them a popular choice for British homebuyers; both those looking for somewhere warm to retire to, and for property investors. As in coastal Spain, the choice is between purpose-built villas and apartments, older houses and flats in towns and villages, and rural properties suitable for conversion.

There are seven islands in the group, but the four biggest are Gran Canaria, Fuerteventura, Lanzarote and Tenerife; each has its busier resorts and quieter, more exclusive areas, with the most over-developed locations including Playa de las Américas in Tenerife and Playa des Inglés in Gran Canaria. The three smaller islands, La Palma, La Gomera and El Hierro, have recently attracted more interest from foreign buyers keen to find something a little more remote than the rest of the Canaries; these may be worth considering if easy access is less of an issue.

Portugal

Portugal's hilly and elegant capital, Lisbon, is one of Europe's truly great cities, with a grid-shaped, historic centre – the Baixa – linked via funiculars to the more laid back, bohemian Bairro Alto and the sophisticated shopping streets of the Chiado; a short tram ride to the east and you are a world away, in the proud yet impoverished ramshackle lanes of the Alfama. Provoked in part by an influx of

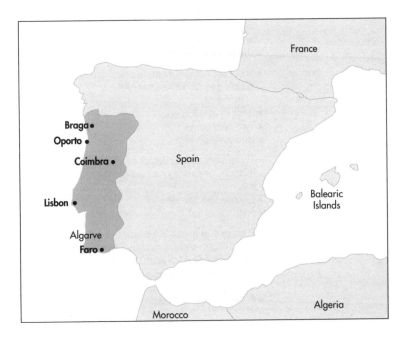

people from Portugal's former colonies in Brazil and Africa, Lisbon is genuinely a cultural melting pot, with a nightlife to match. Flats are surprisingly affordable, but expect to pay a premium if you want the views and carefree atmosphere of the Bairro Alto.

What you can get for your money

Price	Location	Description	State of repair
€66,000	Sagres (Algarve)	• 1,720sq m land plot	Land only
€70,000	Cascais (Lisbon coast)	• 38sq m apartment • Balcony • Walking distance to town centre	Good
€90,000	Lisbon	• Ground-floor city-centre apartment • 50sq m of living space • One bedroom • Patio	Recently refurbished
€95,000	Lagos (Algarve)	• Two-bedroomed country house • 100sq m of living space • 180sq m of land	Needs minor work
From €135,000 (minimum)	Praia da Luz (Algarve)	• Studios and one- to three-bedroomed apartments in a new development • 200m from the beach • Shared indoor and outdoor swimming pools, restaurant, sports facilities • Underground parking	Due to complete 2005
€175,000	Lisbon	• Top-floor apartment in historic building in Bairro Alto with views over the city • 80sq m of living space • Two bedrooms • One bathroom	Excellent
€300,000	Aveiro (on coast, south of Oporto)	• Three-bedroomed detached villa • Includes separate one-bedroomed flat • Garage and gardens • Fully furnished	Good
€493,000	Quinta do Lago (Algarve)	• 80sq m one-bedroomed apartment • On 110sq m plot overlooking the prestigious San Lorenzo golf course • Shared facilities include tennis courts and swimming pools • Private garden and lawned terrace	Excellent

If a city apartment is not appealing, the nearby resorts of Estoril and Cascais may be a suitable alternative – although property is very much in demand here, both among foreign tourists and *Lisboetas* looking to escape the city at weekends and during school holidays. Head inland, and you can find beautiful and remote areas with plenty of property development potential within easy reach of Lisbon airport. Parts of inland Portugal still feel remarkably unchanged by the 21st – or even the 20th Century.

Most Britons buy in the Algarve – the southernmost province of Portugal, which faces the Atlantic but is much more Mediterranean in feel. The Algarve has warm seas and excellent beaches, and is fringed with fishing villages, golf courses and tourist developments – although there are strict government regulations in place to restrict any over-development along the coast. There are a number of purpose-built estates aimed at the expatriate buyer along the Eastern and Central Algarve, the most prestigious of which is the Vale do Lobo. Travel a short distance inland and you can discover the historic and atmospheric towns of Loule and Silves. The most extensive development area lies between Lagos and Faro, but the west coast is not nearly as overrun. The stretch between Sarges and Lagos and the area from Faro to the Spanish border has quiet, semi-secluded beaches, picturesque fishing hamlets, friendly hotels and inns, historical sites, forests and sleepy towns.

Elsewhere in Portugal, the region around the northern city of Oporto, taking in the Minho and the Douro Valley, is also an area worth looking at; to the north of the city, a luxuriant green region stretches all the way to the Spanish border, its coastline dotted with a series of charming seaside resorts.

Getting to Spain

By air

Air Europa flies from London Gatwick to Madrid and Palma

bmibaby flies from East Midlands to Alicante, Barcelona, Malaga, Murcia and Palma.

British Airways flies from Birmingham to Barcelona and Madrid; Edinburgh to Madrid; Glasgow to Barcelona and Madrid; London Gatwick to Alicante, Barcelona, Bilbao, Gibraltar, Gran Canaria, Madrid, Malaga, Palma, Seville and Tenerife; London Heathrow to Barcelona, Gibraltar, Madrid, Malaga and Valencia; and from Manchester to Madrid.

easyJet flies from Liverpool to Barcelona, Madrid, Malaga and Palma; Bristol to Alicante, Barcelona, Malaga and Palma; East Midlands to Alicante and Malaga; London Gatwick to Barcelona, Malaga and Palma; London Stansted to Alicante, Barcelona, Bilbao, Jerez de la Frontera, Malaga, Murcia and Palma; and from Luton to Barcelona, Madrid, Malaga and Palma

Iberia flies from Birmingham to Barcelona and Madrid; Edinburgh to Madrid; London Gatwick to Alicante, Barcelona, Bilbao, Madrid, Palma and Tenerife; London Heathrow to Barcelona, Madrid, Malaga, Santiago de Compostela, Seville and Valencia; and from Manchester to Barcelona.

Monarch flies from Luton to Alicante, Gibraltar, Mahon, Malaga and Tenerife; and from Manchester to Alicante, Barcelona, Gibraltar, Malaga, Palma and Tenerife.

Ryanair flies from London Stansted to Barcelona (Girona), Barcelona (Reus), Valladolid, Murcia, Jerez; from Liverpool to Barcelona (Girona); from Birmingham to Murcia and Barcelona (Girona); from Bournemouth to Barcelona (Girona); from Glasgow Prestwick to Barcelona (Girona).

By sea

Brittany Ferries sails from Plymouth to Santander (journey time 24 hours)

P&O Ferries sails from Portsmouth to Bilbao (journey time 27 hours)

Getting to Portugal

Air Portugal (TAP) flies from London Heathrow to Faro, Lisbon and Oporto; from London Gatwick to Lisbon and Oporto; and from Manchester to Lisbon and Oporto.
bmibaby flies from East Midlands to Faro.
British Airways flies from London Gatwick to Faro and Oporto; and from London Heathrow to Lisbon.
easyJet flies from London Stansted to Faro.
Monarch flies from Luton to Faro; and from Manchester to Faro.

The buying process

Although the language is different, the buying process in Portugal is similar to that in Spain, so the advice given below for Spain applies also to Portuguese property transactions. Specific advice for Portugal is given at the end of this section.

Spain

Whether you want an expatriate 'home from home', or are looking for something a little more authentically Iberian, bear in mind that the process of buying a property in Spain is quite different from that in the UK. Be aware too, that there are also plenty of disreputable players in the property game; proceed with caution and have everything checked out by a lawyer.

Finding a property
The sheer number of purpose-built, coastal apartment blocks and villa complexes, and the fact that the second-home market there has been geared up to UK buyers since the 1970s, means it is extremely easy to find a property to buy in Spain. Finding the right one, however, can be bewildering.

Spanish estate agents (*agentes de fincas* or *agentes de propiedad inmobiliara*) come in many forms, ranging from large developers and property sales companies that specialise in selling holiday homes to foreigners, to smaller, local Spanish agents – often one-man enterprises – and foreign-run agencies or intermediaries. To conduct initial researches and make contact with the larger agencies, you do not even have to leave the UK. Selling holiday homes is such big business in Spain that the bigger developers will often advertise their wares at the growing number of overseas property exhibitions which tour UK cities every year. This is an easy way to find an agent, especially if you are interested in a fairly mainstream, purpose-built property as a holiday home or investment.

But even if you are one of the thousands of Britons looking for a fairly standard Costa property, beware of limiting your search by getting drawn too early into dealing with an agent who represents a single property complex, or a small range of developments.

There are many Spanish property websites – some simply operating as virtual shopfronts for Spanish-based agencies, others offering an all-inclusive service from property selection right through to completion of the purchase. Even if you do not go on to use the services of the company in question, these sites can be invaluable as a source of information and a guide to prices.

If you are planning to look for property when on a visit to Spain, you will find no shortage of agents in the main resorts, and the news-stands of the Costas stock numerous English-language publications carrying property adverts.

If you are looking for something off the beaten track, you may find the local *agente de fincas* rather less visible; as in many rural areas of Europe the quality of their window displays and printed particulars might also leave a lot to the imagination, but developing a rapport with a local agent can, if you are lucky, give you access to an invaluable source of information and local knowledge.

It is important to keep an eye out for dubious practitioners working in the property industry in the Costas. Timeshare fraudsters aside (see pages 24–7), until fairly recently, estate agency in Spain was tightly regulated, with all agents needing to be professionally qualified and in possession of a licence to practise. In practice, especially in the busier resort areas, numerous cowboy outfits had begun to operate – a situation which deteriorated thanks to the Spanish government's desire to capitalise on the success of the property industry, which led them to liberate the industry.

Before 2000, estate agents could only practise legally if they were registered with one of two professional bodies – the Gestores Intermediarios en Promociones de Edificaciones (GIPE) (which has links with the pan-European Confédération Européenne d'Immobilier*) and the Agentes de la Propiedad Inmobiliaria (API)*. Only estate agents who were members of these organisations could have a licence to practise; and licences were only given out to people with the correct qualifications.

Now there is more of a free-for-all, but the best advice is still to look for GIPE and API accreditation when searching for a reputable Spanish agent. Ask for details of this, and of liability insurance and bonds, which should be clearly displayed on all correspondence, contracts and other paperwork. The GIPE has a website through which you can find a list of its members across Spain; the API has a *colegio oficial* in each province, whose number will be in the local equivalent of *Yellow Pages*.

Many Spanish agents are well tuned in to the needs and worries of British buyers and can, if you wish, arrange a 'one-stop-shop' approach to the whole buying process, including everything from recommending a lawyer to providing advice on schools and health services for people looking to move over to Spain permanently. This may suit your circumstances perfectly, but tempting as it may be to hand over everything about the purchase for someone else to manage, make sure you are happy with all aspects of such an arrangement. In particular, ensure that you appoint your own lawyer, and that they are well versed in dealing with both Spanish and British law.

As well as Spanish agents, a host of UK-based agents of various sizes operate in Spain; there are also British people living in Spain who act as intermediaries, helping Spanish property firms tap into the lucrative English-speaking market. These are often not officially Spanish estate agents at all, although many of them offer an excellent service and can cut out a lot of the legwork involved in finding a property in Spain when one is based in the UK and is not used to the Spanish way of doing things. Check that any UK-based agent or Spanish-based intermediary you are thinking of dealing with is a member of the UK-based Federation of Overseas Property Developers, Agents and Consultants (FOPDAC)*.

More than in any other European country, you may encounter 'hard-sell' tactics from Spanish developers – it is not uncommon for them to offer you a 'free flight and accommodation' property inspection trip, whereby you are taken round a holiday estate (*urbanizacion*) or two, buttered up with lunch and a few glasses of sangria and then subjected to an extremely intensive, hard-to-refuse sales pitch. Always be circumspect in your dealings and never sign anything without first getting it checked out by a bilingual lawyer.

Selling property privately is much more common in Spain than in the UK – it is estimated that in some areas, especially in the countryside, as many as a fifth of all property transactions go through without an estate agent's involvement. This is perhaps not surprising when one considers the level of commission estate agents charge – which averages around 6 per cent of the purchase price, but can in some cases reach as much as 10 per cent.

You will find 'for sale' (*se vende* or *en venta*) notices outside properties and in a host of other locations, from supermarkets to bars, clubs and even posted on trees. Strictly speaking the vendor has more to gain from a private sale than does the buyer – most of the time it is they who pay the estate agent's commission – but he or she may set the price a little lower as a result.

If you are able to spend some time in Spain looking for property, time is not too pressing, and your Spanish is good enough, you may want to explore the private route and see where it leads you. But if you do follow this approach, for reasons of personal safety never agree to view a house unaccompanied and if you are interested in the property, make sure you have a good lawyer to check out all the necessary paperwork before you go any further.

At all costs, avoid British sellers who claim to want to sell their property direct to you without encumbering the sale with the niceties of Spanish bureaucracy. There have been cases of UK buyers falling for this trick, whereby they 'buy' a property from a British vendor without the property ever legally changing hands at all – the conman still owns it and the buyer has just given him or her tens of thousands of euros for nothing.

Agreeing to buy

As in many other parts of continental Europe, Spain has a system whereby contracts are signed at an earlier stage than is the case in the UK – so if you are at the stage of viewing properties and do not want to waste everyone's time, including your own, it is important to be ready to commit to a purchase quickly. But whether you are buying a property that has not yet been built, or one that has been standing for hundreds of years, it is vital to have any kind of contract checked out thoroughly by a bilingual lawyer before you make a commitment to buy.

And if, as is often the case with Spanish properties, the seller or his or her agent gives you English versions of Spanish documentation, do not assume they are accurate translations – get the original Spanish paperwork and the English translations checked out at the same time.

Existing properties

If you are buying an existing property – often known as a 'resale', to distinguish it from a new-build villa or apartment – there are three different ways to proceed once you have found a property you want to buy.

The first is to make an offer to buy – a formal, written offer to the seller, stating that you want to buy the property for a stated price, and that you will complete the transaction within a stated period. With an offer to buy you would normally pay a deposit (*arras*) to the estate agent, of around 2 to 5 per cent of the price offered.

The second is a reservation contract, whereby the seller agrees to take the property off the market for a fixed period and sell it to you at the stated price, within the agreed period. Again, you pay a deposit, on the understanding that if you decide not to go ahead with the purchase – apart from under particular, predefined circumstances, written into the contract – you will lose the money. If the seller pulls out, you can claim compensation.

The third and most common form of preliminary contract – which also has the advantage of committing the seller to the deal, as well as you – is the *contrato privado de compraventa*. The *contrato privado* commits both parties to the transaction, so that the seller must sell to you at a stated price, via whatever terms are set out in the contract, and you must buy. You will almost certainly pay a 10 per cent deposit at this point, which you forfeit if you fail to complete. If the seller pulls out, he or she must pay you back double.

The *contrato privado* should contain a number of routine clauses covering, for example, the names of the parties to the contract; a full description of the property, including its land registry entry; details of who is to pay the estate agent what commission; who the notary will be and when the final deed will be signed; and what happens if the parties break the contract.

Issues to cover in the *contrato privado*

- That in legal terms, the property and its boundaries match what you think you are buying.
- That the people you are buying the property from are actually its owners, i.e. it is their names that appear on the local land register (*registro de la propiedad*); it is these people whose names should appear in the purchase contract.
- If there are any existing debts or mortgages against the property, these must be paid by the seller before legal ownership transfers to you, or they become your responsibility.
- That the proper planning consents have been sought, building regulations followed, fines paid and so on.
- Where you are buying a plot of land, that it is properly designated as land permitted to be developed.
- Exactly what is included in (and excluded from) the sale; issues about rights of way and so on.
- Pre-emption rights, for example if the vendor co-owns the property with someone else, who automatically has the right to buy it in preference to you.
- In the case of a new-build, what the arrangements are for stage payments, completion dates and the like.

Depending on the timing and whether or not you have already made a formal offer to buy, your lawyer may have already conducted some preliminary searches; alternatively, you may have gone straight to *contrato privado*, in which case the bulk of the checks on the property will need to take place after you are already signed up to the deal. Standard checks in Spain include a check on the planning status of the property (the *informe urbanistico*); whether or not the seller is the registered owner; and whether it is being sold free of mortgages (both these elements should be revealed by the *nota simple* – property register). Beyond these, it is important to talk in detail with your lawyer about all aspects concerning the nature and location of the property, and how you might choose to use it, so as to identify any other, special enquiries you might need to make.

The contract should, in any case, contain a series of appropriate escape clauses (*condiciones resolutorias*) making clear the circumstances under which you reserve the right to pull out of the transaction and have your deposit refunded. Standard escape clauses might stipulate, for example, that you can pull out if you are unable to secure a mortgage at a particular rate, if the results of the searches are unsatisfactory, if planning permission is not forthcoming, or if the results of a survey (see pages 139–40) are of concern; and that the seller must clear all debts relating to the property before the deed of sale can be signed (see box on pages 134–5).

Newly built properties

Many people buying properties in Spain do so 'off-plan' at a stage when the building has not yet been finished – or not even started. In such cases the initial step, once you have identified the property you want to buy, is to sign a reservation contract, as outlined above. Having reserved the property, you must then agree a full preliminary contract (as above), at which point you may be expected to pay a deposit of as much as 40 per cent of the purchase price. In this scenario, there are several different ways of dealing with the fact that the building has not yet been built.

The preferable one is to buy the land outright, along with whatever the seller has built on it already; and to separately enter into a contract for building the rest of the property, under which you pay by instalments according to the progress of the construction. This approach gives you the security of owning the land from the start, so that if the building company went bust or you were not happy with the way the development was going, you could draw a line under the project at that point and bring in other builders to complete the work.

This type of contract works best where you are buying a property on its own plot of land, rather than as part of an existing development. It suits a more 'bespoke' approach, where you perhaps buy a plot of land from a builder or developer, who at the same time offers to build a house for you.

An 'off-plan' contract is more common, and is typical to villa or apartment complexes, whereby you agree to buy a property once it has been built. Again, you make payments as the building goes up,

Fees and taxes on Spanish purchases

- VAT – Spanish IVA (*impuesto sobre el valor añadido*) – is payable at 7 per cent on newly built properties and land, and on building work if you are doing a self-build. Bear in mind that if you are doing a self-build, you can put in a swimming pool and garage and be charged IVA at 7 per cent as part of the overall project, whereas if you were doing them separately you would have to pay 16 per cent.
- Property transfer tax (*impuesto sobre transmisiones patrimoniales*), which is charged at 6 per cent, is payable on all other purchases.
- Stamp duty of 0.5 per cent is charged on new-builds.
- Notary fees are worked out on the basis of a graduated schedule set by government. For a property costing €150,000 the fee would be around €330. Land registry fees cost a similar amount.
- A local capital gains tax (known variously as *plus valia*, *impuesto de plus valia* and the *incremento de valor de bienes de naturaleza urbana*) is levied on Spanish property sellers, but the convention is that this is paid by the buyer – basically because the tax bill normally arrives after the sale has gone through and the liability stays with the property rather than the previous owner, so if the

but you do not own the property outright until the very end, when the property is finished. Developers prefer this kind of contract, because it makes you dependent on them to finish the job; they often want a schedule of payments on set dates too, regardless of how fast or slow the building work is progressing. At the very least it is worth pushing for payments to be dependent on how much of the property is completed, to give you more leverage.

Shared facilities

If you are buying in a villa or apartment complex, chances are you will be buying into a 'community of owners' (*comunidad de propietarios*). This is a legal entity which exists to deal with shared facilities such as communal swimming pools, lifts, parking areas, external lighting, shared gardens and so on.

The *comunidad* has no impact on your ownership of your own property, which you will own outright. It is simply a mechanism vendor disappears without having paid it, it will be up to you as the buyer to pay it anyway. *Plus valia* is on a progressive scale from 2 to 40 per cent; in most cases the total amount due is fairly low, but if the property has not been sold for a long time and the value has shot up, it can be an unpleasant surprise. To find out how much *plus valia* will be due, contact the town hall. If at all possible you should negotiate for the equivalent amount to be deducted from the purchase price; alternatively, you may agree with the vendor that he or she must pay the tax – but make sure a clause to this effect is written into the contract. Be aware that the tax authorities will still come after you for the money, however, and that you may have to take the vendor to court to prove your point.

- Withholding tax – although it costs you nothing, it is worth noting that if you are buying your property from a person or company not resident in Spain, you must by law withhold 5 per cent of the purchase price and pay this to the tax authorities rather than to the seller. This is then set against the seller's total capital gains tax liability from the sale. This rule does not apply if the non-resident has owned the property for more than ten years (or twenty in the case of a company).

through which all the owners in the development band together to manage and pay for common facilities. Each *comunidad* has a committee which must hold an annual general meeting, and its own rules (*reglementos*) covering everything from use of the swimming pool to whether or not pets are permitted. It also charges fees – which may fluctuate considerably depending on how much maintenance work is required on the site – for which all owners are responsible, as stipulated according to the size of your property.

Make sure you are clear about the restrictions imposed by the *comunidad* into which you are considering buying, and that they fit in with your lifestyle. Many stipulate no use of the swimming pool after 10pm, for example; some are much stricter and say you cannot play ball games in the pool or gardens which, if you are a parent of young children, would probably be enough to put you off buying there completely.

Finalising the transaction

In some senses, and subject to the conditions laid down in it, the *contrato privado* signifies that you own the property, but only in respect of the previous owner having agreed to pass it on to you. What makes the transfer legal in terms of the rest of the world is the signing of the deed of sale (the *escritura de compraventa*).

As in many other European countries, in Spain the legal transfer of properties can only take place through a notary (*notario*), who must be based in offices in the area where the property is being purchased. The *notario* prepares the *escritura* and is responsible for its registration in the property register (*registro de la propiedad)* and tax register *(registro catastral)*; he or she charges fees to the vendor and purchaser, according to a fee schedule set by the government.

In theory it is the buyer who chooses the notary, but in practice – especially where you are buying new property – the seller tends to have a big say in this decision. Often the notary will have been involved in getting together all the relevant information for the developer when he or she bought the land on which to build the development and then split it into separate plots to sell on, for example; so it makes sense for the notary to deal with the subsequent transactions as well. This may sound a little risky, but as long as you have an adequate level of legal advice to protect you, there is no reason why it should be – notaries are neutral observers of property transactions rather than acting for either party.

During the period between signing the *contrato privado* and signing the *escritura* – theoretically between four and eight weeks but often longer than that – your lawyer will carry out all the agreed checks on the property, and sort out all the necessary documentation for the finalisation of the deal. In the meantime, you will need to arrange all the finances so that everything is in place for the deed to transfer on the agreed date.

All property owners in Spain, whether resident or not, must obtain a tax identification number, *número de identificación de extranjeros* (NIE), from the local tax administration office or police station – you will not be able to pay your taxes or register your property without it. Tax is an issue to be particularly aware of when buying a property in Spain. As explained on pages 134–5, there are numerous taxes payable whenever property is bought and sold, and as a result there has been, as in Italy, a tradition of under-declaring property values.

The authorities are coming down much harder on under-declaration than in the past, although few would deny that it still occurs to some extent. These days, the Spanish taxman can normally be relied upon to turn a blind eye as long as the under-declaration works out at less than about €15,000 or 20 per cent of the real value (as assessed by the tax office). Under-declaration is illegal, so lawyers' advice is always to avoid it at all costs. If the authorities catch you out, they can force you to pay the tax you have dodged, with interest and penalties; they can also insist on buying the property from you at the price declared in the *escritura*.

Building your own property

Unlike in many other countries, where the emphasis tends to be on restoring old property, in Spain there is a big market for land where you can build your own home. Many estate agencies offer plots of vacant land (*parcelas*) for sale as well as existing properties. Building your own property is considered relatively economical in Spain when compared to restoration work – the table overleaf gives an idea of costs. Bear in mind that land tends to cost anything from around €30 to €150 per square metre.

Before you start negotiations, however, it is vital to ask your lawyer to investigate the proposed plot thoroughly – this will include examining the title of the land and checking out its planning status. The relevant town hall will have a town plan, *plan general de ordenacion urbana* (PGOU), which will indicate which zone your proposed property would come into. Normally the PGOU is approved every four years, and any interim changes in them must be publicly posted and approved, with a chance for affected property owners to protest or makes claims.

If your land is located in an existing and approved *urbanizacion*, you should have no problems gaining a building permit, but you must check – and check that the *urbanizacion* is, indeed, approved. You can find out by asking to see the *proyecto de urbanisation* and the *plan parcial*, at the town hall.

Buying land in areas that are already fairly built up should generally present no problem, because such land is likely to be clas-sified as *fincas urbanas* – which means planning permission should be fairly easy to obtain. However, purchasing land in a rural area can prove rather more problematic – if it is classified as a *finca rustica* it will not be classified as building land, and normally only fairly large areas of agricultural land will be allowed building permits; on a practical level there may be other problems too – it may be extremely difficult and costly to arrange connection to water, electricity, sewage and roads, for example.

Typical building costs in Spain

The following figures, produced by the Fundacion Instituto de Propietarios Extranjeros (FIPE)* – a group for foreign property owners – relate to the construction of a modest house in Catalunya (which is considered relatively expensive as compared to areas such as the Costa Blanca), built in May 2003.

Item	Cost (per sq m)
Land movement	€5.41
Foundations	€21.85
Structures	€55.35
Drainage	€9.21
Bulky brickwork	€131.71
Brickwork on roof and waterproofing	€36.45
Brickwork for façade	€25.51
Brickwork for flooring	€25.43
Brickwork indoors	€15.94
Plasterwork and ceilings	€25.76
Locksmith	€3.83
Carpentry outdoors	€20.47
Carpentry indoors	€24.78
Venetian blinds	€10.31
Plumbing	€16.08
Sanitary ware	€11.21
Electrics	€16.96
Stove and kitchen	€12.60
Glasswork	€4.81
Painting and stucco	€16.41
Other	€8.54
Total	€498.62
Insurance	€9.97
Architect's fee, building permits	€67.31
Total cost per square metre	€575.90 plus IVA (7%) = 616.21

Watch out for local planning laws too, which in Valencia, for example, are so geared towards the needs of the tourist industry that private property owners (including you, if you buy there) can be forced to sell parts of their land to developers creating new *urbanizaciones*.

It is fairly common for *parcelas* in *urbanizaciones* to be offered for sale; if you are buying land of this type, make sure the sale price includes all services (water, paved road, electricity and sewage for example) to the border of the plot you are considering. Get your lawyer to check all the relevant permissions for the land – and surrounding areas – extremely carefully; and, as explained above, if you are buying from a builder or developer under a deal whereby they will also construct the property, make sure you get legal title to the land itself straight away and that the contract allows you to get rid of them and bring in another team.

Once your lawyer has made all the necessary checks, he or she should be able to give you the go-ahead to buy the land on the basis that there is no reason why you should not obtain a building permit (*permiso de edificar*). The next stage, while you are also going about buying the land, is to engage an architect or builder to produce a set of plans and detailed specifications for the building (known as a *memoria de calidades*). For a list of qualified Spanish architects – and of UK architects operating in Spain – contact the Consejo Superior de los Colegios de Arquitectos de España (CSCAE)★.

Many larger builders have 'off the shelf' designs for various types of home, which you may wish to use or adapt; they will also manage and oversee the entire project, if you wish. Whether you are going for the 'off the shelf' approach or going it alone by paying an architect to draw up your own design, the *memoria* will form part of your contract with the builder, so make sure it is right before you commit.

Depending on how much time you have at your disposal, and whether you are able to be in Spain to oversee matters, obtain as many building quotes (*presupuestos*) as you can, and make sure that the eventual contract you agree is absolutely clear about what is included in the price and what is not.

Negotiate a reasonable date for completion of the work, and agree that if this is not met, the builder will pay you a set amount per day for being late. It is customary to pay a proportion of the total building price upfront, and to hold back between 5 and 10 per cent of the price until after the work has been done, to allow for any 'snagging' problems.

Once the project is complete, you will need a fistful of paperwork, including a *boletín de instalaciones eléctricas* from the electrician, a *certificado de fin de obra* from the architect and a *cédula de habitabilidad* from the town hall (to certify the building is fit to live in). To inscribe the house on the plan of your plot lodged with the land registry, you will need to get your notary to prepare a *declaración de obra nueva*.

Restoring old property

A minority of foreign buyers in Spain opt for older properties, such as a village house or a traditional farmhouse built around a courtyard (*cortijo*). If you fall into this category the first action you will need to take is to instigate a survey of the property. Restoring property can prove so expensive that sometimes you would be well advised to knock the original building down and build a new one from scratch.

Depending on where you are in the country and any personal recommendations you may have received, you might wish to employ a Spanish surveyor to examine the building.

Spanish surveys tend not to be as comprehensive as British ones, but some Spanish surveyors are more geared towards the British market. Unless their English is exemplary, you will need to arrange for translations, which can add to the expense. Expect to pay between €700 and €2,000 for a survey. Alternatively, you could use one of a growing band of British surveyors that has relocated to Spain to serve UK buyers. Make sure they have sufficient experience of Spanish building techniques to give you a meaningful appraisal of the building, however – and that they have indemnity insurance to cover provision of Spanish reports. Taking into account the fact that the report will not need to be translated, costs are comparative to those of Spanish surveyors.

If the renovation work you are proposing involves changes to the outside of the property, you will need to obtain a building licence (*licencia de obra*) from the town hall; your lawyer will get this for you.

Portugal

If you are planning to look for a property through an estate agent in Portugal, look for a state-licensed one (*mediador autorizado*), who should be able to prove his or her status by showing you his or her AMI number. As in Spain, use a bilingual lawyer and preferably one who has experience of both the Portuguese and UK systems. Lawyers must have an *asses* number; if in doubt, contact the Portuguese Chamber of Commerce in the UK, which will provide a list of qualified lawyers and an information pack on buying abroad.

The first concrete step towards a purchase is called a promissory contract (*contrato promessa de conipra e venda*). A legally binding contract between vendor and purchaser, this spells out the terms of the sale, agrees on payments and confirms your commitment via a deposit, which is usually no less than 10 per cent of the total purchase price. If you break this contract – subject to the provisos laid down in it – you forfeit your deposit. If the seller reneges, he or she must pay you twice the amount of the deposit.

The documents needed for any property sale to go through are the title deeds (*certidao do registo predial*); a *caderneta urbana* from the tax office, which acts like an ID card for the property, defining its size, the borders of its land and a rateable value; and, assuming the property was built after 1950, the licence to show that it complies with all relevant building regulations (*licenca de habitacao*).

The notary (*notano*) will also need your fiscal number (*numero de contribuinte*) in order to register you for payment of property taxes (*contribuicao predial*). As in Spain, the *escritura* is the legal deed of conveyance between the vendor and buyer, and is carried out by the notary, who registers the deed and pays the relevant taxes.

The biggest issue when buying in Portugal has traditionally been a punitive property transfer tax known as SISA. Under the SISA regime, the first €80,000 of the registered purchase price was tax-free and everything over that amount was charged at rates that went as high as 10 per cent. The tax had to be paid prior to completion of the purchase.

For tax-avoidance purposes, a tradition developed whereby many Portuguese properties in the higher price ranges were made available for purchase 'offshore'. The idea was that a company registered in a tax haven (like the Channel Islands or Gibraltar for example) owned the property as its sole asset, so instead of buying the property, you bought the company – thus the property itself never transferred to you, and you avoided SISA. There was also no capital gains tax on the sale, and no death duties.

In the last few years the Portuguese government has cracked down on this offshore loophole by tightening regulations around such companies; imposing a presumed minimum rental income for income tax purposes; and establishing special, higher rates of *contribuicao autarquica* for properties owned in this way. As a result, some property owners have transferred their offshore companies to different tax jurisdictions, most notably the US state of Delaware; others are, expensively, transferring the property into their own names, thus incurring the new transfer tax (see table below) and capital gains tax along the way.

In June 2003, SISA was replaced with a new transfer tax known as *imposto municipal sobre as transmissoes* (IMT) (see box below), which is progressive and so penalises people buying more expensive properties the most. On a property costing €140,000 it would cost €2,100, for example; on a property worth twice that, the tax would be €12,000 – nearly six times higher. IMT is charged at 15 per cent on property owned through an offshore company based in a black-listed jurisdiction, including the Channel Islands and the Isle of Man. For further information see page 152.

The new Portuguese property transfer tax

Value of property	Tax rate (%)	Allowance to be deducted from percentage calculation
Up to €80,000	0	None
€80,000–110,000	2	€1,600
€110,000–150,000	5	€4,900
€150,000–250,000	7	€7,900
€250,000–500,000	8	€10,400
More than €500,000	6	None

Financial matters

The headline prices of many properties in Spain and Portugal may make purchasing property look extremely tempting, when you compare them with what you get for your money in the UK. But you still need to think carefully whether you can afford to own a second home and the best way to finance your property purchase. Most importantly, take independent financial advice – if necessary from several sources – before going any further.

Mortgages

The first choice when buying in Spain or Portugal is whether to take out a euro mortgage or re-mortgage your UK home and raise finance that way. Whichever approach you take, you are likely to need a substantial amount of capital to kick-start your purchase.

Spanish and Portuguese lenders will generally lend up to 80 per cent of the value of the property, but 75 per cent or less is more common. Just because some British lenders are happy to entertain 100 per cent loans does not mean the same loan-to-value ratios are available everywhere.

To be really safe, and taking into account the high transactional costs when buying in these countries, it probably makes sense to borrow only two-thirds or less of the total cost of the property, if at all possible. Bear in mind also that there is usually a lower limit of around £20,000 on the amount lenders will lend; some will even refuse to lend on properties worth less than a certain amount, or in more obscure locations.

The vast majority of Spanish and Portuguese mortgages are lent on a repayment basis, although some specialist providers may agree an interest-only deal; most are for 15 years, but occasionally 25-year loans will be considered – so long as they are fully paid off by the age of 70, or sometimes 65. Fixed rates are the norm.

As in France, Spanish and Portuguese lenders will assess you according to your ability to service the loan. As a rule of thumb, they will look at your net income (your earnings after tax and national insurance have been deducted), divide it by three and say that this amount should cover all your existing monthly outgoings plus the proposed repayments on the new mortgage. Existing outgoings are classed as mortgages, loans and any maintenance payments – credit-card repayments do not count. If you are applying for a joint loan, both incomes will be taken into account. So if your joint net monthly income is £3,000 and you have a mortgage on your UK property that costs £500 a month, and a car loan that costs £200 a month, the lender would look at the first £1,000, take off £700, and consider offering you a loan with repayments of up to £300 per month.

Generally speaking, lenders will not consider rental income for mortgage purposes, unless you are renting out a property to permanent tenants rather than for holiday lettings. If you buy somewhere with a solid rental income record, you may be able to persuade a lender to take this into account.

As in the rest of the euro currency zone, Iberian mortgage rates are generally lower than in the UK at the moment, but do remember that payments will fluctuate with the sterling/euro exchange rate – and that these fluctuations can be substantial. If you are taking out a euro mortgage, shop around to make sure you are getting a good exchange rate; specialist currency dealers are likely to give you a better rate than a high-street bank. It is also possible to 'forward buy', which means agreeing to buy all your euros for the next year at a price agreed in advance – this has the advantage of certainty, but obviously means you can gain or lose according to what happens to the exchange rate during the period of the deal.

Negotiating a re-mortgage on your UK property may be a cheaper option than a foreign loan in terms of set-up costs, especially if you stay with the same lender; you will not need any extra life insurance; and particularly if you are on a fixed-rate deal, the cost of the loan will be much more predictable, rather than fluctuating with the exchange rate. Interest rates will almost certainly be higher, however, and if you run into serious problems, your main home will be at risk – so borrowing through a re-mortgage is probably a sensible approach only if you are borrowing relatively small sums.

Renting your property out

Whether you are buying in Spain or Portugal, the levels of letting income you can achieve will vary enormously according to the location of your property, but also to its condition, the facilities it offers, and a whole host of other considerations – noise, position in relation to the sun, proximity to beaches and so on.

Spanish/Portuguese lettings: possible income and expenses

Type of property	Low season (Oct to Feb)	Mid season (March to May)	High season (June to Sept)
Two-bed bungalow or apartment	£150 per week	£225	£300
Three-bed bungalow or apartment	£175 per week	£250	£350
Two-bed villa with pool	£200	£300	£450

- Typical annual running costs (including taxes) for a small- to medium-sized villa in a popular area: around £1,500–2,000 per annum.
- Example of costs of employing a villa management company: complete management package costs 20% of gross rents, with cleaning charges on top, of €50–70 for two- to four-bedroomed properties; key-holding around €90 a year; one-off call-out charges, for example to meet maintenance staff, €45.

Sources: Anchorage Villas; Citrus Iberia Ltd

Unless you are planning to move to Iberia yourself and are therefore thinking about buying two properties close to each other, which you can oversee, it is important also to factor in the cost of running the property as a lettings business. Paying other people to do this work can eat into profits substantially.

The table opposite shows some examples of letting incomes for typical properties in the Costa Blanca; similar properties in the Algarve or Costa del Sol might be expected to command higher letting incomes – especially those on golfing complexes. Some figures are provided here; see also page 189 for more detailed information on costs in Italy – which are likely to be comparable.

Inheritance issues

A big issue to think about when buying in Spain and Portugal is who should own the property; it is also imperative to make a will in the country you are buying in, and to adjust your English will to take into account your foreign one. Because the inheritance laws and taxation regimes in Spain and Portugal are so different from those in the UK, making the wrong decision about whose name or names to put in the title deeds can cost your loved ones a great deal of avoidable inheritance tax; and failing to make a Spanish or Portuguese will to cover your new home could also mean your property is distributed in a way you did not intend. It is essential to take legal and tax advice from professionals with in-depth knowledge of both regimes, and to think carefully about all your options, before making any decisions.

Spain

In Spain, the biggest problem is that you are obliged by law to leave at least two-thirds of your property to your children when you die. This may well be what you intend to do anyway, but it can cause serious problems, especially if you have children from previous marriages, and even more so if you and your partner are not married.

Under Spanish law, a surviving spouse keeps all the assets they brought to the marriage, half of the goods acquired during marriage, and all personal gifts or inheritances that have come directly to them (depending on their *regimen matrimonial*, see page 147). So each spouse owns one half of the property and when one dies, only half of the Spanish property needs to be disposed of.

However, of this half only one-third can be freely disposed of, under what is known as the law of obligatory heirs (*herederos forzosos*). This law states that when a person dies leaving children, the estate is divided into three equal parts. One of these thirds must be left to surviving children in equal parts. Another third must also be left to the children, but the person making the will can decide how to divide it; and any surviving spouse also has a life interest in it, so if it includes a house, for example, the child who inherits it cannot dispose of it freely until his or her surviving parent dies, because the surviving parent holds what is called a *usufructo* over the property. The final third of the estate can be left to anyone. If, as a foreigner residing in Spain, you die without a will, your estate in Spain will be distributed according to this law.

If, however, you have made a will, the Spanish law provides that the disposal of any assets you have in Spain will be governed by your own national law, not that of Spain (remember, this does not mean you avoid Spanish inheritance taxes, however), regardless of whether you are actually resident there.

Strictly speaking, there is a complication here because English (and other British) laws state that real property such as land, houses and apartments must be disposed of according to the law of the country where that property is located. So in other words, Spanish law says English law will apply, and English law says Spanish law will apply.

But in practice, non-Spaniards are allowed to make a Spanish will bequeathing their Spanish property to any person of their choice, so long as they declare that their own national law is ruled by the principle of free disposition of property by testament; and so long as inheritance tax is paid on the property when it passes on. Remember, though, that while this is standard practice, it is not strictly in agreement with the law – so if, for example, you chose to leave the property to your favourite son, thus cutting out your daughter from her inheritance, she could contest the will and win her share of your estate.

The other crucial aspect to all this is that you must, as well as making a Spanish will, make a UK will to cover any assets you have back home. The UK will must state clearly that it disposes only of your UK assets, and the Spanish will must state clearly that it disposes only of your assets in Spain; otherwise you can end up with two wills, each stating that 'everything' goes to two different people.

Before you even make your will, you need to be clear about what assets you are talking about passing on, which will depend at least partly on in whose name the property is registered.

As in France, one of the issues you must decide on when you sign the *escritura* for the property you are buying is what you want your matrimonial regime (*regimen matrimonial*) to be.

The *regimen matrimonial* governs how you as a married couple wish to deal with your finances, and there are two options: common ownership of assets (*comunidad de bienes*) or separate ownership (*separacion de bienes*). Under the first approach (*comunidad de bienes*), all assets acquired after the marriage – even if they are put in one party's name – belong to both. Under the second (*separacion de bienes*), each spouse is entitled to own assets in their own name, and the other has no automatic claim over them. So if you were to opt for *separacion de bienes* and put the Spanish property solely in your spouse's name and he or she then died, you would have no automatic right to inherit it. It is important to think carefully about which approach you wish to take here, so seek plenty of advice. It is very difficult to go back on this once you have signed on the dotted line.

An option well worth considering if you have adult children (with whom you get on) is to give them the money to buy part of the property and add them to the title. In terms of tax, this can – so long as you arrange it all properly so as to avoid gift tax – save you a lot of money because you only own a quarter, fifth or whatever of the property, instead of half; meaning only that part will be taxable.

An alternative is to put the property entirely in the names of your children but retain a life interest (*usufructo*) for yourselves. This would allow you to live there and only pass the property on after the two of you have died. Again, you would have to make sure this gift was administered properly so as to avoid gift tax.

Bear in mind also that if the unforeseen happened, and your child or children died without heirs, you could find yourself inheriting the property back and having to pay inheritance tax as a result.

There are also various other ways of owning property which can, in particular circumstances, be worth thinking about – buying through a Spanish company and using trusts, for example. As always, take specialist advice to find out the best way to structure ownership for your specific situation.

All this would be academic, of course, if inheritance tax in Spain were not as punitively high as it is (see below). The highest rate of tax is 81.6 per cent, after all; and there is no IHT exemption between husbands and wives.

Inheritance tax rates – Spain

Asset valued	Tax rate (%)
€0–7,993.46	7.65
€7,993.46–15,980.91	8.5
€15,980.91–23,968.36	9.35
€23,968.36–31,955.81	10.2
€31,955.81–39,943.26	11.05
€39,943.26–47,930.22	11.9
€47,930.22–55,918.17	12.75
€55,918.17–63,905.62	13.6
€63,905.62–71,893.07	14.45
€71,893.07–79,880.52	15.3
€79,880.52–119,757.67	16.15
€119,757.67–159,643.83	18.7
€159,634.83–239,389.13	21.25
€239,389.13–398,777.54	25.5
€398,777.54–797,555.10	29.75
More than €797,555.10	34.0

The following multipliers are used to factor up the above rates, according to the 'closeness' of the person inheriting, and their overall pre-existing wealth

Net worth of inheritor (€)	Group 1: parents, children, spouses	Group 2: second or third-degree relatives, e.g. siblings, cousins, nephews	Group 3: others (including non-married partners)
0–402,678	1.00	1.59	2.00
402,679–2,007,380	1.05	1.67	2.10
2,007,380–4,020,770	1.10	1.75	2.20
More than 4,020,770	1.20	1.91	2.40

Portugal

Succession law in Portugal is not as prescriptive as in Spain; the inheritance tax (*imposto sobre as sucessoes e doacoes*) regime in Portugal is also undergoing reform so as to make things less punitive for spouses and children who inherit. Until recently the system distinguished, like that in Spain, between different levels of 'closeness' in relationship between the donor and recipient, although their existing wealth did not form part of the calculation.

As of January 1, 2004 you can leave property to surviving spouses, children and parents, and they will not have to pay any inheritance tax; if you leave it to others they must pay a flat-rate stamp duty (*imposto de selo*) of 10 per cent. This change came in along with a host of changes to Portuguese property law, described on pages 142 and 151.

Other taxes arising from your purchase

Spain

Residential property tax (impuesto sobre bienes inmuebles)

This tax, known as IBI, is a local tax charged simply by virtue of the fact you own a residential property and use it yourself, or have it available for your use. It is paid in advance by the person who occupies the property on 1 January, so if for instance you buy a property in June, the first six months of this tax should already have been paid. IBI is calculated by the local council, on the basis of the notional rental value (*valor catastral*) of the property.

Other taxes

These include refuse tax (*basura*) and other one-off taxes, which can be raised by town halls for particular projects or budget shortfalls. Altogether, IBI and other taxes should add up to less than €700 a year for a fairly large house, and proportionately less for smaller properties.

Income tax on rentals (impuesto sobre la renta de no residentes)

Whether or not you are, for tax purposes, resident in Spain is a surprisingly complex question, as is whether or not you are 'ordinarily resident' in the UK and therefore, in theory, liable for tax under both regimes. In both cases, take specialist tax advice in advance of making any decisions about whether or not to emigrate, how much time to spend in a property abroad, and the like. Paying unnecessary tax can become an expensive hobby when you buy property abroad.

In simple terms, if you are a Spanish resident you will, as in any other foreign country, become liable for Spanish income tax on your worldwide earnings – this will include any rental income on Spanish property. Income tax rates currently range from 15 per cent on the first €4,000 up to 45 per cent on anything above €45,000. And as a non-resident, the simple fact of owning a Spanish property renders you liable for income tax on any rental income it generates (there is in fact an advantage in being a resident in this respect, because residents now pay income tax on only 50 per cent of rental income received).

Tax on rental income for non-residents is charged at a flat rate of 25 per cent of gross rents; depending on how much you are likely to earn from renting the property out, it can be worth setting up a business in order to claim back reliefs and allowances.

Even if you do not rent your property out, the Spanish authorities tax you on the basis that you do – they calculate a notional income based on 2 per cent of the *valor catastral* of the property, or 1 per cent if the *valor* has been adjusted since 1994. This is then taxed at 25 per cent.

Wealth tax (patrimonio)

Unlike in France, where wealth tax only kicks in at a very high level, you do not have to be particularly wealthy to pay Spanish *patrimonio*. Non-Spanish residents are liable for wealth tax on their assets in Spain, minus any Spanish mortgages or debts secured against the property. The rates are as follows.

Value of assets	Wealth tax rate (%)
€0–167,129	0.2
€167,129–334,253	0.3
€334,253–668,500	0.5
€668,500–1,337,000	0.9
€1,337,000–2,673,999	1.3
€2,673,999–5,347,998	1.7
€5,347,998–10,695,996	2.1
More than €10,695,996	2.5

Capital gains tax

Spanish residents pay 15 per cent capital gains tax; non-residents pay 35 per cent. There is a complex system of allowances, which your tax adviser should be able to explain to you – but in simple terms, you need to have owned a property for around five years before they significantly reduce your CGT liability. Bear in mind that there is a separate, local version of capital gains tax (*plus valia* – see pages 134–5) payable when you buy a property; this is not, contrary to popular belief, one and the same. Also, remember that if you are buying your property from a person or company not resident in Spain, you must by law withhold 5 per cent of the purchase price and pay this to the tax authorities rather than to the seller (see page 135). This is then set against the seller's total capital gains tax liability from the sale. This rule does not apply if the non-resident has owned the property for more than 10 years (or 20 in the case of a company), however.

Portugal
Income tax on rentals
As a non-resident any income from Portuguese sources, including property rentals, is taxable. Current rates of income tax range from 12 per cent on the first €4,182 of income to 40 per cent on any income over €52,277. If you own a property through a company, you will pay at a fixed rate of 25 per cent.

SISA and its replacement
This infamous transfer tax on properties, was replaced on January 1, 2004 by the imposto municipal sobre as transmissoes (IMT). This is, crucially, charged on the market value of the property, rather than the declared price – meaning potentially big charges on transfers. Land for building is charged at a flat rate of 6.5 per cent, and property owned through offshore companies will pay a flat rate of 15 per cent. The fact that IMT is charged on the market value also means that vendors must pay capital gains tax on the difference between the value stated when bought, and the new value when sold.

Municipal property tax (contribuicao autarquica)
This tax, now being gradually replaced, was calculated according to the registered value of the building concerned. For rural properties it is charged at 0.8 per cent, and for urban properties 1.1 to 1.3 per cent. The tax is being replaced by a new one called the *imposto municipal sobre imoveis*, part of the aim of which is to redress the balance between old and new properties, so that rates on new properties are likely to fall relative to those on old ones – especially where their rateable value (*valor tributavel*) is historically low. Taxes are likely to be levied at 0.2 to 0.5 per cent on new properties, and at 0.4–0.8 per cent on older ones (based on a corrected *valor tributavel*). Property

151

held by offshore companies will be charged at 5 per cent as a punitive measure for 2004. It will also be assumed that such properties are being rented out, resulting in a further charge of one fifteenth of the rateable value.

The reform of this tax is partly a response to the problem of under-declaration of values that has been endemic to Portugal, as in Spain and Italy. If the tax department (*Finances*) doubts the declared value of the property, it will have the power to revalue it; the local town hall will also have first option to purchase for the declared price if it feels it is too low.

It is expected that in some cases during the revaluation period – which could take up to ten years – the *valor tributavel* will be corrected by factors of 40 or even higher; although owners will not be expected to pay an increase in IMI of more than €60 a year. The system will be revised again in 2008.

Capital gains tax

This is chargeable on 50 per cent of the gain for non-residents; in the past this could be avoided if you owned the property through an offshore company, but take advice on the tax efficiency of this in the light of recent changes to the SISA regime (see page 142). If you are a Portuguese resident and sell your property, 50 per cent of the capital gain is taxed as income, unless it is your principal residence and the sale proceeds are reinvested in another property within a certain time limit. There is no wealth tax in Portugal.

Living in Spain and Portugal

Registration documents

Any foreigner moving to Spain will need a foreigner's identification number or NIE (*número de identificación de extranjero*), which will be used on a raft of official documents, including the *escritura* when you buy a property. To get an NIE you need to fill in a form and show your passport at the Office for Foreign Nationals (Oficina de Extranjero).

You will also need a social security card (*cartilla de seguridad social*), which will contain your personal social security membership number. Once you have obtained this you can take it to a local health centre to be assigned to a doctor and obtain a health certificate (see pages 158–9).

If you want to prove that you live in Spain you can register with the local council (*ayuntamiento*) by presenting them with the rental contract for your accommodation or an electricity or water bill, or similar to prove that you live there.

If you wish to stay more than three months in Portugal, you must apply for a residence permit, which will be issued by the Immigration and Border Control Department (Serviço de Estrangeiros e Fronteiras). A residence permit can only be refused for reasons of public policy, public safety or public health. Unemployment, for instance, or even a criminal record, is not a good enough reason to refuse you a permit.

Using a *gestor*

Bureaucracy in Spain and Portugal, as in Italy, is legendary in its complexity. Paperwork can be extremely daunting even if your linguistic skills are impressive, and it is little wonder that a whole category of professional has sprung up in response – that of the *gestor*.

The *gestor* has no English equivalent; essentially his or her job is to act as an intermediary between you and the state when dealing with red tape. He or she can tell you what procedures you need to follow in order to achieve whatever it is you want to achieve (and this could be something as simple as applying for a vehicle registration); often a *gestor* can even supply you with the relevant forms.

More importantly, if you authorise a *gestor* to do so, he or she can act on your behalf – effectively, he or she will stand in the queue so you don't have to (although it should also be noted that queues are often substantially shorter if officialdom knows it is dealing with a *gestor* as opposed to an inexperienced-looking foreigner). He or she will also act as an accountant, book-keeper and small business adviser, if you so wish.

Gestores are not legally qualified, but look for one who is licensed. You should be able to find recommendations from people in the local community, who should know of a *gestor* who speaks English. Alternatively, just look around for *gestorias* on the high street or in the local equivalent of *Yellow Pages*. The Spanish and Portuguese use *gestores* routinely, even for seemingly simple things like renewing their passports, and you may find them invaluable in helping you set up utility contracts, open bank accounts and the like. It cannot be over-emphasised just how much easier they can make your life. A good one is well worth the expense.

If you are buying property in Portugal as a non-resident – and especially if you are doing so through an offshore company – you must by law appoint a fiscal representative to deal with your tax and financial affairs. Usually your lawyer or *gestor* can arrange this for you.

Work

As in the rest of the European Economic Area, UK citizens have full rights to participate in the Spanish and Portuguese labour markets – but do not be deceived into thinking that this means you will find your ideal job easily. If you want a career rather than just a job you will almost certainly need near-native language skills to get on in the workplace; and even if you are professionally qualified back at home, do not assume these qualifications will translate directly to Iberian equivalents.

The European Employment Services Network (EURES)★ (see Chapter 4) can be a useful source of information before making the leap of moving to Spain.

In terms of official job-seeking resources in Spain, look out for *oficinas de empleo*, which operate as both job centres and benefits offices. Bear in mind that you will probably stand more chance of gaining employment if you are officially resident. Temping agencies in Spain are called *empresas de trabajo temporales*, and they are policed in such a way that they should, in theory at least, provide temporary placements that could lead on to more long-term employment; in other words they can be a genuinely useful source of work experience rather than just a source of dead-end, short-term contracts. Additionally, national and local newspapers and English-language publications often carry classified jobs sections.

If you wish to set up as self-employed, you would be well advised to make use of a *gestor*'s services. Be prepared for significant expenses upfront, too; the first thing you need to do is register at the local tax office (*agencia tributaria* or *hacienda*) and pay a 'tax on economic activities' (*impuesto sobre actividades economicas*), which can cost you several hundred euros for each activity you intend to pursue. You will also need to register to pay NI contributions; the *gestor* can be very useful in advising you on the best way to handle this without making unnecessary contributions.

Tax

As explained earlier in this chapter, there are numerous tax liabilities that arise by virtue of your ownership of property; remember also that if you move permanently to Spain or Portugal you will be liable for tax on your worldwide income.

Spain in particular is a high-tax economy, with tax rates ranging from 15 to 45 per cent according to income band; the lowest and highest rates in Portugal are 12 and 40 per cent respectively. Spain also has a wealth tax ranging from 0.2 per cent on the first €167,000 up to 2.5 per cent on wealth over €10.7 million; although allowances for residents mean that if your house is worth less than €150,000, if you move over there permanently you are unlikely to have to pay very much.

It is well worth exploring all the tax implications of a move or purchase abroad well in advance of searching for the property of your dreams; investing sensibly in good advice can save you a lot of money in the long run.

Banking

Whether or not you plan to move to Spain, you will need a Spanish bank account; for this you will need proof of your identity and *estado civil*, Spanish postal address, and NIE tax code. There are two types of bank in Spain – clearing banks (*bancos*) and savings banks (*cajas de ahorro*). As in the UK, there is little difference between the two these days, with savings banks now offering more day-to-day accounts as well as interest-earning accounts.

As a non-resident you will probably need to open a 'foreigner's account' (*cuenta extranjera*). A wider range of accounts, including deposit accounts, is available to residents; sweeper accounts such as those on offer in the UK are also available. There are no cheque guarantee cards in Spain; sometimes you will be asked for your passport or residency card instead, but as a whole people take it on trust that you will not issue them with a bad cheque – which is, in fact, a criminal offence.

Some people on the Costa del Sol choose to bank offshore in nearby Gibraltar, thus benefiting from high-interest, tax-free accounts and then simply bringing the money into Spain by driving across the border and back again. Strictly speaking, concealing an offshore account from the Spanish tax authorities is illegal, although it is rare for customs officials to check so thoroughly as to spot any suspicious-looking amounts of money.

Pensions

Many people assume that they can retire to Spain or Portugal in much the same way as they would in the UK. But one major difference is that if you become a resident in Iberia, your pensions – including your state pension and your tax-free lump sum (tax-free in the UK, that is) – are taxable there. The only exception is government service pensions, such as police or teachers' pensions, which are tax-free in Spain and Portugal – but not so in the UK.

Careful planning, whereby your pension is treated as an annuity, can reduce your pension tax liability by as much as four-fifths in Spain and two-thirds in Portugal. The earlier you start planning for it, if you think you want to retire abroad, the better: financial planning, using other investments as well as pensions can help, but this involves in-depth knowledge of the UK and Iberian systems, and their interactions.

Remember too that if you move abroad before retirement age, your UK pension entitlement will be frozen; and depending on how many years' NI contributions you have made, you may or may not be eligible for a UK pension when you do retire – you will therefore need to decide whether or not you want to make additional payments from your new country of residence.

As with legal matters, there is no substitute for good advice about tax. This may cost you dear in terms of initial outlay, but could pay great dividends over the medium and long term.

Schools

Spain

In Spain, pre-school education (*educacion infantil*) is available for children up to six years of age, but is entirely voluntary. The government guarantees there will be a sufficient number of places to ensure schooling for those who request it. Nursery schools and crèches (*guarderias*) are widely available in towns and cities, although they are in strong demand, as in most developed countries.

Primary education (*educacion primaria*) is compulsory and free of charge between six and twelve years of age. It is organised in three cycles of two years each, and subjects are similar to those studied in the UK; Spanish children normally learn English from the age of eight.

Secondary education (*educacion secundaria obligatoria*) is also compulsory, and is free; it lasts for four years after primary education, which means pupils begin this stage at 12 years of age and finish at 16. It provides the necessary education to study for the school-leaving certificate (*bachillerato*) or intermediate vocational training.

As in the UK, the final stage of secondary education is voluntary and lasts for two years, and is normally undertaken between 16 and 18 years of age. Students who have gone down the *bachillerato* route and who want to go onto university must take entrance exams (*selectividad*) to enter higher education.

There are three types of school in Spain:

- public schools, which are publicly owned and accountable to the different autonomous communities (regional governments) and are free of charge
- state-subsidised private schools, that satisfy a series of requirements and are subsidised by the state. These are free, though some charge fees that cover clothing, academic materials and so on; this may vary from one establishment to another, but the amount is always small
- private schools, which are privately owned establishments, the cost of which depends on many factors such as the enrolment fee, whether monthly payments and services are included or not, e.g. transport, refectory, special classes, sports facilities and so on. Costs are lower than in the UK, ranging generally from €200 to €500 per month.

School timetables are different from those in the UK, with nursery and primary schools often having a three-hour break in the middle of the day and then finishing after 5pm, and secondary schools generally finishing at 2.30 or 3pm.

Portugal

In Portugal, pre-school education takes children from the age of three to the age of six, although it is non-compulsory, as in Spain. There are public- and private- sector providers.

Portuguese elementary education is universal and compulsory and comprises three sequential cycles covering a total of nine years (from the age of six until fifteen). There are public, private and international schools, as in Spain.

Secondary education in Portugal is delivered by secondary schools and professional schools. Both types enable entrance to university, although the secondary schools are more academic in nature. University degree courses last for between four and six years; there are also more vocationally based polytechnics.

To enrol your child in school, contact one of the schools in your area or get in touch with the Regional Director of Education (Direcção Regional de Educação).

Private schools should be certified by the Ministry of Education, and can be expensive. There are international schools in Lisbon, Oporto and the Algarve, but they are very expensive and the possibility of admittance is restricted. Contact the British Embassy or Consulate to find out more details.

Health

Spain

As in the rest of Europe you are, as an EU resident, entitled to emergency treatment in Spain if you have an E111 form. If you stay longer than three months, however, this cover runs out and you could be faced with some costly medical bills – so buying a good travel insurance policy is a very wise first move. Bear in mind also that the E111 does not cover you for private hospitals or doctors; 40 per cent of medical treatment in Spain is private.

If you move to Spain, you need to sort out social security contributions through your employer if you are working; if you are a pensioner in the UK you are entitled to the equivalent of what a Spanish pensioner would get (via form E121); if you are self-employed, check out how you stand in terms of previous National Insurance contributions – ask for form E106.

The Autonomous Communities (regional governments, for example covering Andalucia) now have their own departments of health, rather than everything being run nationally; lists of hospitals and health centres can be obtained from the local equivalent of *Yellow Pages*. Having said this, the state acts as guarantor of the quantity and quality of provision in any part of national territory through the Spanish national health system.

Portugal

In Portugal, the official services for providing healthcare to the population are also organised into a national health system, the Serviço Nacional de Saúde (SNS), managed by the Ministry of Health, comprising health centres and public hospitals.

As in other countries, the E111 will cover you for emergency treatment; private travel insurance is also a wise precaution, especially if you are planning to spend more than three months in the country.

In order to benefit from the healthcare provided by the SNS if you actually move to Portugal, once you have started working you should register with the health centre (*centro de saúde*) in your area of residence, taking with you a valid identity document or passport, social security beneficiary's card and a supporting document as proof of residence.

You will then get an SNS identification card (*cartão de identificação de utente do SNS*), and will be assigned a family doctor (*medico de família*).

The health centres provide general practice/family medicine, public healthcare, nursing, vaccination and some diagnostic examinations.

For each consultation or any healthcare provided by the SNS, you will pay a small amount, called the moderating tax (*taxa moderadora*), for example €2.50 for a health centre appointment. You do not pay for inpatient care, however.

As well as these public services, there are various private and professional healthcare institutions, for which you need private medical insurance to cover what can be huge bills.

Insurance and utilities

Most Spanish homeowners have a multi-risk household policy, which covers the building itself, its contents and any civil responsibility that lands on the owner (continente, contenido, and riesgo a terceros respectively). Insurance is normally higher for holiday homes.

Car insurance types are similar to those in the UK; and in respect of home and motor policies, the same principles also apply in Portugal.

In many parts of Spain and Portugal, mains gas is a rarity; electricity blackouts are also fairly common, especially in rural areas. If you are in the south, be prepared to consider air conditioning a necessity within a short space of time.

Chapter 7

Italy

Italy has been described as Europe's most complex and alluring destination and there is little doubt that, with its sunny climate, beautiful scenery, fine wines, cultural heritage and relaxed attitude to life, the country has a particular appeal for UK residents.

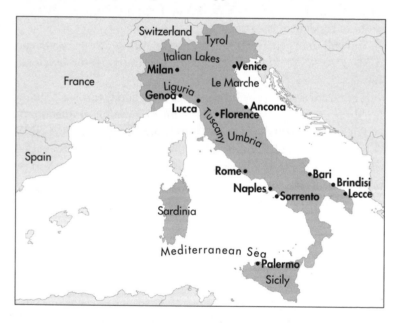

Where to buy

More than two million British people visit Italy each year, with the five most popular regions being Veneto (which includes Venice), Tuscany (which includes Florence), Lazio (which includes Rome), Lombardy (which includes Milan) and Campania (which includes

Naples). Growing numbers of Britons have been purchasing holiday and retirement homes since the pioneers first bought up parts of Tuscany in the 1960s.

Tuscany, with its rich array of historic monuments, remains the firm favourite, but there are 21 other regions in Italy, each with its own distinctive identity. From the bilingual German–Italian Alpine region of Trentino Alto-Adige and the industrialised heartland of Lombardy in the north; to the rolling hills of Tuscany and Umbria in the middle; and on to the defiantly independent Naples and Sicily in the south – Italy has something for all tastes.

Comparison of prices across Italy

Region	Town	New or restored house		House for restoration	
		minimum price per sq m	maximum price per sq m	minimum price per sq m	maximum price per sq m
Abruzzo	Chieti (centre)	€1,300	€1,800	€400	€800
Calabria	Cosenza (centre)	price not available	price not available	€465	€620
Emilia-Romagna	Bologna (centre)	€3,100	€3,870	€1,810	€2,220
Lazio	Rome (Trevi)	€4,900	price not available	€3,000	€5,355
Liguria	La Spezia (centre)	€1,300	€1,600	€1,000	€1,400
Lombardy	Como (Citta Murata)	€2,170	€3,360	€1,050	€1,800
Le Marche	Macerata (suburbs)	€1,500	€1,750	€800	€930
Sicily	Palermo (centre)	€1,290	€1,810	€520	€775
Tuscany	Siena (centre)	€3,400	€5,200	€2,450	€2,550
Umbria	Terni (centre)	€1,700	€2,000	€550	€700
Veneto	Venezia (Giudecca)	€2,500	€4,000	€1,500	€2,500

Source: Federazione Italiana Agenti Immobiliari Professionali (FIAIP)

Tuscany

Rome and Milan may be the 'brains' and 'brawn' of the modern, industrialised Italian republic, but Tuscany – the cradle of the Renaissance – is its cultural heart. Packed with cultural delights and artistic treasures that have inspired everyone from Lord Byron to Tony Blair, Tuscany's beautiful towns and cities include Florence – the region's capital – Siena, Pisa and Lucca. The region even gave Italy its national language, thanks in no small part to Dante's seminal literary masterpiece, *The Divine Comedy*, which was written in Tuscan dialect.

Even outside the cities, the region has much to offer property seekers, especially those on the lookout for somewhere with rental potential. Tuscany's medieval villages and secluded hill-top houses are perched among some exquisite landscape. The thickly wooded hills, verdant vineyards and secluded farmhouses of the Chianti wine region are probably the best-known portion of the sun-blessed Tuscan countryside. The first wave of expatriate UK residents and second home-owners moved in as long ago as the early 1960s, hence the area's nickname 'Chiantishire'.

To the south of Chianti, the area to the west of a line from San Gimignano in the north-west, through Siena and on to Montepulciano in the south-east, features classic Tuscan landscapes – vineyards, olive groves, cypress avenues and fields full of sunflowers swaying gently in the breeze – as well as beautiful towns and villages such as Montalcino and Monteriggioni. The area around Arezzo and Cortona to the east is also appealing but relatively unexplored, and in the north, the mountainous regions above Lucca are also worth closer examination.

However, Tuscany is more than just rolling hills. In the early 1800s, Livorno became Italy's first commercial seaside resort and the region has a long tradition of seaside tourism. It has a long and varied coastline – including sandy beaches and pebbled coves – that stretches from the more established northern resorts such as Massa and Viareggio, to the low-hilled, coastal strip around the southern town of Grosseto and Napoleon's place of exile, the beautiful island of Elba.

What you can get for your money

Price	Location	Description	State of repair
€55,000	Near Barga, north of Lucca	• One-bedroomed detached cottage on hillside • 45sq m of living space • 0.6 hectares of land	Needs restoration including new roof
€93,000	Sansepolcro, north-east of Arezzo	• Two-bedroomed house over three floors plus cellars • 120sq m of living space • 60sq m outbuilding • 0.2 hectares of land	Needs major restoration
€200,000	Near Viareggio, west of Lucca	• Two-bedroomed cottage on one floor with external portico • 15km from sea. • Two-storey outbuilding plus one hectare of land	Restored
€1,650,000	Chianti, near Siena	• Luxury villa including two separate apartments, with five bedrooms and three living rooms • Over 500sq m of living space, and 0.5 hectacres of land • 40sq m outbuilding • Swimming pool	Fully restored

Umbria

Umbria, often referred to as the 'green heart' of Italy, is a land-locked region of wooded hills and valleys, punctuated by several classic hill-towns – fortified in pre-Roman times by the mysterious Umbrii tribe and, in the towns such as Perugia and Orvieto west of the River Tiber, by the Etruscans. Urban highlights include Orvieto's cathedral, considered one of the finest Gothic buildings in Italy, picturesque Gubbio, and the graceful medieval town of Spoleto, once the capital of the Holy Roman Empire.

The region also contains St Francis' birthplace, Assisi, with its superb Giotto-frescoed basilica, recently rebuilt after it collapsed in an earthquake. There are two Umbrian national parks – the Parco Regionale del Monte Cucco and Parco Nazionale dei Monti Sibillini, which continues over the border into Le Marche and is popular with UK buyers. Lake Trasimeno is the largest inland stretch of water in the country.

For many years considered a backwater but now enjoying a revival as Tuscany's cheaper and less crowded neighbour, Umbria has more recently become a popular choice for foreign house hunters. It is also jiving its way onto the cultural map by means of major events such as Umbria Jazz, Italy's premier annual jazz festival, held in Perugia every summer.

What you can get for your money

Price	Location	Description	State of repair
€65,000	Tuscan border, near Sansepolcro	• Two terraced cottages • Potential total of five bedrooms, three bathrooms plus living space • Garden	Needs major restoration
€95,000	Near Citta di Castello	• Tobacco tower and barn • 100sq m of living space • 7,000sq m of land	Complete rebuild needed
€100,000	Near Todi	• Two-bedroomed hillside house • 50sq m of living space plus 105sq m terrace • Includes furniture	Converted
€310,000	Near Perugia	• Farmhouse over three floors • Total of 18 rooms • Two-bedroomed apartment on top floor • One hectare of land including 100 olive trees plus other fruit trees • Large terrace • Planning permission for swimming pool	Top-floor apartment converted; rest of house requires major restoration

Le Marche

Le Marche ('The Marches' in English) forms the eastern seaboard of central Italy, between the regions of Emilia-Romagna to the north and Abruzzo to the south. The region has a strong economy, and the relaxed way of life there, combined with rich natural resources, mean its 1.5 million inhabitants have the highest longevity in Italy.

From the relatively narrow coastal plains the land rises sharply to the peaks of the Apennines, which form a natural boundary with Umbria and Tuscany to the west. The inland mountainous zones are mostly limestone and are noted for bare peaks, rushing torrents, dramatic gorges and cave complexes. The highest point in Le Marche is Monte Vettore (2,476 metres) in the Sibillini mountains – now part of a national park stretching westwards into Umbria. Many parts of Le Marche, including the huge upland plain of the Piano Grande in the west, are havens for flora and fauna.

Nearer the coastal plain there are fertile, rounded hills topped by ancient fortified towns in the Tuscan and Umbrian mould – most notably Urbino in the north and Macerata and Ascoli Piceno further south. The areas around these towns, and the smaller villages in the shadow of the Monti Sibillini, are a good bet for properties to restore – ideal if you want the splendid isolation of a house in the hills but with easy access to the coast. The villages of Piticchio and Ripatransone are also worth a look.

This stretch of the Adriatic coast has long sandy beaches, but apart from the limestone Conero peninsula, it is virtually all flat. As well as the bigger, touristy beach resorts such as Gabicce Mare, Pesaro, Senigallia, and San Benedetto del Tronto, there are plenty of smaller, rockier resorts running down from Monte Conero, just south of Ancona.

What you can get for your money

Price	Location	Description	State of repair
€50,000	Near Belmonte Piceno (one hour to Ancona)	• Two-storey stone/brick building • Over 150sq m of living space • Separate outbuilding for wood storage • 2,000sq m of land	Needs partial rebuild plus restoration throughout
€70,000	Amandola	• Two-bedroomed apartment • 70sq m of living space plus terrace	Fully restored
€107,000	Sarnano	• Farmhouse over three floors • 200sq m of living space • 2,000sq m of land	Total restoration needed
€290,000	Fermo	• 18th-century castle • 400sq m of living space • 1 hectare of land • 5km from the sea	Structurally sound but needs internal restoration including rewiring

Liguria

Liguria is a thin strip of land sheltering on the seaward side of the mountains that divide Piedmont from the coast. It runs from France in the west to Tuscany in the east, and its capital is the grand and ancient port of Genoa, reputedly the birthplace of Christopher Columbus. The region has for many years been the seaside playground of the rich and famous Milanese, and grand houses dot the coast, which is largely rocky and in many parts, such as the famously exclusive Portofino, inaccessible by car.

What you can get for your money

Price	Location	Description	State of repair
€114,000	Imperia (town centre)	• One-bedroomed fifth-floor apartment (no lift) • Attic for conversion to second bedroom	Fully restored
€150,000	Prela	• Detached house converted into two apartments • One apartment has one bedroom, the other two bedrooms plus terrace	Fully restored
€272,000	Riomaggiore	• Two-bedroomed house over three floors • 70sq m of living space, plus terrace • 100m to sea • In conservation area in Cinque Terre National Park	Fully restored
€580,000	Imperia (outskirts)	• Modern, detached four-bedroomed villa over two floors • Two bathrooms • Garage, cellar and large basement • Terrace and garden • Space for swimming pool	No work needed

To the west of Genoa is the Riviera di Ponente, or Riviera di Fiori (so called because this is major area for flower growers) – a mecca for Italian families during the summer in resorts that include the once-elegant San Remo and the more modest Albenga and Finale Ligure. To the east runs the rugged Riviera di Levante, which takes in the Cinque Terre – five tiny fishing villages, including Portofino, accessible only by train, boat or on foot, set high above the dramatic

Ligurian coastline. There are numerous picturesque villages, such as Portovenere, where coloured houses perch precariously above the sea.

Inland, up steep, winding roads and tracks, lie the terraced hillsides scattered with tiny medieval villages, vineyards, olive and fruit groves that make up the Ligurian interior. If you are looking for a hillside bolt-hole set back from the crowds on the rocks below, it might be worth looking around Diano Castello, Varese Ligure, Ortonovo or Dolceacqua.

Abruzzo and Molise

If you are hoping your property hunting might throw up a hidden gem, Abruzzo and Molise – two of Italy's most unspoilt regions – might just be where to find it. With dramatic scenery ranging from vast, untamed mountain plains, through quiet valleys and hill villages to the long, sandy Adriatic coastline, Abruzzo possesses four national parks and has huge potential for the second home-owner.

The region contains Gran Sasso, the Apennines' highest peak, around which there are 22 skiing resorts, an array of atmospheric towns such as L'Aquila and Sulmona, numerous outlying villages and a fine coastline – low and sandy in the north and steeper in the south. In some areas, stone-built sheep farms carved into steep hillsides, sometimes three, four or even six rooms high, one on top of another, are ripe for conversion.

In Abruzzo and Molise, properties can be much cheaper than in Tuscany or Umbria, and these regions have mountains, hills and sea. The locals have been fairly slow to catch on to tourism – in 2001, Abruzzo was only half as popular as Le Marche among UK tourists, for example, and fewer than 1,000 Britons visited Molise. There is nothing like the demand for holiday rentals as there would be further north and west, then – but, luckily for the house-hunter, the prices reflect this.

If you are tempted by properties in seaside resorts, try the northern province of Teramo; for atmospheric fishing villages, consider San Vito and Fossacesia to the south of Chieti, where traditional fishing huts built on piles (*travocchi*) are still in use today.

Ferries from Pescara, the sophisticated main town – just 80 miles down the coast from Ancona – take you to Croatia. The eastern connection is continued in Molise, where in isolated villages an

Albanian–Italian dialect incomprehensible to most Italians is spoken – this is a legacy from Albanian émigrés more than six centuries ago, and a sign of how remote parts of this region are.

What you can get for your money

Price	Location	Description	State of repair
€32,000	30 mins south of Pescara	• House on three floors • Cellar with vaulted ceiling	Has new roof but rest of building needs restoration
€80,000	Near Pescara	• Two-storey farmhouse • Over 240sq m of living space • 700sq m garden • Near small lake and 10 mins from the sea	Needs restoration
€250,000	30 mins west of Pescara	• Two-storey house • Over 250sq m of living space • Seven large rooms over two floors • Garden and terrace • Cellar • 200m from sea	Fully restored

Puglia to Calabria

As a general rule, the further south you go in Italy, the hotter it gets, and the cheaper the property. That is certainly the case with Puglia, the heel of Italy's boot, where it is still possible to buy a *trullo* (a conical farm building known only in this part of Italy and possibly of north African origin) – admittedly one that needs considerable work to make it habitable – for a few thousand pounds.

Puglia is not all remote farmland, however. Italians and Germans have been holidaying here for decades, so there are plenty of bungalow-filled tourist villages as well as a number of historically interesting towns, including Bari, Lecce, Ostuni and Martina Franca. The region is littered with Byzantine architecture, in many areas interspersed with more ancient menhirs and dolmens, which contrast with the blindingly white local houses.

From Brindisi you can get ferries to Corfu and the Greek mainland, and in fact, geographically, southern parts of Puglia seem more Greek than Italian; in parts of the region a language similar to modern Greek is even spoken. Areas to consider if you want a

Greco-Italian feel to your holiday property include Martarano, Martignano, Soleto and Zollino. For a home with solid year-round letting potential, look at San Foca, Roca Vecchia or Otranto – a Byzantine city overlooking some of the best sea in Italy. Le Murge, meanwhile, is an undulating plateau in the centre of the province. The Gargano promontory to the north plays host to some of the best sea and sand anywhere on the Adriatic.

The most southerly part of the Italian mainland comprises Basilicata and Calabria – marginalised, impoverished southern provinces that could hardly be further, both scenically and metaphorically, from the industrialised plains of the north of Italy. The beautiful Tyrrhenian coastline, which includes charming, relatively undiscovered resorts such as Tropea and Scilla, creates a heady mix for property hunters prepared to go further off the beaten track. Calabria's capital, Reggio di Calabria, is just 20 minutes by ferry from Sicily, and if you fly to Rome you can get an internal flight to Lamezia, around 50 miles north of Reggio.

What you can get for your money

Price	Location	Description	State of repair
€7,000	Cisternino, Puglia	• Rustic *trullo* in panoramic position • Olive grove	Needs complete restoration
€48,000	Ostuni, Puglia	• *Trullo* with two cones • Outbuilding • 55sq m of living space • 4,000sq m of land • 3km to sea	Needs complete restoration
€62,000	Scalea, Calabria	• House converted into two one-bedroomed apartments • 75sq m of living space • 12sq m terrace	Converted and furnished
€330,000	San Nicola Arcella, Calabria	• 5,000sq m of land • Planning permission for two houses, made into four two-bedroomed apartments, each of 88sq m • Terraces and gardens	Yet to be built

Sicily

Sicilians would be the first to point out that their island is a separate entity from the rest of Italy, and with bustling Palermo, chic

Taormina and historical gems such as Siracusa and Agrigento to offer, it is easy to see the origins of their pride. Temperatures in Sicily can be around the 30°C mark for half the year. There are few areas in the world so rich in history – Sicily having been invaded successively by the Greeks, Romans, Arabs, Normans, French and Spanish before it finally became part of a unified Italy in the nineteenth century.

Geographically the coastline varies from rocky cliffs and stacks in the north, to sandy beaches and azure seas in the south and east of the island; and from a grey, volcanic interior in the north and east, presided over by Mount Etna, one of the world's largest volcanoes, to greener, gentler slopes in the south. Parts of it are heavily industrialised, however, such as the coast between Siracuse and Catánia.

Renowned for the overwhelming generosity of its people but tainted by a seemingly inextricable link with the mafia, Sicily has developed a tourist industry only in the last couple of decades. A gastronomic and wine lover's delight, it is big enough to have a culture and character all of its own – and this is reflected in higher property prices than might otherwise be expected in the south of Italy. Houses and apartments are still affordable, however, and the international airports at Catánia and Palermo make Sicily a good bet for British property hunters.

What you can get for your money

Price	Location	Description	State of repair
€68,000	Piazza Armerina	• Two-bedroomed hillside villa • 65sq m attic • 25sq m terrace • Garage • 2,500sq m of land	Needs interior decoration
€130,000	Messina	• Two-bedroomed town apartment • 105sq m of living area • Balcony • Courtyard • Garage • Walking distance from sea	Fully converted
€250,000	Sciacca	• Four-bedroomed house • Two terraces • Two storage rooms • 600sq m of land • 200m from beach	Newly built

---

Getting to Italy

British Airways flies from London Gatwick to Bologna, Genoa, Naples, Pisa, Rome (Fiumicino), Venice and Verona; from London Heathrow to Milan and Rome (Fiumicino); from Birmingham to Milan, Rome, Turin, Venice and Verona; and from Manchester to Milan, Rome and Venice. New routes to Bari, Cagliari and Catania from London Gatwick from March and May 2004.

bmi files from London Heathrow to Venice and Milan (Linate).

bmibaby flies from East Midlands and Cardiff to Milan (Bergamo); and from East Midlands to Pisa.

easyJet flies from London Stansted to Bologna, Milan (Linate), Naples, Rome (Ciampino) and Venice (Marco Polo); from London Gatwick to Milan (Linate); and from Bristol and East Midlands to Venice.

Ryanair flies from London Stansted to Alghero, Ancona, Bari, Bologna, Genoa, Milan (Bergamo), Palermo, Pescara, Pisa, Rome (Ciampino), Trieste, Turin, Venice (Treviso) and Verona (Brescia).

The buying process

Whether you want a luxurious Tuscan villa with pool, a Milanese *pied-à-terre* or a Puglian ruin with potential, there are essentially three stages to go through when making a purchase.

The first stage is to select a property and establish that you want to buy it. The second stage involves drawing up a private contract with the seller, known as the *compromesso*. At the third stage – finalising the purchase deed, known as the *rogito* – the sale is made public and ownership of the property transfers to you.

Especially if you are buying a property that includes agricultural land, Italian property law can, like that of most countries, become complex – so it is important to feel confident that the people acting for you are doing so in your best interests, and that you know what is going on. The process is a good deal easier if you speak good Italian yourself but, if you do not, it is extremely helpful to have a trusted friend or a lawyer who can check the credentials of the people you are dealing with, assist with negotiations and make sure the purchase is progressing satisfactorily.

Finding a property

Particularly if your Italian is not up to scratch or you are searching for property over a wide distance, you may want to find a property through one of the growing number of English-speaking property consultants that specialise in selling Italian homes to buyers from the UK and elsewhere. Many of these operate a bespoke or 'one-stop shop' service, handling everything from finding you a property to organising viewings and sorting out finance. Alternatively you may wish to go through an estate agent (*agente immobiliare* or *mediatore immobiliare*) that you have found when on a visit to the area in question. Larger towns will have several agents to choose from, and the better agents will be keen for your business.

Whichever route you take, it is important to choose an agent carefully and make sure you are happy with the level of service they provide. This is especially important because in Italy you as the buyer must pay some of the agent's commission (*provvigione*) – generally the buyer and seller each pay around 3 per cent of the purchase price, although this varies from province to province.

Check the credentials of the agents with whom you are dealing. As in other countries, the vast majority of Italian estate agents are trustworthy, but you could stumble across one who wants to exploit the fact that you are a foreigner. Remember that it is relatively inexpensive to set up an impressive website full of beautiful photographs of Italian properties – whether you are a reputable, qualified estate agent or not.

Under Italian law, all bona fide agents must be listed in the *ruoli* – a register of licensed *agenti immobiliari* and *mediatori immobiliari* held at each local chamber of commerce (*camera di commercio*). Since 1989 agents have only been able to gain a licence if they follow a specific course and pass an exam. Each member of the *ruoli* must lodge with the chamber of commerce specimens of the modules he or she use in his or her work, such as sales mandates.

In recent years, larger chambers of commerce, normally in the larger cities, have begun to establish centralised property databases (*borse immobiliari*) which contain listings of properties offered for sale through accredited estate agents. Using the *borsa* is free and allows you to request a search for the particular kind of property you want, safe in the knowledge that the agent through which it is offered has a licence to practise.

UK-based agents selling Italian property normally link in with *agenti immobiliari* in the area in question, so find out where they operate from and you can check their credentials in the same way.

There is nothing to stop unscrupulous people setting themselves up as estate agents, but under Italian law they will be liable to fines and penalties, and most importantly, perhaps, you are under no obligation to pay any agent who has not been registered by the chamber of commerce.

The professional bodies for Italian estate agents are called the Federazione Italiana degli Agenti Immobiliari Professionali* and the Federazione Italiana dei Mediatori e Agenti in Affari, so if they are members you will have the comfort of knowing they are covered by an indemnity insurance scheme, should you need to make a claim against them. These bodies, and the UK-based Federation of Overseas Property Developers, Agents and Consultants (FOPDAC)* – which represents UK estate agents who operate abroad, are, in turn, members of the Confédération Européenne de d'Immobilier (CEI)*, which operates a code of practice for estate agents across continental Europe. If you are unlucky and feel you have been treated unfairly or have received substandard service from an estate agent, you can complain to the *Commissione di Vigilanza* at the local chamber of commerce, who should take your complaint seriously.

Another way of finding a property is, of course, to do it yourself – through friends or contacts, perhaps, or by spotting somewhere on sale privately through a small ad. This approach has the advantage of saving you money in estate agents' fees – although a good estate agent could easily save you much more than this in the long run, in fact – but you need to tread carefully because, if the seller is not genuine, the next steps in the buying process could, if handled incorrectly, cost you dear.

Agreeing to buy

Once you have found a property you wish to buy, the next step is normally to make a written offer. This document, a *proposta d'acquisto irrevocabile*, which can be a letter you write yourself or, more commonly, a standard form supplied by the estate agent which you sign, is binding on your part for a specified period – normally from seven to fifteen days.

It sets out the price and terms of your offer, making clear that the property must be sold as seen and free of encumbrances, and on the assumption that the property is free of any mortgages or other debts – which remain attached to the property rather than the seller, unless this is agreed before contracts are signed. You or your agent must send two copies of the *proposta* by recorded mail, and if the seller agrees to the sale, he or she signs both and returns one to you. At this point neither party can change their mind about the price. Before you decide to go ahead, you should take legal advice. See page 175 for more on appointing an Italian lawyer.

It is customary to pay a deposit at this stage – but it is important to make clear in the *proposta* that this money is being paid as an *acconto*, which means it will be set against the purchase price and will be returned to you if, for whatever reason, the purchase is not concluded. Italian law requires all parties to a transaction to act in good faith, and it relies on everything being written down, so while it may seem premature handing over money before you have done searches, surveys and so on, you are protected providing the *proposta* is filled out correctly.

If you are buying a new-build property, especially through a developer, you may be asked to make a 'booking' (*prenotazione*) for a particular property and pay a deposit. This is extremely rare, but if you agree to do so, make sure you have a written contract expressly stating that the payment you have made is an *acconto* and is therefore returnable if the purchase does not go ahead.

Once you have established that you want to buy the property, and that the seller agrees to sell it to you, the two of you must work towards agreeing a contract. It is important to realise that whereas in the UK it is lawyers or legal executives who do all the conveyancing for house purchases, in Italy this is a job that can be done through several different people.

Increasingly estate agents, who have previously concentrated purely on introducing buyers and sellers, are branching out into conveyancing. In the UK around 90 per cent of house sales go through estate agents, while in Italy the figure is closer to 50 or 60 per cent, so in an attempt to attract custom, many agents will now handle everything from initial introductions to arranging a mortgage, helping you agree a contract (*compromesso*) and sorting out the paperwork in readiness for the transfer of the property (*rogito*). So you might get your estate agent to conduct all the searches for you. The agent may, as part of his or her service, appoint a *geometra* – a professional who is a cross between a surveyor and an architect – to do them on your behalf. Alternatively you can appoint a *geometra* directly.

Additionally, you would be well advised to appoint an Italian or Italian-speaking lawyer to act on your behalf, both to oversee the buying process and to sort out a will that makes proper provision for passing on your property under Italian inheritance law – which differs from that in the UK in several respects, one being that property cannot be passed solely to a spouse, but must be shared among any children.

Whichever way you proceed in handling the purchase, your starting point should be to get hold of the seller's purchase deed (*rogito*) from when he or she bought the property.

The aim of the searches at this stage is to make sure the property you want to buy is as it has been described, that it meets various legal requirements, that it can be sold to you without breaching anyone else's rights, and that there are no debts attached to it, which – unless investigated and dealt with – would devolve to you when it becomes yours. All these searches will, unless you specifically request otherwise, be repeated by the notary before completion of contracts, but for peace of mind it is sensible to explore all the potential problems before signing a *compromesso*, to protect yourself from losing the hefty deposit you are about to put down. If it turns out after you have committed money that the seller was not acting in good faith, you could have a lengthy court battle on your hands to get it back.

Your estate agent, lawyer or *geometra* will conduct a range of searches on the building, and on the seller him- or herself, through means of a detailed credit search called the *visura ipotecaria*, which Italians liken to a financial X-ray. It is worth noting that if you are taking out a mortgage on the property, your lender will do a *visura ipotecaria* automatically. The searches will check, amongst other things, that:

- the property exists and is as described, and belongs to the seller, who must also have a valid title to sell it. If, for example, the seller is married and shares finances with their spouse (*comunione di bene*), as is the usual case, or if he or she inherited the property along with several other family members, a sale will not be possible without the consent of all parties

- there are no third parties' rights, mortgages or other encumbrances affecting the property
- the property meets all relevant planning and building regulations, and has a plan approved by the local authority (*comune*). Compliance with planning and building regulations has been a particular issue in Italy since 1985, when a planning amnesty (*condono edilizio*) was introduced – and sellers should have applied for, and be able to produce, documentation to absolve them of any breaches dating back that far
- there is a certificate stating that the property is fit for human habitation (*certificato di abitabilitá*) – this is essential if you plan to let the property
- the seller has complied with all the relevant Italian tax legislation – if not the property may be legally unsaleable unless the taxes due, plus fines, are paid
- where the seller is self-employed or a company, the seller has not been declared bankrupt (*fallito*) and that there are no such applications pending
- where the property is in a block of flats (*condominio*), all service charges should have been paid
- details of any agreements about access and use of communal spaces are provided.

If you are buying from a building company or developer, it is important for the contract to protect you if the firm goes bust – otherwise you might not be able to get your money back, as well as losing the house.

If you are buying in a rural area, your agent will need to ensure that no one has 'pre-emption rights' over the property. All buildings in Italy are registered on one of two registers – the urban and rural registers. Despite its name, the urban register actually lists most residential buildings, even those in the middle of nowhere, while the rural register lists purely agricultural property.

Under Italian law, if you are buying agricultural land, neighbours who are registered farmers – in layperson terms, this means 'proper' farmers whose living comes from agriculture, rather than anyone with a chunk of land and a few sheep – have 'pre-emption rights', which means they should be offered first refusal to buy neighbouring land if it comes onto the market. So your agent must inform anyone with such a claim of the proposed sale and give them 30 days in which to exercise their right.

In most cases, the house itself and up to around 3,000 square metres of land will be exempt from pre-emption rights because even if it was not already on the urban register, it will be once you buy it as a residence – so only land beyond this might be affected. It is worth remembering that in fact it should be possible to 'urbanise' the entire land, but this could prove expensive tax-wise because land of more than 3,000 square metres would bring the property into a 'super deluxe' category of *rendita catastale* (see page 181).

Assuming any such third parties do not want to buy the land, you will need to get them to sign a declaration to the effect that they do not want to buy it at any price. One approach is to invite them to the completion ceremony (see page 180) and get them to sign the deeds to this effect. Often a small payment will be expected in return, but think of this as a small price to pay compared to the alternative – anyone with pre-emption rights who was not given first refusal and found out about the sale at a later date, could insist on buying the land at the value declared on the *rogito*, which – as explained on pages 180–1 – will be much lower than what you will have actually paid for it.

When all the searches have been completed satisfactorily, you can move on to agree the terms of the contract (*compromesso*), including the price, the amount of the deposit payable on exchange, and the date of completion. If necessary, special terms may have to be inserted into the contract to deal with particular problems revealed by the searches. The *compromesso* can include as much or as little information as you like, but there are a number of points it should cover as a minimum (see box overleaf).

There are two different ways of paying the deposit required at the *compromesso* stage. One is to pay a *caparra confirmatoria*. This way, if you decide not to proceed with the purchase, you lose the deposit – and the seller has the right to take you to court and force you to complete the purchase. If the seller decides not to proceed, he or she must pay you double your deposit and you, similarly, have the right to force the sale. The other approach is to pay a *caparra penitenziale*, which is retained or paid back twofold in case of default as with a *caparra confirmatoria*, but which gives neither party the right to take the other to court and force the deal.

What must be included in a *compromesso*

- Identification of the parties (full names, place and date of birth, passport number, nationality, tax identification number – in the case of companies which are selling, they must provide their value-added tax number, and their legal registration number).
- Indication of the location of the property in question.
- Identification in the national register of lands or urban areas. In the case of segments of property, the seller must undertake to obtain at his or her expense, their identification (*frazionamento*) in the national register. This must take place before the final sales agreement with the notary.
- In the case of land and/or for portions of buildings, the agreement must be accompanied by a map from the register, which will be signed by both parties.
- Verification of the seller's title to the property.
- Verification of whether any limitations exist to the title, for example judicial or bank obligations, inheritance or property rights, rights to first choice of purchase, or any other limitations that reduce or in some way curtail the right to full title of the property. The seller must commit him- or herself to eliminating such limitations prior to, or simultaneously with, the final sales act.
- Identification of all servitudes that might weigh on the property (roads, trails, pipelines and so on that pass through the property) and those from which the property should benefit (access to water from nearby natural sources or wells, rights of passage, and rights to access to pipelines and so on).
- Building licences issued after 1967.
- Building licences in the process of being issued: in the case of purchase of a building to be constructed, agreement to purchase and total payment must be conditional on the issuance of the required licence.
- The sales price, indicating the amounts paid at signature (or at various successive moments) and the balance to be paid at the time of the final sales act.
- The date established for the final sales act. This must be at least 60 days after the private sales agreement.

The normal practice is to pay a *caparra* of up to a third of the purchase price, although this is negotiable. While it might be tempting to push for a lower amount, this can be counter-productive, especially if the property is likely to be appealing to other potential buyers. If you have paid a fairly small deposit and the seller then receives a higher offer for the property, it may prove economical for him or her to pull out of the sale, pay you twice the deposit, then accept the higher offer and proceed with the other buyer.

Finalising the transaction

The *compromesso* is a private contract between buyer and seller, but to become the official owner of the property, you must make the deal public by completing a purchase deed (*rogito*), for which employing a notary (*notaio*) is essential.

Notaries are public officials and are the only professionals entitled to transfer legal title to properties in Italy. They act impartially rather than for either party to the transaction. Their role is:

- to verify what is being sold, to whom, and with what authority
- to ensure that all taxes due on the property have been paid
- to ensure that the building is not in breach of any laws or regulations
- to ensure that the property is unencumbered by debts or other parties' rights
- to draft the *rogito*, assuming there are no other problems.

Notaries' searches will often duplicate those already carried out by your estate agent, *geometra* or lawyer. Two days before completion they do a final check to make sure the seller has not raised any finance using the property as security.

Good notaries are extremely thorough, and nothing will get past them. You may wish to use the same *notaio* who transferred the property when the seller originally bought it, thus saving some legwork – but then again, you may prefer to find your own. Often your estate agent will recommend a good *notaio*.

It is worth noting that it is possible to instruct a *notaio* to simply witness a contract, but he or she would do so only on the basis that you and the seller accept responsibility for any problems resulting from it – so be cautious of a seller who tries to get you to speed up the transaction by simply running a contract past the *notaio* at the eleventh hour.

In order to complete the transaction you will need to organise the money for the purchase, including the notary's fees and the taxes payable (see box below). You must also provide an Italian tax code number (*codice fiscale*) – rather like a National Insurance number – which you obtain from the local tax office.

The *rogito* must be signed by both parties in person. If you are not fluent in Italian you must by law pay for a translator, so that everyone is clear that you are fully informed about what you have agreed to. If you are unable to be present you can, in fact, send a representative – your Italian lawyer, perhaps – but if so you must have given him or her power of attorney (*procura*). On completion, the notary will register the sale at the local land registry (*ufficio dell' agenzia del territorio*, formerly known as the *ufficio del catasto*), forward all the taxes arising from the transaction and deal with the formalities relating to the discharge of any outstanding mortgages on the property.

The administration of property transactions in Italy is structured in such a way that tax evasion is commonplace, and it is important to understand this before you embark on this final stage in the

---

Fees and taxes on Italian property purchases

Assuming the property is in the urban building register, you must pay taxes that add up to 10 per cent of the taxable value – that is, the *valore catastale* – rather than the amount you are actually paying. The 10 per cent is made up of 7 per cent registration tax (*imposta di registro*), 2 per cent *imposta ipotecaria* and 1 per cent *imposta catastale* – these are effectively fees one pays to register the property transfer. If it is in the rural register you must pay a total of 18 per cent.

In both cases the *imposta di registro* is reduced to 3 per cent, and you pay nominal *imposte ipotecaria* and *catastale* of €129 each, if the property will be your main home (*prima casa*). To qualify as a *prima casa*, you must take up residence in the property within 18 months of completion and not sell it, or move away from the area (that is, the local council area or *comune*) within five years. If you end up breaking either of these conditions, you must repay the 8 per cent difference

---

buying process. Under Italian law, the *rogito* must record the taxable value of the property (*valore catastale*), which is fixed by the state according to the size of the building and other factors. The *valore catastale* will be very much lower – perhaps by a factor of four or five – than the price you are actually paying for the property, which has already been agreed in the *compromesso*. It is worked out by multiplying the *rendita catastale* – a valuation worked out for tax purposes using a formula based on the size, location and quality of the flat, which is uprated by 5 per cent to account for inflation since 1996 (the date of the last census) – by 100.

It may seem fraudulent to declare a price that is so much lower than the price you are paying, but common practice dictates that as long as the price you declare is at least as high as the *valore catastale*, the notary will be satisfied. He or she is not therefore interested in the size of the cheque you hand over to the buyer – although in practice this may in fact be, subject to your agreement, several cheques, or a mixture of cheques and cash, because having declared that they have received only the amount of the *valore catastale* for the property, the seller must of course then be careful not to have huge sums of money identifiable by the tax authorities passing through his or her account.

---

and pay a small fine. *Prima casa* discount does not apply if the house is classed as luxury (*di lusso*) in the *rendita catastale*.

The Italian equivalent of value added tax – *imposta sul valore aggiunto* (IVA) – will be payable if you are buying from a builder or developer, at a rate of 10 per cent. This is reduced to 4 per cent for a *prima casa* but goes up to 20 per cent if the property is *di lusso*. If IVA applies, the *imposta di registro* is reduced to a nominal fee of €129, as are the *imposte ipotecaria* and *catastale*.

Italy's equivalent of capital gains tax was abolished in 2002, and inheritance tax is also no longer charged (see page 194).

Notaries' fees are fixed within a band by law. Part is a fee for the public element of their work, and part for practice expenses. If you feel you have been overcharged, you can have the bill assessed by the Consiglio dei Notai, which is the professional body of notaries. A typical bill would be around 1.5 per cent for a property worth €100,000.

Restoring old property

If your property needs restoration work of any kind, you will need to engage the services of an architect or *geometra* to run the project. Every town of any size will have several to choose from, and most estate agents will be happy to recommend one. In the same way as you would in the UK, always ask to see examples of the architect's or *geometra*'s previous work to assure yourself that he or she is experienced in the kind of job required.

Before they are qualified to run their own practice, *geometri* must complete five years' training, followed by several years' apprenticeship and a state exam, at which point they can enter the official *geometra* register, held at the *collegio dei geometri* in each province. As well as listing all qualified *geometri*, the *collegi* also set guideline fees, so if you feel you are being overcharged, it may be worth checking.

A new, more structured system for dealing with planning permission and building regulations was introduced in July 2003, alongside changes to the tax regime in October 2003. Under this new system, there is for the first time a national guideline – the *Testo Unico dell'Edilizia* – that summarises the regulatory structure under which the planning authorities at regional and local council level should operate. The *Testo* stipulates five categories into which building and restoration work falls, although it leaves local councils considerable flexibility to interpret these, so it is vital to employ an architect or *geometra* who understands the specific approach of the council in the area you are buying in.

Which category your project falls into is important because it determines how much IVA you must pay; it also affects what form of planning approval is needed from the council, and the related fees payable; in turn, this affects how quickly or otherwise you might be able to proceed with the work. The categories are as follows.

- ***Manutenzione ordinaria*** This is for relatively light projects. In most councils, this will include work such as painting inside walls, changing floors or replacing a boiler – things where you are not changing the structure of the building in any way. There are variations between councils, however – Milan will allow you to change internal (non-supporting) walls under this category, for example, whereas Bologna would put this in the next category (see below). External rendering and painting is included by most councils, but while in Milan and Bologna you must use materials and colours similar to what was there previously, in Florence it is enough to choose from a range of colours approved by the council.

- **_Manutenzione straordinaria_** This is for bigger projects where you are modifying structural parts of the building (without changing the overall volume or use of the building); or where you are adding plumbing or electrical services. Examples of what might be included in this category are: adding windows where there are currently walls, building steps, raising the height of floors, installing central heating from scratch, complete rewiring.

- **_Restauro e risanamento conservativo_** This relates to work done on historic or artistically valuable properties, so long as it does not involve changing the overall volume of the building. Councils will allow old buildings to be renovated and will normally be happy for you to replace more recent adaptations, so long as the conversion has respect for how they were originally built. If you plan to demolish and/or rebuild, the plans must demonstrate that you are rebuilding to the same overall plan and volume.

- **_Ristrutturazione edilizia_** This relates to rebuilding work or projects that will increase the volume of the building, such as loft or basement conversions; and to projects involving a change of use, for example from office to residential. In some councils, including Florence, this category would also be used for projects that increase the height of buildings.

- **_Ristrutturazione urbanistica_** This relates to major projects that would bring about considerable changes to the urban landscape, for example the construction of a housing estate or an inner-city redevelopment.

From October 2003, IVA of 20 per cent has been payable on all projects falling into the first two categories above, and 10 per cent on the rest. Prior to October 2003, 10 per cent was payable on all building work.

Rules about the kind of permit you need in order for your project to go ahead have also changed. Until June 2003 there were five kinds of permit, but after a transition period the aim is for these to be slimmed down to just two (see below). The pre-reform structure was as follows:

- **Nessun permesso** – no permission is needed for projects falling into the *manutenzione ordinaria* category.

- **Autorizzazione edilizia con silenzio-assenso** – this approach allowed your architect or *geometra* to submit plans to the council, signed by you and him- or herself, 90 days before work was due to commence, and if the council raised no objections in that time, work could proceed. It could be used for projects involving historic or artistically significant buildings, or for those in the *manutenzione straordinaria* category. This was abolished as of June 2003.

- **Dichiarazione di inizio attivita senza pagamenti da parte del cittadino** (also known as DIA) – this is an alternative whereby, 30 days before starting work, the architect or *geometra* submits plans underwritten by a declaration that what he or she is doing is in line with all the various regulations. The council may raise objections, and if it does not give you permission it must give a proper reason why. If you are restoring a historic property, you also need approval from the *soprintendenza* who represents the equivalent of something like National Heritage in the UK. There is no fee for a DIA.

- **Dichiarazione di inizio attivita con pagamento da parte del cittadino** (also known as **super-DIA**) – this is like the DIA except there is a payment attached. The *super-DIA* is used for all projects involving *ristrutturazione edilizia*, and is an alternative to the *permesso a costruire*.

- **Concessione** or *permesso a costruire* (*permesso* as of June 2003).

The new rules streamline planning permission into two alternatives – the DIA or the *permesso*. The DIA approach has the advantage of speed, but all the responsibility for the changes you make to the property falls on your shoulders, and the council can at any time – including beyond the initial 30 days when it may raise objections to the plans – require you to make alterations to bring the property into line with planning and building regulations. If you apply for a *permesso*, on the other hand, the responsibility shifts to the council and in theory, if there were problems with the project you could hold it liable. This means that, although in theory the council should give you an answer within 60 days, in practice it can take six months or more to gain approval for the work.

The other point to remember is that, whichever approach you take, you must get a *certificato di agibilitá* for all work you have done that involves creating living quarters. This certifies that the work done passes building standards relating to issues such as light, security and energy efficiency. To obtain a certificate you must present relevant documentation to one of the new *Sportelli Unici dell' Edilizia* – centralised planning offices set up at councils across Italy. Failure to do so results in a fine of nearly €500.

For work in the first category, there has been no need to submit plans to the *comune*, although you as owner have the responsibility to ensure work complies with planning and building regulations. For work in the second category, the *geometra* may submit a relatively informal application and in this case, work can begin immediately, with the *geometra* exercising his or her judgment of its appropriateness in the knowledge of what line the *comune* would take.

For major work, your plans must be submitted for authorisation by the local *comune*, signed by yourself and the *geometra*. You must pay a fee to the *comune* and it normally takes at least 90 working days to receive authorisation from the time the request is presented – which could of course delay your decision about whether or not to buy the property in the first place.

Special rules apply if the property you are buying falls under a definition of '*beni culturali*'. This is very rare and applies only to buildings that form part of Italy's cultural heritage. As one might expect, gaining permission to restore such buildings can be an extremely long and drawn-out process and involves getting approval from the Fine Arts Commission (Commitato di Belle Arti). It is also vital to note that, even if permission is granted and you decide to go ahead with the purchase, the state has a right to buy the property from you within 60 days of the sale being completed – and at a price determined by the state, rather than by the purchase price you have agreed.

As in the UK or anywhere else, the costs of restoring an Italian property can vary enormously from property to property, but for a very rough estimate, assume it will cost at least €1,200 to €1,500 per square metre, or nearer €2,000 for new buildings or extensions. Be aware however, that if you emigrate to Italy and are paying income tax (IRPEF), the government will often give you tax relief on some restoration costs. This arrangement has been in place in some form for the last six years, and has recently been extended to 31 December 2004.

It means that Italian taxpayers can offset 36 per cent – over a period of ten years – of the cost of work falling into the *manutenzione straordinaria, restauro e risanamento conservativo* or *ristrutturazione edilizia* categories, or for any work done to improve the security or safety of the property, against IRPEF, up to a maximum of €17,280 (i.e. 36 per cent of €48,000). If you think you may be in a position to claim this relief, ask your *commercialista* for advice.

If you are restoring a property while continuing to reside elsewhere and wish to have the project entirely managed on your behalf, there are many specialist firms set up to do just that. You have the option of paying professionals by the hour, or a fee calculated as a percentage of the overall conversion cost. If paying hourly, you might, as an example, expect to pay €50 an hour for a *geometra* to produce plans and oversee the project; assistants managing particular aspects of the work or keeping you updated on progress might cost around half that. It might cost you around 5 per cent of the conversion cost to have a firm manage the architectural design, material specifications and sourcing, secure planning permits and other official approvals, plus a further 10 per cent for project management and interior and exterior landscaping.

Bear in mind that it rarely pays to do any refurbishment work on the cheap, and this can be particularly true in Italy, where planning laws are strict. The best local builders will, by necessity, enjoy good professional relationships with the local *geometra* and *comune* officials; and none of them will take kindly to foreigners pitching up with ideas that go against the character of the local area. It is important to take advice on everything from the size of swimming pools to the use of local materials if you wish to gain approval for your refurbishment. In Tuscany, for example, different colours of roof tiles may be recommended, depending on whether or not they will be set against a backdrop of bright yellow fields of sunflowers.

And remember that, just as in the UK, planners in Italy have the power to force you to redo any work that is substandard or in contravention of planning guidance; or, in extreme cases, to order the building to be pulled down.

Financial matters

Mortgages

Where the property you are buying is already subject to a mortgage, or if you will be buying with the assistance of a mortgage, it is essential to deal with all the necessary arrangements before signing the *compromesso*. If the seller has a mortgage and/or there are other loans attached to or secured against the property, you will need to agree with the seller that these will be paid off, and the corresponding entries on the local land register cancelled before the *rogito*. This will require the assistance of the *notaio*. If you so wish, it may be possible for you to 'take over' the mortgage (*accollo del mutuo*), with the agreement of the seller and his or her lender, but it would be vital to check the state of the repayments and the terms of the original mortgage agreement if you went for this option.

It is possible for UK buyers to arrange an Italian mortgage, but do not expect to find the range of mortgage options on offer at home, because the mortgage industry is still relatively young in Italy. You are unlikely to get a mortgage for more than 75 to 80 per cent of the property value, especially if it is for a second home. Italian mortgages also tend to run over a shorter repayment period, which can make the monthly cost prohibitively high – a 15-year term would be typical.

A big disadvantage of euro mortgages is that they are subject to the vagaries of the currency markets, so as the sterling/euro exchange rate varies, so do your repayments. Actually making the repayments is also more expensive, because unless you are able to take the money over to Italy each month in person, you will have to arrange an electronic bank transfer through your UK bank.

If you do apply for an Italian mortgage, the lender will assess your eligibility on the basis of your ability to service the loan. The general guideline is that out of your net income, 35 per cent should cover existing outgoings and the monthly repayment on the Italian loan. So, for example, if you have a net monthly income that translates to €2,000, and have a current mortgage that costs €500 and no other outgoings, the lender would take into account 35 per cent of the income, that is €700, and would consider lending you a sum with a monthly repayment of up to €200.

If you are self-employed, income is assessed as the average of the last three years' net income. If you are employed, a lender will base your income on your payslips and the amount that is credited to your account monthly. Your outgoings will be deemed to include liabilities such as mortgage or rent in the UK, personal loans and child maintenance payments.

Lenders will generally not lend on a property that is going to be let out permanently, so 'buy to let' arrangements, now common-place in the UK, are unlikely. The reason is that the Italian legal system treats tenants much more favourably. So it can be extremely difficult to get rid of unwanted tenants, meaning that if you were to default on the loan, the lender would be left with a complicated legal case on its hands.

Proposed rental income from holiday lettings to friends will not be considered as part of your income for mortgage purposes, but lenders should agree to this, especially as having visitors should ensure it is more secure and any maintenance problems can be spotted and dealt with more quickly.

One alternative to an Italian mortgage is to re-mortgage your UK home. This can be a relatively cheap way of raising the cash you need, but you may not be able to get a re-mortgage for more than 75 per cent of the Italian property's price. Remember that you risk losing both homes if you cannot maintain the repayments.

Another option is to take out a second mortgage with a UK lender. Several high street lenders and specialist brokers now offer mortgages overseas. You will often have to have at least a 20 per cent deposit. There will generally be a minimum level of loan and, as with any other mortgage, your income and existing borrowings will be taken into account. Taking out a second mortgage allows you to use the Italian property as security, which means your home in the UK is not at risk.

Insurance

Any mortgage you take out on an Italian property will require you to arrange adequate life insurance. As well as this, adequate insurance cover to protect the property itself is strongly advisable. Your mortgage provider may include buildings insurance in its package, but otherwise you will need to arrange separate cover.

Similarly you will need to arrange home contents insurance, making sure you are covered all year round – whether or not you are in residence.

Most big Italian insurers offer buildings and contents insurance, and in general, insurance premiums are relatively cheap, but you may prefer to arrange cover through a specialist broker or insurer in the UK. Make sure you take out a policy that includes emergency travel expenses if you need to fly out following a disaster, and if you intend to rent out your home make sure the policy includes public liability cover, just in case your tenant has an accident and tries to sue you.

Renting your property out

Specialist Italian rental firms stress that good-quality, well-positioned holiday homes less than two hours from an airport can bring in a gross return on your investment of between 6 and 10 per cent a year. So a €500,000 house in Tuscany might earn you some €30,000 to €50,000 gross a year, for example.

Estimated costs of letting a three-bedroomed property with pool in Tuscany for 20 weeks a year

Item	When letting (20 weeks a year)	When not letting (32 weeks a year)
Cleaning (20 times)	€1,900	
Laundry: sheets and towels (20 times)	€600	
Gardener (every 2 weeks)	€100	€100
Welcome pack	€30	
Management costs of pool	€450	€450
Management of heating system	€80	€80
Cleaning for the new season	€250	€250
Renewal of pans, glasses, etc.	€250	
Electricity bills	€800	€800
Gas bills	€500	€500
Rubbish disposal	€153	€153
Water bills	€250	€250
Fire insurance	€220	€220
ICI (council tax)	€220	€220
Flowers and plants	€200	€200
Products for cleaning, light bulbs, etc	€150	€150
Dry cleaning of blankets / covers	€80	€80
General maintenance	€300	€300
Total costs	€6,533	€3,753

Source: Tuscany Now

But, if you are letting your property out regularly, remember to factor in maintenance costs, which could eat up a large proportion of your rental income. Keeping swimming pools in good working order and, in many areas, maintaining wells so as to guarantee an adequate water supply in the summer months, can prove to be expensive ongoing costs. Unless you have a trusted friend in the area who can manage the property for you – cleaning and checking it, meeting guests, sorting out keys, tending the garden, for example – you will also need to employ a managing agent. Some estate agents can arrange all this for you, and there are companies that specialise in managing properties for foreign owners. But expect to pay a premium for it – charges can be as high as another 20 per cent of the net income from the property.

A leading rentals company specialising in Tuscan properties esti-mates that the owner of a small three-bedroomed property with a pool would incur the costs per annum outlined in the table on the previous page, some of which arise simply from maintaining the property to a high standard, regardless of any lettings.

Living in Italy

The chances are that the property you buy in Italy will be a holiday home that you will only use for short periods of the year. But you may want to live there for extended periods, or move out to Italy more permanently. If so, you may need to think carefully about how you could earn a living there, and how you and your family would access public services.

Work

If you plan to work in Italy, you will not normally, as a national of the European Economic Area (EEA), need to obtain a work permit or a visa before you arrive. A full UK passport qualifies you to enter Italy for up to three months to look for work or set up in business – although you may be asked to prove that you have adequate finances to cover you for the duration of your stay and that the cost of your return journey is secured.

Once you get there, you must apply for a resident's permit (*permesso di soggiorno*), and you will need a worker's registration card (*libretto di lavoro*) to entitle you to undertake most types of work. UK nationals working in Italy have the same rights as Italian nationals with regard to pay, working conditions, access to housing, vocational training, social security and trade union membership. Families and immediate dependants are entitled to join them and have similar rights.

If you want to work on a self-employed basis, you will still require the *permesso di soggiorno*, and you will need to specify exactly what type of occupation or profession you propose to pursue. If you intend to establish your own company, there is a separate registration procedure to be complied with.

To apply for a *permesso di soggiorno*, which is valid for three months, you must report to the local police headquarters (*questura*) upon arrival or, in small towns, the *commissariato*, within seven days of arrival. If you do not manage to find work in this time, you must renew your *permesso* through the local police, or the *questura* in large towns and cities. All renewals must be made on special document paper (*carta bollata*) which you can buy from most tobacconists (*tabaccherie*).

The worker's registration card (*libretto di lavoro*) is required for most types of work, and can be obtained through your employer or the town hall (*municipio*) whether or not you require one. The *libretto di lavoro* is similar to a P45 in the UK, and is kept by your employer until you leave his or her employment.

Finding work

There are several ways you can go about finding employment in Italy:

- Use the European Employment Services Network (EURES)* (see Chapter 4).
- As an EU citizen, you have free access to the services of the Italian employment service. The Italian equivalent of an employment office is a *sezione circoscrizionale per l'impiego e il collocamento agricolo* (SCICA). The address of your nearest SCICA will be in the telephone directory, listed under *Ufficio del Lavoro e della Massima Occupazione*.
- Newspapers can be another source of jobs. The major newspapers in Italy include *Corriere Della Sera*, *La Repubblica* and *La Stampa*, and financial dailies include *Il Sole 24 Ore* and *Italia*

Oggi. There are two fortnightly English-language periodicals which cover the Rome area and carry job pages – *Wanted in Rome* and *Metropolitan*. International newspapers such as the *International Herald Tribune* carry advertisements for management, technical and other professional staff.

- Another source of possible contacts in Rome, Florence, Bologna and Milan is the *English Yellow Pages* – a directory that contains listings for English-speaking professionals, businesses, organisations and services. You can buy this from newsagents and bookshops in the cities concerned.

- If you are a member of a professional association or union, it may be worth contacting it to see if it knows of any relevant vacancies or opportunities in Italy. At the very least it may have contacts with its counterparts in Italy, who could prove helpful sources of information or advice. Chambers of commerce (*camere di commercio*) may also be worth a visit.

Once you have a job

Depending on the kind of work you choose to do, you may or may not need a contract of employment. National collective agreements (*contratti collectivi nazionali di lavoro*) are drawn up every three years in each economic sector by the unions and the employers' organisations. Usually the terms and conditions of employment are set out in these agreements and you will therefore not need an individual employment contract. This will not be the case if you are doing part-time or fixed-term work, however – under these circumstances you should be offered a contract setting out the terms and conditions of employment. Make sure you understand, and agree to, what it says before you sign.

Most employment sectors have their own legal minimum wage, which is set every three years. All employees receive an extra month's wage in December, and in some sectors the annual salary is divided into 14, 15 or 16 payments. The standard working week is 40 hours with a legal maximum of 48 hours. Overtime, which cannot be demanded of any employee, is paid at a rate of 130 to 150 per cent of the normal hourly rate, although many unions have agreed bans on overtime. Annual leave ranges from 25 to 30 days, depending on length of service. In addition, there are also ten statutory public holidays.

Setting up in self-employment

EU legislation gives all EU citizens the right to set up as self-employed persons anywhere in the EU. But it is worth checking if there are any special registration requirements for your particular profession. An Italian consulate office here or the Camera di Commercio, Industria, Agricoltura e Artigianato (CCIAA) in Italy, should be able to help. If you are registered as self-employed in the UK and take up work on a self-employed basis in Italy, you may be exempted from paying Italian social security contributions for up to 12 months, providing you continue to pay National Insurance contributions at home. To qualify for this exemption will need to obtain form E101 from your local tax office.

Tax

If you emigrate and work in Italy you will be liable for Italian income tax (*imposta sul reddito delle persone fisiche*). The Inland Revenue defines you as non-resident in the UK if you live abroad for 183 days or more a year, not counting days of arrival and departure

You will have already obtained a tax number (*codice fiscale*) from your local Italian tax office (*ufficio imposte diretto*) in order to buy your property in Italy, and if you take a job you must give this to your employer and IRPF will be deducted at source. Tax offices are listed in the telephone directory under *Uffici Finanziari*.

Even if you are a non-resident in the UK, you must submit a UK tax return stating the details of your Italian property, and you could be liable for income tax on any income it generates. As with other EU countries, there is a reciprocal agreement which means you will not be charged twice for the same tax. Check with an accountant to make sure you know how to handle your affairs in the most tax-efficient way possible.

The other taxes you will encounter in Italy are:

- *imposta sul valore aggiunto* (IVA) – the Italian equivalent of VAT, which is currently charged at 19 per cent. For further information on this, contact your local *ufficio provinciale imposta sul valore aggiunto*
- *imposta comunale immobili* (ICI) – the equivalent of council tax, which is calculated on the value of any property that you may have, with the rate varying from 4 per cent to 6 per cent of the

valore catastale; householders also pay separate rates for rubbish disposal (*nettezza urbana*) and water rates (*acquadotto comunale*). The *comune* will tell you what the current charges are. If the property is unfit for habitation it could qualify for a 50 per cent reduction. ICI is paid in two instalments in June and December.

- Import taxes – you may have to pay import taxes on certain items if you are moving household goods to Italy.

As in most countries, the Italian tax system can be complicated, and it is worth noting that many Italians – and not just those who are self-employed – employ the services of an accountant (*commercialista*) to administer their tax affairs.

Banking

To open an Italian bank account, you will need your passport; proof of address in Italy (including a residence certificate – il certificate di residenza – and utility bills); proof of income; birth certificate; and a reference from your home bank. The best approach may be to arrange things with an Italian bank which has offices in the UK (London), and can liaise with a local branch in Italy on your behalf.

Pensions and retirement

Retiring to Italy has become a more attractive option since Italy abolished inheritance and gift tax (imposta sulle donazionie) in 2001. You can now leave your property to relatives up to the fourth degree; and up to €150,000 per legacy to anyone else; tax free.

Health

The Servizio Sanitario Nazionale (SSN) runs the Italian National Health Service, which has a reciprocal agreement allowing all EU citizens free urgent medical treatment. To make sure you are eligible for this, fill in an E111 form, available from UK post offices. If you need medical treatment, go to the foreigners' office (*ufficio straniero*) in your nearest local health authority (*azienda sanitaria locale*) and exchange it for a booklet covering your temporary stay (normally valid up to three months).

But an E111 only entitles you to the most basic care and may not cover you for many forms of treatment, so if you are using your property as a holiday home, it is advisable to take out travel insurance – perhaps an annual policy if you are likely to visit several times each year – to cover you whenever you visit.

If you emigrate and work in Italy, you will be paying Italy's equivalent of National Insurance contributions, which qualify you to register with the local *unita sanitaria locale* (USL) and obtain a national health number. Self-employed or freelance workers should first register with the local *istituto nazionale di previdenza sociale* (INPS). USL addresses can be found in the local newspaper or the *TuttoCitta*, a supplement that comes with telephone directories.

Once you are registered with the USL, the next step is to register with a family doctor (*medico convenzionato*), who will issue you with prescriptions and referrals to specialists. A list of doctors, local national health centres and hospitals should be available from your local USL. First aid (*pronto soccorso*) at casualty departments is direct and free of charge for every citizen who needs urgent assistance. You may also get free help for less urgent problems, but some Italian regions have decided to charge for this non-emergency service.

If you are retiring to Italy, provided you have residency there, you are entitled to the same rights as Italians – although it is worth bearing in mind that many Italians take out private health insurance.

With private insurance, you are free to choose any doctor or specialist and be treated in private hospitals (*cliniche*), sometimes avoiding a long wait for a specialist appointment or surgery. Accommodation is considerably better than in state hospitals, and visiting hours are usually unrestricted. Treatment can be very costly though, so it is important to check beforehand whether your insurance company will cover you for the particular type of treatment proposed.

Schools

As in the UK, all children are entitled to a free state education in Italy. Currently, children aged three to six can attend state nursery school (*scuola infantile*), although this is not compulsory. State nursery schools are free and offer full-time care and education.

Compulsory full-time primary education is provided in the primary school (*scuola elementare*), which caters for students aged six to 11 years. All children who have reached the age of six at the beginning of the academic year (1 September) or who will do so by 31 December of that year, can enrol in the *scuola elementare*.

At the end of primary school children take a leaving certificate (*diploma di licenza elementare*), before going to a *scuola media inferiore*, from age 11 to 14. At 14 they take an exam leading to a second leaving certificate (*diploma di licenza media*), which qualifies them to go on to a *scuola media superiore*.

At upper secondary level (*scuola media superiore*), students study a range of subjects within broad streams, depending on their interests. For each stream there is a nationally determined curriculum, with core subjects including Italian, history, a modern foreign language, mathematics and physical education. Students leave secondary school at 19 to enter employment or proceed to university or other higher education.

Reforms introduced in 2003 and being phased in over several years will bring the starting age for nursery down to two and a half, and for primary school down to five and a half. Primary and lower secondary education will run for eight years, at the end of which there will be an exam.

If you would prefer your child or children to be educated in English, there are a range of English-language schools across Italy, but these are fee-paying. To find out more contact the European Council of International Schools (ECIS)★.

Utilities

The national electricity company is Ente Nazionale per l'Energia Elettrica (ENEL). Before supply is allowed, an inspector must call to check that your wiring is up to standard.

Most cities and large towns are supplied mains gas by the Società Italiana per il Gas (ITALGAS). For more rural areas you will need a gas tank or gas bottles.

Water supply is under the control of the local *comune* and each one has many rules and regulations concerning its usage. Many areas in Italy have fluctuating water supplies and in some areas, cuts in the supply can be frequent.

The telephone system is run by four companies – Telecom Italia, Albacom, Wind and Infostrada. Arranging a telephone to be installed can take up to two months.

With all the utilities you must be prompt in paying bills or face getting cut off within a matter of days.

Chapter 8
Florida, USA

There can be a tendency to dismiss Florida as simply playing host to that most commercialised of attractions, Disney World. But it is almost as impossible to generalise about the 'sunshine state' as it is to make sweeping statements about Spain, France or the UK. Florida is generally split into seven geographical regions, with the major ones for home buyers being the central region, which contains Orlando, Disney World and Universal Studios; the south-east region, which stretches down from Palm Beach to the Florida Keys and contains Miami, Key West and the 600,000-hectare Everglades National Park; and the south-west region, which houses all the sophisticated gulf resorts, like Naples and Venice – this is a large region for retiring millionaires and attracts a good many artists and writers too.

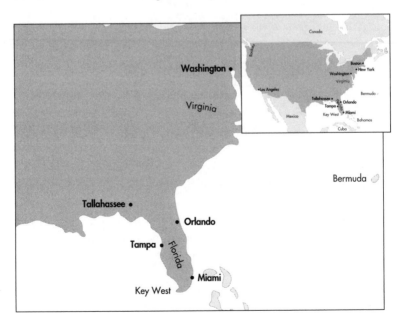

Where to buy

What you can get for your money

Price	Location	Description	State of repair
$110,000	Alachua (north-west coast)	• Two-bedroomed villa • Internal area 91sq m • Two bathrooms • Shared facilities, including pool • Parking space	Not yet built; for sale off-plan
$179,900	St Petersburg (central west coast)	• Two-bedroomed condo • Internal area 99sq m • Two bathrooms • Parking, shared pool and spa • Balcony	Built 1988; may need interior decoration
$200,000	Miami Beach (south-east coast)	• One-bedroomed high-rise condo, built 1971 • Garage and lift access • Balcony	Newly renovated
$264,000	Orange County (central Florida, near Disney World)	• Four-bedroomed, villa • Internal area 185sq m • Three bathrooms • Part of a 500-home new development with sports facilities and park	Not yet built; for sale off-plan
$425,000	Lee County (south-west coast)	• Two- to three-bedroomed villa in gated community • Internal area 370sq m • Two bathrooms • Three-car garage • Beach access, fitness club and golf membership	Built 2000
$995,000	Pinellas County (central west coast)	• Five-bedroomed architect-designed house in gated community with golf course • Internal area over 370sq m • Four bathrooms • Three-car garage • Heated pool • Backs on to a private lake	Built 1994; may need some minor redecoration

Property prices vary enormously within Florida, with the lower prices tending to be further north, where the climate is less attractive than in the middle and south of the state. Some of the most beautiful parts of the state are on the south and central west coasts, where the climate and 150 kilometres of beaches can be superb. The crowded area of Pinellas County, on the central west coast, claims an average of 360 sunny days a year. The north has its attractions too, however, and the north-west coast in particular boasts some spectacular open beaches and the Apalachicola National Forest, an extremely well preserved wilderness.

In most parts of Florida you will find no shortage of new-build gated communities with levels of specification choice, security and shared facilities practically unknown in the UK; and their resale equivalents. Average house sizes are substantial by British standards, too. Old properties in need of 'remodelling' are also available, but bear in mind that if there is major structural work to be done, it can often be cheaper simply to demolish and rebuild.

Getting to Florida

By air
American Airlines flies from Heathrow to Miami.
British Airways flies from Heathrow to Miami; Gatwick to Tampa and Orlando.
Virgin Atlantic flies from Gatwick to Orlando; Gatwick to Miami; Manchester to Orlando (May to November only)

The buying process

Given what we know about how litigious a society the USA has become, it is surprising how many people buy property in Florida without obtaining independent legal advice. It is much more sensible to do so, as using a lawyer can protect you against everything from being overcharged to buying a property which has undisclosed short-term rental restrictions. Just because you can read the small print in an English-speaking country, this doesn't make you a qualified lawyer!

Finding a property

Around three-quarters of people in Florida buy and sell their homes through real-estate agents, brokers or 'realtors' (see overleaf). These professionals are different but all are regulated, so make sure you only deal with licensed ones.

Under Florida law, anyone who deals in real estate must be licensed, although agents who are employed directly by a single developer or builder need not be licensed. If you use a UK-based agent, they will not normally be licensed in Florida, which is not a reason to avoid them but do make sure the agents they are dealing with in Florida are themselves licensed.

Real-estate agents, brokers or salespeople should be state-licensed, which means they will have passed exams and are covered by indemnity insurance – this would compensate you for losses brought about by their errors or omissions. All licensed agents must conform to a code of practice set out by the Florida Real Estate Commission. Ask to see licences – if the agent is a professional, this should cause no embarrassment.

If you want to protect yourself still further, go for an agent or broker with the title 'realtor'. To use this term, a realtor must be a member of a local real-estate board affiliated to the National Association of Realtors (NAR)*, which has a code of ethics; to be a member, he or she must have completed a course of study. Being able to complain to the NAR if necessary gives you another layer of protection.

A concept practically unknown in Europe but much more widely used in the USA is that of the 'buyer's broker' – that is, a real-estate agent whom you employ to find you a property. There are several ways for a buyer's broker to make his or her money – he or she may charge you a fee, for example, or they may charge you nothing and negotiate with the seller or their broker to split the seller's commission.

There are three ways in which real estate can be bought and sold in Florida. If the agent is employed solely by either the buyer or seller, this is called 'single agency'. Alternatively an agent can work for both the buyer and seller as 'dual agency'. Or the agent can work as an independent intermediary as 'transactional agency'. Under Florida law a broker must disclose in writing on what basis he or she is acting, but there are differences in how they can operate. Crucially, a broker acting on a 'single agency' or 'dual agency' basis must disclose all relevant information to his or her client, whereas one working as a 'transactional agency' only has a duty of honesty and fair dealing.

Remember also that if you make an enquiry or offer and are talking to an agent who is working for the seller, by law he or she must report everything you say – so play your cards close to your chest or the seller will be told immediately what your top price is.

Agents charge an average of 6 per cent on real-estate sales – when both buying and selling brokers are involved, they split the commission. All commission is paid at completion and not before.

You will find that most estate agents in Florida offer the same properties as each other. This is because there is a 'multiple listing service' – a kind of broker network whereby selling agents publicise what they have on their books, and other agents can then earn half the commission if they are the ones to find the buyer. Some properties will be offered exclusively through one agent, though, and it is certainly the case that agents are biased towards properties listed exclusively with them, because it means they do not have to split the commission with anyone else.

Around a quarter of property sales in the USA are handled directly between the buyer and seller, which means the seller saves on commission and can – in theory at least – pass some or all of this saving onto the buyer. If you do go down this route, it is worth having the value of the property independently appraised.

Arranging a survey

As in the UK, it is advisable to have a survey done whenever you are buying a property other than a newly built one (which will be covered by a warranty, although in fact some people advise still having a survey done, in case any shortcuts have been taken with the building). Termites and other wood-boring insects are commonplace in Florida, so there is a particular reason to have a survey done.

It is unusual to carry out a survey (normally known as a 'house inspection' in the USA) before signing contracts, so it is essential to insert a clause in any contract that makes the purchase dependent on a satisfactory inspection report (see page 203).

Make sure you are clear about what is included in and excluded from the survey; you may need to pay extra if you have specific worries that need checking out. Average home inspections cost around the same as they would in the UK, or may be cheaper. To find a certified and licensed inspector, look for one who is a member of the American Society of Home Inspectors (ASHI)★; check that he or she has professional indemnity insurance too. Many inspectors offer one-year guarantees.

Agreeing to buy

Once you have seen a property you like and haggled your way to an agreed price, it is common practice to make an initial deposit of a few thousand dollars as a goodwill gesture to show that you are serious about proceeding with the deal. You must then make a formal offer. This process is much more binding than in the UK and involves sending the seller a full purchase contract setting out how much you are prepared to pay for the property and under what circumstances. If you are buying with a spouse, partner or other parties, you must all sign at this stage.

Unlike in the UK, many home sales in Florida take place without lawyers being involved – or at least not in the sense in which we would understand it. The conveyancing process is often done by what is called a 'title insurance company'. Basically such firms examine the public records to make sure the seller owns the property, and assuming this search comes up satisfactorily, they will insure the property against a third party making a claim to it (apart from according to exceptions laid out in the policy). It normally takes a month or two to prove the title.

However, as a UK buyer and first-time US property purchaser, you are strongly advised to engage your own lawyer, in which case make sure he or she is a title insurance agent and can therefore provide a full conveyancing service, rather than having to sub-contract to a title insurance firm.

Using a lawyer means you can get him or her to draft and manage a purchase contract at the same time – request quotations for title certification, preparing of contract documents, fees for closing (completion) and any notary fees (which may be necessary if certain of the closing documents need to be witnessed). Especially given that there is no language barrier between the UK and USA – apart from in a terminological sense – you are probably best advised to employ an experienced local lawyer, rather than one based in the UK, to act for you. On the other hand, you may wish to engage a lawyer with experience of both UK and Florida jurisdictions, or to separately take advice from a UK lawyer about how the US purchase might impact on your interests here.

Any conditions on the purchase must be included in the contract from the start (see box opposite) and bear in mind that, unlike on this side of the Atlantic, in Florida verbal contracts are not worth the paper they are not written on.

What the contract must include

Basic clauses

- Names of parties to the contract
- Description of the property (its legal description rather than just its address)
- Purchase price, including details of where the money will come from (for example, *x* amount of deposit, *y* amount of mortgage, *z* capital from the buyer)
- Details of what is included in and excluded from the sale
- Closing (completion) date.

Standard clauses, examples of which include the following.

- Details on access to and from the property
- Statement that the seller conveys the property 'by statutory warranty deed', i.e. he or she owns the property and has the right to sell it
- Statement that there are no easements or restrictions on use of the property, for example limitations on renting the property out
- Termite inspection clause (insisted on by many lenders) stating that there must be an inspection and that if damage is discovered, the seller must pay a percentage of the purchase price to repair the damage
- Proof of clear and good title to the property, free from third-party claims.

Contingency clauses allow one or both parties to escape the contract. Typical examples include the following.

- Valuation ('appraisal') by the lender must not be below the agreed purchase price
- Financing details – usually the buyer must apply for a loan within a set period and must be turned down by the lender in order for the contract to be cancelled, so the contract will be quite specific about the criteria on which you as buyer are looking for a loan; as long as these are met, you must go ahead
- Home inspection – it is always advisable to make a sale contingent on a satisfactory inspection
- If you need to sell a home in order for the purchase to go ahead, you must make this a condition of the contract.

The buyer will probably send back a counter-offer changing some of the terms in the contract, and you can then send that back and so on, until both parties are happy. Depending on the circumstances, this process can go on for some time, after which you agree terms, pay a deposit – normally 10 per cent of the purchase price – and then proceed towards completion (or 'closing' as it is known in the USA).

You pay your deposit to what is known as an 'escrow agent', usually selected by your estate agent but subject to approval by all parties. This agent is responsible for compiling and checking the documents and ensuring the transaction can 'close' within the period specified in the purchase contract. Make sure you know what happens if either side pulls out of the deal – generally speaking, if either side pulls out, the other can force them to go through with it.

As well as making sure the contract covers you against every eventuality, your lawyer (or title insurance agent) must check that:

- the property belongs to the seller
- the seller has legal authority to sell the property
- there are no pre-emptive rights or restrictive covenants on the property
- there are no plans to build anything that could affect the value or enjoyment of the property
- the property has all the necessary building permits and planning permissions
- there are no debts attached to the property
- title insurance is forthcoming (this will be insisted on by lenders).

Finalising the transaction

You will already have agreed a closing date in your purchase contract. Before closing, the closing agent will check that all the conditions contained in the contract have been fulfilled. He or she will also collect any fees or taxes due, witness the signing of the deed of sale and arrange for the registration of the property in your name in the local property register.

You must be ready to pay the balance of the purchase price on the date of closing, along with other payments due, such as closing costs, taxes and insurances. You must pay in cash or a cashier's cheque (banker's draft). You will get a closing statement which sets out all the costs and fees for which each party to the transaction is responsible.

In the USA, property is sold subject to the condition that you accept it in the state it is in at the time of closing. For this reason, and to make sure you protect yourself against unscrupulous sellers, do a final check of the property immediately before closing, taking your broker and/or lawyer with you. You should have a detailed inventory of what is included in the sale – check that all this is in place and if it is not, make sure an appropriate amount of the purchase price is held back. If you find out after signing that things are missing, you will not really have any redress.

Taxes and fees on property purchases in Florida

In total you should allow around 5 per cent of the purchase price to cover the following:

- legal and notary fees
- inspection fees
- title search and insurance premiums
- transfer fees (recording of the purchase in the official records)
- property taxes
- community fees
- mortgage fees (generally around 3 per cent of the mortgage amount), including application fee, credit report fee, lender's legal fees, appraisal fee, lender's title insurance fee, and so on
- homeowner's insurance premiums.

Buying a newly built property

Many UK buyers opt for newly built properties in Florida, largely because of the perceived ease of purchasing somewhere that does not need restoration or refurbishment. The usual procedure is to buy a 'custom-built' property off-plan; here you are buying a plot of land in a development and commissioning the developer to build a property for you, according to one of a set range of standard floor plans and specifications. In theory at least, most homes should be built within six months of you signing the contract.

When you buy off-plan you will normally be expected to pay a holding deposit of up to around $2,000 to reserve a lot, after which you will have a cooling-off period of 15 days before signing the purchase contract, at which point you would normally pay a 5 per cent deposit.

You may also have the option of a 'turn key' service, which means you buy absolutely everything from the builder, including furniture, appliances and even cutlery – in effect, everything you would need in order to let the property out to tourists.

As with other properties, it is vital to do a pre-closing inspection when buying a new property, and for any problems to be rectified before you close the deal. There should also be a six-month period after the purchase, during which you can get any problems sorted out.

Restoring old property

As in the Spanish Costas and other holiday home-oriented regions, there is a distinction between new and 'resale' property, with the latter often providing better bargains as well as, of course, the ability to actually see what you are buying rather than a mound of earth and a computerised or artist's impression of what your property might look like.

Many older properties may need some work doing on them, however – this is known as 'remodelling' in the USA. If you will be letting the property out, the costs of remodelling can be set against the income tax payable on those earnings, and against capital gains tax when you sell. You should be able to get a mortgage that includes an element for remodelling; alternatively, banks offer home-improvement loans as in the UK.

Do some research on the kind of work you are having done – in some cases, contractors must be state licensed; check also whether they have third-party insurance and provide a warranty. There are plenty of disreputable builders, so take recommendations from people you can trust (your lawyer for example); or contact the local chamber of commerce for a list of contractors. If your property is in a condominium (see below) take particular care to check any restrictions or covenants imposed by the condominium association, as well as making sure any work complies with the Florida building code.

Community properties

Properties through which you own a share of common elements, like gardens, leisure facilities or whatever, are extremely common in the USA, particularly in Florida. Such properties may be apartments (often known as condominiums or condos), townhouses or detached homes on a private estate.

There can be pros and cons to owning such properties. On the plus side, they are often more secure; they offer the possibility of a ready-made social life; and you do not have to arrange everything, like pool maintenance, yourself for example. On the minus side, they can be noisy; there can be restrictive rules and regulations you must abide by; and fees for shared facilities can be expensive.

In some cases, whole town or village centres are built as part of the housing development, creating an entire new neighbourhood. If you are buying in an established development it is well worth talking to the locals about how successfully these arrangements have been handled, to get the inside track on what you are letting yourself in for.

There is a variant on the condo concept, called a cooperative (or coop), whereby you do not own your apartment in quite the same way; instead you own a number of shares in a non-profit-making corporation, depending on the size of your property. You pay towards a mortgage for the whole building, taxes, employee salaries and expenses, according to your number of shares. All the various owners of the coop have a power of veto over any potential new owners.

Always check the level of condo or coop fees carefully before you make an offer on a property of this type; they can be prohibitively high, especially in cases where the headline price of the condo appears to be unusually cheap. Also make sure you are clear about the rules and regulations in force at the development, especially if you are planning to let your property out – it is not uncommon for there to be restrictions on short- or long-term rentals.

Mobile homes

Mobile homes are more common in Florida than in any other US state – there are more than a million of them, in fact. Prices tend to be around half or two-thirds of the price of an equivalent-sized built home; apart from that, there is little difference between buying a mobile or buying a built home, except that you must rent or buy piece of land (a 'lot') to keep it on. There will be a monthly charge for maintenance, facilities and management, as with any other kind of community property.

Financial matters

Financing your purchase

As with purchases in the UK, your main choice when deciding how to finance a house purchase in the USA is whether to go for a US mortgage, or to remortgage your UK property.

The main advantages of remortgaging are ease – you do not have to pay legal or Land Registry fees if you add to your existing loan, and you may even avoid arrangement fees; and the fact that you will pay UK interest rates, which are presently lower than those available to foreigners in the USA. You also avoid the set-up costs involved with taking out a US mortgage (these can be as high as 2 per cent of the size of the loan), and you do not have to deal with the vagaries of the dollar/sterling exchange rate, which can have an enormous impact on capital values and the cost of monthly repayments.

The advantages of taking out a US loan are rather less obvious, but a significant one is that if you find you cannot afford repayments, while you may lose your US home your UK home will not be affected. Taking this approach also means you can build up a US credit history, which can help you raise further finance in the future. You can also reduce your tax liability if you will be making money from rental income – because you can offset the cost of the mortgage interest against income received for tax purposes.

If you opt for a US loan you will generally not be able to borrow more than 70 to 80 per cent of the market value, meaning you will need access to a sizeable amount of capital in order to make the purchase. If you pay less than a 20 per cent deposit, lenders will insist that you have a mortgage life insurance policy, although this can normally be cancelled once an agreed proportion of the mortgage has been paid off.

US lenders, like those in the UK, may lend on the basis of an income multiplier, usually limiting loans to a maximum of three times your salary; alternatively they may look at your gross monthly income and limit your monthly repayments to 30 per cent of it. If you have substantial savings or investments and are self-employed, you may think about a non-income status mortgage for 65 to 70 per cent of the market value.

It can take as long as three months to get approval for a US mortgage, and mortgage fees can vary between 0 and 4 per cent of the loan amount. The typical loan period in the USA is 30 years, but mortgages over 10 to 15 years are available; as in the UK, if you can afford the repayments, these can make good financial sense over the long term.

When you buy a new-built property, the builder will normally pay most of the mortgage fees, and if you buy without a mortgage they should offer a cash discount of around 2 per cent because of what they will save on closing costs.

As a non-resident you must usually make advance payments of three to six months' worth of mortgage payments too, and similarly for property taxes and insurance premiums. If you are buying from a non-resident of the USA, you are usually obliged to pay 10 per cent of the purchase price, as a withholding tax, to the tax office, so that the seller cannot disappear without paying at least some capital gains tax.

Renting your property out

The first question to answer if you want a property in Florida to generate letting income is whether or not you are permitted to rent it out. In a general sense, non-US residents are able to use their homes for up to six months of the year, and to rent them out for the rest of the time.

But – and it is a big but – in many parts of the state (in some areas whole counties and in others, specific communities) there are restrictions against short-term rents (normally of 28 to 30 days or less). When you are buying property in Florida it is imperative to check this from the outset. Rental restrictions are a major topic of debate in the state; they are more of an issue in condos but whole areas can be 'zoned' so that short-term rentals are not allowed. Court rulings and lawsuits change the situation every day, and the best advice is that if you absolutely need to generate letting income in order to afford your overseas property, look somewhere other than Florida.

Bear in mind also that there are tight safety regulations for all properties used for rental in Florida; you must register the property with the state and apply for a licence, which must be displayed in the home. You must have safety equipment including approved fire extinguishers, smoke detectors and two locks on front and back doors. If you are discovered letting a property without a licence you can face extremely punitive fines.

On top of all this, you must pay sales tax on all property rentals of less than six months' duration (see page 211), and in some counties you will also be liable for extra taxes such as tourist development and tourist impact levies. You will also be liable for US income tax on rental income, although if you elect to be taxed on a 'net' basis you can offset all expenses against this.

You will also need to think carefully about the cost of managing the property. Assuming a 70 per cent occupancy rate (36 weeks of the year) – which is high – one company estimates that a four-bedroomed villa in the 'Disney' area of Orlando could generate rent of around $24,000 a year; the expenses to keep the place going would cost around $11,000, leaving you with an estimated profit of around $13,000 to cover the mortgage (see table below). This estimate does not, however, include anything to cover management fees for services such as 'meeting and greeting', key holding, providing welcome grocery packs, laundry and changeover cleaning; and on-call availability.

Basic running costs and potential holiday-home income in Florida

	2-bed condo	3-bed villa	4-bed villa
Pool, yard, shared facilities maintenance	$100	$275	$275
Utility bills	$125	$230	$250
Cleaning	$100	$120	$130
Repairs and replacements	$25	$25	$25
Community association	$50	$36	$36
Taxes and insurance	$100	$150	$200
Total per month	$500	$836	$916
Total per year	$6,000	$10,171	$11,112
Rent per week	$384	$524	$664
Rent per year (70% occupancy)	$13,977	$19,074	$24,169
Profit per year	$7,977	$8,903	$13,057
Profit per month	$665	$742	$1,088

Source: Florida Countryside. NB these figures exclude mortgage payments and fees for management of lettings

You may well have friends in Florida who are prepared to help out with some or all of this, but they are unlikely to remain friends for long if you call upon them to do so without paying them a decent amount for their time and effort. Paying a professional to do all these things could easily cost you another $500 a month – eating away at whatever profit you might otherwise have generated.

Property taxes

Real property tax is the equivalent of UK council tax – it is levied on property owners to pay for services like education, police, fire, library services, waste disposal and social services. It is worked out on the basis of the property's current market value, which is set by each county every three years; within each county, different municipalities can charge taxes at different rates. They tend to range between 1 and 3 per cent of the property value per year. If you are a resident you can claim a 'homestead exemption' of $25,000 off your home's value; there are also reductions for senior citizens and people with disabilities.

Tangible personal property tax is a county tax levied on business assets, which also includes items contained in properties that are rented out; you must keep receipts for all major items of furniture, appliances and so on. It is charged at the same point as real property tax. With both taxes, you get discounts for paying your bills within a set period, and there are penalties for late payment.

Intangible tax is a state tax imposed on people with intangible assets (mainly shares, bonds, annuities and the like, but also including mortgages on properties outside the USA) of more than $20,000. It is charged at $1 for every $1,000 of assets.

Sales tax (the US equivalent of VAT) is levied at 6 per cent in Florida, although some counties impose a surtax of up to 1.5 per cent on top. It is charged on the first $5,000 of the actual purchase price, so it varies between $300 and $375. Sales tax, payable to the state of Florida, must be paid on short-term property rentals of less than six months, and some counties impose tourist taxes (payable to them) of 2 to 5 per cent on top. All this means you must get a sales tax certificate number from the Florida tax department before you let property out; as with other taxes there are strict rules and deadlines for filing of tax returns, and penalties for late payment.

Capital gains tax (CGT) for non-residents is usually charged at 30 per cent on qualifying assets; any improvements you have made to the property, plus selling costs and depreciation will be taken off the selling price to work out the net gain. A withholding tax of 10 per cent is held back from the gross selling price, to be set against your total liability.

If you are a resident, CGT varies from 8 to 18 per cent but if you are selling your main home the first $500,000 of house value (for a married couple) is exempt.

Inheritance and gift taxes

As a non-resident, you must pay inheritance tax (more commonly known as 'estate tax' in the USA) on the value of property located in the USA at the time of your death. Transfers between spouses are exempt from tax, as is the first $65,000 of your estate. The highest rate of estate tax was 49 per cent for 2003. This will reduce gradually to 45 per cent by the year 2009.

It is vital to take advice on inheritance issues in advance of making any decision about buying a property in Florida. You must ensure the property is in the right names (single owner, joint owners, joint owners with children, children's names only and so on) from the start.

You need to make two wills as well – one for your UK assets and one for those in the USA. Having a Florida will for your assets there speeds up the execution of your estate; it also enables you to state, if you so wish, that you want your estate there dealt with according to UK law (assuming you have UK domicile). If this is not stated, it will be assumed that US law should apply.

Living in Florida

Most people from the UK buy property in Florida purely for holidays, although some also see the 'sunshine state' as a good financial investment. For some, the love affair proves more permanent, although this can prove more problematic than one might expect.

Immigration rules

Perhaps the biggest difference between the USA and Europe when it comes to buying property is that it is much more difficult to plan to live over there permanently. While EU subjects have the right to live wherever they want within the EU and have the state treat them like natives, the immigration rules mean it can be extremely difficult to become a resident of the USA.

However, there are circumstances in which it is achievable, as follows.

- If any members of your immediate family are US residents or citizens you may be entitled to residency, although it can take anything from a year to ten or more to get through the waiting list. You will achieve residency quickest if you are marrying a US citizen or are the minor child of one.
- If you travel to the USA with a 'B' visa (B1 for business people, B2 for tourists), you can stay up to six months at a time, although you cannot simply stay there six months, go home for a week then come back.
- If you enrol on an academic programme, you can enter the USA on a student visa, which allows you to stay for the duration of the programme. You will have to show you have sufficient funds to pay for tuition and living expenses without working.
- You can get a visa of indefinite duration for the purpose of setting up a business in the USA. This is called an 'E' visa. It is possible to have your US real-estate investments considered an enterprise, although you will generally need to own more than one property, or be in the process of buying more than one, to qualify. You will need an experienced US immigration lawyer to get you in this way, and it is best if you explore all this before actually making a purchase so that you can, if necessary, change the way you are buying it.
- Non-US businesses can transfer executive personnel to the USA to operate the US branch, affiliate or subsidiary operation. This provision is meant for multinational companies but works for small businesses too; there are limits on how this 'L' visa can work, however.
- An 'H' visa is a long-term visa for professional workers (normally people with degrees or equivalent experience) who have a particular skill that an employer needs and is prepared to pay you a salary for, that is the same as, or higher than, that paid to US citizens in the same area. If the employer is a start-up

company, you are not required to provide financial details, but by the end of three years you need to show that the company has enough income to pay your salary.

- If you have an L or E visa, your spouse will be entitled to work in the USA in any job.

Applying for any of these visas, except the tourist and student ones (B2), can be expensive and it is advisable to employ a specialist immigration lawyer to make the application on your behalf, because otherwise you may miss out on important details pertinent to the process and end up having your application denied. Legal help may cost several thousands of pounds, however, so you need to be serious and fairly confident about your application before you start.

Work

You may be thinking about buying in Florida because your employer is about to transfer you there, in which case you already have a job lined up. If this is not the case, then although you may feel at more of an advantage as an English speaker trying to find work in the USA, the reality is that the economy in Florida is very much geared towards tourism. So if you do not have anything else in the pipeline, the summit of your career aspirations there is likely to be working in a relatively lowly paid job in the service industries.

One of the most common ways for non-US citizens to find their way into working in Florida without having to submit to such drudgery is to buy a business, thus qualifying for an E visa (see immigration rules above). If you are doing this, you will need to have money to invest in the company – you will normally only be able to raise finance for around 25 per cent of the total value.

You may wish to employ a licensed business broker to find a business on your behalf, do the negotiating and arrange for an E visa, but shop around and do be careful, because there are disreputable people working in this field. You will certainly want to engage a lawyer to act on your behalf as well. If you do go down this route, try to be realistic about what you are doing and do not get carried away. Would you be setting up a business in this field in the UK? Do you know anything about it? Are you prepared to put the necessary work in to make this business work? Have you done enough research to be confident that it stands a chance of success?

If the answer to any of these questions is no, the best advice is to walk away and think again. Otherwise you may just end up with a very expensive visa application and an impoverished lifestyle.

Tax

In the USA there are several forms of income tax, the most important being federal income tax, which is charged in bands at 15, 28, 31, 36 and 39.6 per cent. In some states you would also have to pay state income tax, but Florida is one of the few that does not levy such a tax.

The USA has a double-taxation treaty with the UK, in much the same way as EU countries do, so depending on your domicile and where you are resident, you should pay tax to only one jurisdiction. If in doubt, seek advice from a tax specialist.

Health

If you are visiting, living or working in Florida, one of the first things you must sort out is some kind of health insurance. If you need to use the US health system and are under-insured, the medical bills you could face could be astronomical.

Anyone staying for up to six months should have a comprehensive travel policy or an international health policy to cover you at home and in other countries, including the USA. Most international policies cover you for repatriation should it be necessary, and for your body to be shipped back home if the worst happened and you died over there. Check the details of the policy carefully, though; look at what excesses are in place, make sure the annual limit on medical costs is at least $2,000,000, and check whether the insurer will settle the bills direct with the health provider in the USA, or reimburse you.

Most US residents have health insurance paid for partly or wholly by their employers, but there are estimated to be more than a million Americans with no or inadequate health insurance. People aged 65 and over, and people of any age with disabilities, are covered by the publicly funded health scheme Medicare.

If you are planning to move to the USA and do not fit into any of these categories, check out the cost of healthcare in advance – it may be so expensive that it puts you off the whole venture. A policy for a typical family of four could easily cost $1,000 a month or more; if anyone in the family has pre-existing illnesses they will be excluded from cover, and there will be excesses of, for example, $10 for each routine visit to a physician and $1,000 for each in-patient hospital admission. There may be a limit of, say, $50,000 on what the insurer will pay out in a year, or a lifetime limit of $1 million.

Insurance and utilities

Insuring your home in the USA is not just a sensible precaution against burglars and accidental damage – it is an essential protection against life in the most litigious society on the planet. Homeowners' policies generally have two elements – casualty insurance, to cover losses to your home or personal possessions, suffered by you as a result of man-made or natural causes; and liability insurance, to cover you against financial responsibility for injuries to third parties on your property, or that can be attributed to your property. Extra cover for hurricane, earthquake or flood damage is expensive and can, in some parts of Florida, make you think twice about buying in the first place – so check out the risk of damage, and the likely insurance premiums, before you buy. Insurance for holiday homes is, not surprisingly, more expensive, and many insurers will suspend cover if the place is uninhabited for more than 30 or 60 days.

As for liability insurance, $1,000,000 is recommended as the minimum cover necessary, although many policies will only go up as far as $100,000 with their standard policies. It is not unknown for people in the USA to sue for millions of dollars because they slipped on someone's garden path, for example. US courts seem to work on the assumption that everyone must have liability insurance, and make settlements that can be huge.

Although gas is relatively cheap compared to electricity in the USA, be prepared for some high utility bills if you plan to spend any time there. As a foreigner starting an account with utility firms you are likely to have to pay security deposits in order to have your services switched on, and these can add up to several hundred dollars. Air conditioning is common but expensive. Water is also metered, so you may find your bills spiral during the hot summer months.

Chapter 9

Emerging markets

Being in a position to think about buying a property in France, Spain, Portugal, Italy or the USA may seem exciting enough to most Britons, but these are reassuringly familiar holiday destinations. For bargain hunters, investors and people who thrive on doing things a bit differently, there are numerous other countries also worth considering. All it takes is a bit of imagination, a dash of pioneering spirit and – perhaps even more than when dealing with 'standard' countries – a very thorough lawyer.

The Mediterranean

Cyprus

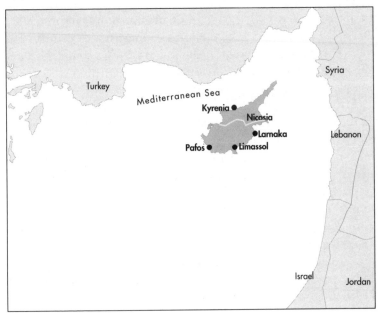

Cyprus has been a popular tourist destination among the British, and other north Europeans, for many years now. The island has two international airports (Larnaka and Pafos), low tax rates, a low crime rate and a high standard of living. Many Greek Cypriots also have excellent English. These factors have contributed to the Greek portion of Cyprus becoming a haven for British people wanting to retire to sunnier climes.

The country is now poised to join the European Union in May 2004, a development expected to accelerate recent growth in the economy. The Cypriot government has also relaxed its laws on ownership of businesses by foreigners so that members of the EU can own a business in Cyprus outright – making it more possible for UK residents who want or need to carry on earning a living to emigrate to the island.

The property market is buoyant, with prices rising by an estimated 10 to 15 per cent during 2002/03; mortgages are now available from a range of sources, including at least one of the major Greek banks. If you are a non-Cypriot, you are entitled to freehold ownership of one property, a villa or an apartment or a piece of land up to 3 *donums* (4,012 square metres). If you are of Cypriot origin there are no restrictions.

The basic buying process is not dissimilar from that in the UK, except that even paying a nominal deposit of £1,000 to £2,000 makes the deal legally enforceable; on signing a proper contract you must pay up to 30 per cent of the full price. The contract is then deposited at the land registry and both parties proceed towards completion.

At the moment all foreigners buying property in Cyprus must be granted approval to do so by the Council of Ministers. To make a purchase you will need to provide a bank reference, a character reference and details such as criminal records, proof that the land size is within the required limits, that only one home is owned in Cyprus, and that you have enough money to keep yourself. Approval can take up to a year. If you decided to buy in advance of gaining approval (as a result of being pressurised by the vendor, for example) and approval was not granted (although it always is, provided you meet the criteria laid out above) you could re-apply and would be able to live in the house for 17 years before you had to sell it.

By law in Cyprus all registered estate agents must do searches on their properties and must inform clients of any legal encumbrances, mortgages or problems relating to the property.

You must pay property transfer tax of 3 per cent on the first 50,000 Cypriot pounds, 5 per cent on the next 50,000 Cypriot pounds and 8 per cent on anything above that; plus stamp duty at 15 pence per 100 Cypriot pounds up to 100,000 Cypriot pounds and 20 pence thereafter. An annual immovable property tax also applies; the first 100,000 Cypriot pounds, worth of the property is exempt and anything after that is charged at 2, 3 or 3.5 per cent. Capital gains tax is charged at 20 per cent, but there are generous exemptions; inheritance tax is levied only on non-residents.

UK retirees are taxed on a flat rate of 5 per cent on pension and investment income brought into Cyprus, with exemptions totalling 4,000 Cypriot pounds per person.

Getting to Cyprus Fly to: Larnaka or Pafos.

Examples of property prices in Cyprus

- One-bedroomed off-plan apartment in Limassol, close to town centre, air-conditioning and underground parking: £52,000 (sterling).
- Two-bedroomed apartment five minutes outside Pafos; shared pool, air-conditioning, fully furnished: £84,000 (sterling).
- Newly built three-bedroomed house 10 kilometres from Larnaka and 2 kilometres from beach, with private pool, air conditioning and landscaped garden: £140,000 (sterling).
- Four-bedroomed, two-bathroomed detached house near Tala, with private pool, air conditioning, mature gardens, pond and water feature: £260,000 (sterling).

Greece

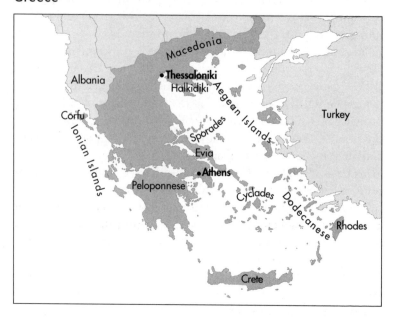

Three million UK holidaymakers visit Greece each year, but until recently very few bought property in mainland Greece or on its 2,500 islands. Before 1991 foreigners were banned from buying there. All that changed with EU entry, although restrictions still apply for non-EU citizens who wish to buy in border areas such as the Eastern Aegean, the Dodecanese islands, Crete and Rhodes and parts of northern Greece.

The buying process in Greece is similar to that in much of the Mediterranean, but there are widespread problems with local red tape. There has not been a great tradition of property-related paperwork, which means disputes can arise over who actually owns a particular property. An old whitewashed village house that has probably been in a Greek family for generations may be fraught with difficulties, for example. For local people, this is less of a problem because they probably know who is the legal owner, or at least are better placed to sort out a dispute, but foreign buyers need proof of ownership – particularly if they need to raise finance in order to pay for it.

What British buyers should obtain is a title deed stating clearly who owns the property. But often you may have to rely on a law that says anyone in possession of a property for 20 years is considered to be the owner. In the absence of deeds, the vendor should provide evidence that he or she has been there for 20 years – this can be easier said than done but, assuming the evidence is available, it will result in the local council producing a certificate proving ownership.

Such proof of ownership is vital as protection against other people who may have a claim to the property – especially in a country where lots of people do not make wills, and where many people emigrate when they are fairly young and return to their homeland at a later stage. Put yourself in the hands of an English-speaking local lawyer, who will know about any local laws and local interpretations of laws; he or she will carry out searches to check the property's title before you go any further.

Generally speaking you will need to pay 10 per cent on signing of a pre-contract agreement; you are tied in from this point (unless problems occur, as anticipated in the contract) and will lose the money if you pull out. The seller must pay you back double if he or she pulls out. You must pay a purchase tax to the Greek government, which will be 9 to 11 per cent of the 'tax assessed value' of the property; allow a total of at least 12 to 15 per cent above the purchase price in order to cover legal fees and so on.

Examples of property prices in Greece

- Newly built, two-bedroomed apartment on island of Kos (southern Sporades), with built area of 60 square metres, terraces and sea views, 12 kilometres from beach: €75,000.
- House on island of Kythnos (Cyclades) with two bedrooms and two bathrooms (two hours to Piraeus); built area 70 square metres, land of 660 square metres, 2 kilometres to beach: €117,000.
- Restored country house on island of Kalymnos (Dodecanese) with all-round sea views; 90 square metres on two levels; 5,000 square metres of land including olive, pine and palm trees; sold furnished: €146,000.
- Architect-restored farmhouse in Arkadia (south-east Peloponnese); 130 square metres on 700 square metres of land including olive grove; courtyard, sea views; three bedrooms, two bathrooms plus separate guest apartment: €270,000.

According to Greek law, if a plot of land is not within the town plan and if there are no forest or archaeology restrictions, permission to build can be granted for any plot of a minimum of 4,000 square metres. Permission can be granted for plots of land of 2,000 square metres or less, if they are located within the planning zone or with frontage to the principal municipal road. Inside villages, towns and cities, planning permission can generally be granted for any plot. Building permits can only be obtained through registered architects or engineers in Greece and cost about 4 to 5 per cent of the total cost of the building.

Getting to Greece Fly to: (mainland) Athens, Kavala, Thessaloniki; (islands) Corfu Town, Heraklion (Crete), Chania (Crete), Rhodes Town, Kefallinia (Kefalonia), Kos, Limnos, Mytilini (Lesbos), Samos, Zakinthos.

Malta

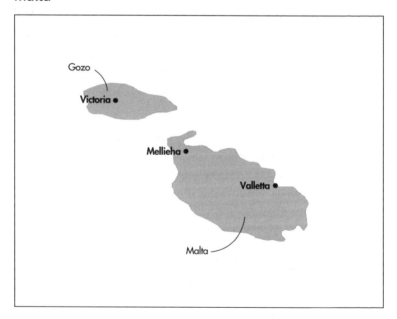

Malta has been a popular holiday destination for UK residents for many years, and small numbers of British people have been retiring to it and its neighbouring island Gozo – largely attracted by the climate, the favourable tax regime (permanent residents pay 15 per cent income tax and 5 per cent inheritance tax) and the nation's Anglophile culture.

Interest in property on the islands has been rising more recently, however, especially since Malta announced its intention to join the EU – an event which is likely to occur in May 2004. Malta's concern that EU status would result in an increase in demand for property, thus pricing native Maltese and Gozitan families out of the market, led the government to negotiate special arrangements relating to people buying second homes.

Prior to May 2004, foreigners can purchase one property in Malta or Gozo after obtaining the relative permit. Once the islands are in the EU, citizens from other member countries who want to buy a holiday home will still need an authorisation and will only be able to buy one flat (which must be worth more than 30,000 Maltese pounds – approximately £51,000) or one house (which must cost more than 50,000 Maltese pounds – around £85,000).

If you move to Malta permanently you can buy any property irrespective of value. Once you have lived there for a continuous period of at least five years, or if you are buying property connected with business activities, you may, if you wish, buy more than one property.

Getting to Malta Fly to: Valletta.

Examples of property prices in Malta

- First-floor one-bedroomed apartment in a holiday complex in Bahar ic-Caghaq (resort on northern coast, halfway between St Julians and St Paul's Bay); enclosed terrace, shares a large garden and communal pool: €70,000.
- Three-bedroomed apartment on third floor of a complex in St Julian's; two open balconies, lift access and own garage: €145,000.
- Three-bedroomed bungalow in Kercem (Gozo); with own garden, pool and garage: €374,000.
- Beautiful town house in Valletta, in need of minor restoration; features private courtyard, stone staircase, high ceilings, original floor tiles, etc; six bedrooms, three large receptions, huge cellar, sea views: €625,000.

Turkey

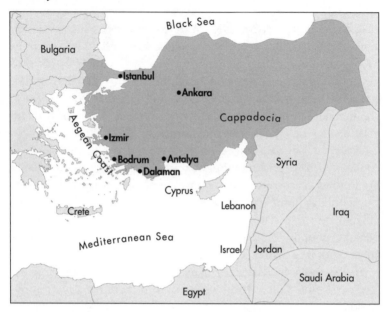

Although not much more than ten years ago Turkey was little-known in the UK as a holiday destination, nearly a million British tourists now go there every year. Add to this Turkey's increasing attempts to modernise its way into the European Union – it first applied for membership 30 years ago and has been an official candidate since 1999, though has yet to reach the shortlist – and it is easy to see why Turkey is hotly tipped as an investment for anyone who wants a place in the sun at minimal cost.

Whether or not Turkish property values ever rise to EU levels, the trend certainly appears to be upward, and although earthquakes and bombings do nothing to assist the tourist industry there is little doubt that in terms of its natural resources, the country matches Greece as a tourist destination.

Buying a property in Turkey is easier than one might expect, so long as you buy in towns rather than rural or military zones. The process is similar to that in most southern European countries, although there are the same potential problems with lack of clarity about property and land title, and it is important to have confidence in your lawyer to sort these out, especially if you are buying off-plan from a developer.

A purchase tax of 4 per cent is payable; there are also annual property taxes to be paid, at a rate of 0.1 per cent for houses and 0.3 per cent for developed lands. New properties are exempt from the annual property tax for five years. All properties are subject to revaluation every five years for tax purposes. You must also pay the estate agent's commission, which is normally around 3 per cent.

Getting to Turkey Fly to: Ankara, Antalya, Bodrum, Dalaman, Istanbul, Izmir.

Examples of property prices in Turkey

- Three-bedroomed apartment in Altinkum (2 hours to Izmir), 80 square metres, on second floor of purpose-built block: £19,000 (sterling).
- Ground-floor newly built apartment in Fethiye, with two bedrooms and two bathrooms, plus three balconies and shared pool: £45,000.
- Villa in Bodrum, with two bedrooms and two bathrooms, 85 square metres, on two floors plus terrace of 20 square metres: £51,000.
- Three/four-bedroomed riverside villa in Gocek (25 minutes to Dalaman airport); on plot of 800 square metres, with permission to build a second house or pool; terraces on ground and first floors: £115,000.

Balkan States

The end of hostilities in the former Yugoslavia has combined with a gradual opening up of the south-eastern corners of Europe, to create a great deal of interest among investors in some parts of the Balkans. An abundance of natural beauty and affordable property could be a winning formula – but tread carefully and think hard about what you are buying and why, rather than focusing purely on the low prices.

Bulgaria

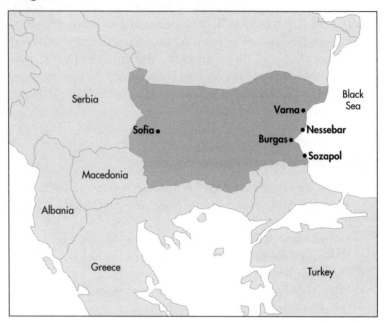

One of the poorest countries in Europe, Bulgaria has had a chequered history. A dominant force in the Balkans during the medieval period, Bulgaria endured four centuries of rule by the Ottoman Empire, then finally gained full independence in 1908. The Second World War brought Soviet occupation, the end of the monarchy and, in 1948, the start of 41 years of unbroken Communist rule.

Since 1989 the country has been gradually moving away from its Cold War past, and is working towards membership of the EU, with 2007 touted as a possible entry date.

Under Bulgarian law, foreigners can buy buildings but not land – so for foreign nationals the most common method to buy property there is to set up a company, which can then own the land. As time goes on, the law should change as the country opens its doors fully in line with EU regulations. There are rules and regula-tions about how such a company must establish and run itself, but the basic process is similar to setting up a company in the UK.

Bulgaria's biggest selling point is its Black Sea coastline, which used to be a popular destination among Soviet apparatchiks and is already beginning to attract sizeable numbers of tourists from the UK and other western European countries, particularly to coastal towns such as Varna and Borgas and the resorts of Nessebar and Sozapol. Another attraction is Veliko Turnovo, the medieval former capital, accessible via Sofia. There are also mountainous regions, giving the country its other claim to fame, as a haven for winter sports.

So far the country has focused on developing package tourism, so letting income might not be as solid as in some countries because the bulk of visitors will already have accommodation arranged. But there is great potential for capital appreciation – and for enjoying a friendly, proud and unusual nation on the latest of a long series of cultural journeys.

Getting to Bulgaria Fly to: Sofia or Varna.

Examples of property prices in Bulgaria

- Apartment in residential block in Black Sea port/resort of Borgas: 62 square metres of living space: €18,000.
- Four-bedroomed three-storey villa in village near ski resort of Borovets, on a plot of 400 square metres with a mature garden: €26,000.
- Five-bedroomed three-storey villa in spa town of Velingrad; two kitchens, two receptions, marble floors and fireplaces; walled garden: €51,000.
- Two-storey villa and guest cottage near Varna; total of seven bedrooms plus garden and second-floor balcony: €53,000.

Croatia

The Croats' warmth and sense of unity remain undiminished, despite the traumas of the 1990s. The country's unique natural resources – a strip of nearly 1,800 kilometres of beautiful coastline, dotted with more than a thousand islands basking in the clean, clear waters of the Adriatic – should carve out an enduring appeal as a holiday destination for tourists with an appreciation of the finer things in life. Seaside apart, a hotchpotch of baroque, Habsburg, Venetian, Roman and medieval influences shape Croatia's towns and villages, as well as the jewel in its crown, the stunning city of Dubrovnik.

It is possible to buy property in Croatia as a foreigner, but it is not easy because you must first get the approval of the Ministry of Foreign Affairs (MFA). In Croatia the ultimate proof of ownership is entry of the owner's name in the local 'land book' on that specific property, and the local courts will not allow a foreign citizen to be entered in land books without the Ministry's approval.

To obtain it, you need to submit a written request signed by you and drafted by your lawyer, the sales contract, an excerpt from the land book for the particular property, proof of citizenship for both buyer and seller (with any photocopies notarised by a Croatian public notary), and certain other documents. You must pay a 10 per cent deposit to the notary at this point. Once a letter of approval is received from the MFA, you pass on the balance of funds; an application is then made to register the transaction in the land book.

It can take anything up to a year to get approval, and there is also a backlog of some years for entering properties into the land book. Vendors are understandably reluctant to wait while all this is sorted out. One way around the problem is to set up a Croatian company – which has the same property-buying rights as a Croatian citizen – and buy the property through it, but this has tax implications, so research your options thoroughly and take trustworthy legal advice.

Getting to Croatia Fly to: Dubrovnik, Pula, Split, Zagreb.

Examples of property prices in Croatia

- Stone house of 58 square metres, 50 metres from the sea in the centre of the old town in Vis, South Dalmatia; for conversion, with yard measuring 165 square metres: €58,000.
- One-bedroomed apartment with sea views in Rovinj (old town); 38 square metres of living space plus balcony, fully renovated and sold furnished: €70,000.
- Two-bedroomed apartment in Dubrovnik, just behind the old town; 82 square metres of living space plus 30 square metres of terrace: €120,000.
- Castle for renovation on outskirts of Dubrovnik; 9,000 square metres of living space; set in 16,000 square metres of grounds: €600,000.

Slovenia

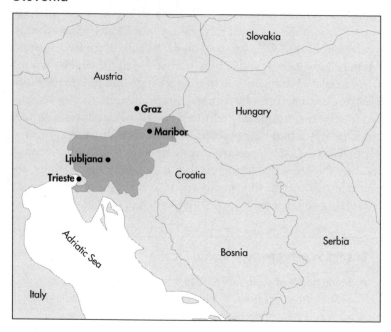

Slovenia is a tiny country often referred to as the 'Balkan Switzerland'. It has just two million inhabitants, and is one of the more prosperous parts of the former Yugoslavia. It borders Italy, Austria, Hungary and Croatia and contains a tiny stretch of Mediterranean coastline, as well as beautiful lakes and mountains. Having escaped the latest Balkan conflict virtually unscathed, Slovenia already has a standard of living higher than Greece and this is likely to rise further when it joins the EU in May 2004 – the first and only part of the former Yugoslavia to do so.

This country could be a prime candidate if what you want is an unspoilt holiday home destination with good letting potential, whether in the coastal region; the capital, Ljubljana; or the more northerly skiing region around Maribor (accessible via Austria's Graz airport as well as via Ljubljana). Over the last few years the Slovenian property market has been opening up to foreign investors for the first time, but the process is slow, and obtaining even the most basic information, about property for sale and how to go about buying, can still be difficult – so Slovenia is probably one to watch rather than to jump at.

Prices are more closely aligned to EU levels than many of the country's more impoverished fellow EU aspirants in Eastern Europe, but they offer good value for money. Like its southerly neighbour Croatia, Slovenia has more to offer the British buyer than just potential for rapid capital appreciation.

Getting to Slovenia Fly to: Ljubljana, Graz, Trieste.

Examples of property prices in Slovenia

- One-bedroomed vineyard house with kitchen, wine-pressing room and cellars in Trnovska vas (wine region in eastern Slovenia) in a development area; total land area 1,970 square metres: €34,000.
- Two-bedroomed house on two floors, located near river in village of Braslovce (mid-Slovenia); 100 square metres: €65,000.
- Two-bedroomed sixth-floor flat in the centre of Ljubljana, built in 1976; 80 square metres of living space, parking, balcony: €145,000.
- Spacious four-bedroomed designer flat in Ljubljana (Moste district), built 1995, 151 square metres of living space: €320,000.

Eastern Europe

In the last ten or so years, the grand old cities of Eastern Europe – previously hidden from Western eyes by the Iron Curtain – have begun to sell themselves as tourist destinations. And experts predict that, as the enlargement of the European Union takes hold from May 2004 onwards, at least one of them will emerge as the financial and commercial 'capital' of what used to be known as the Eastern Bloc.

The Baltic States' capitals – Tallinn (Estonia), Riga (Latvia) and Vilnius (Lithuania) certainly have appeal as city break destinations, as does the Slovak Republic's elegant capital, Bratislava, and Poland's second city, Kraków. As money flows in to even things out across an enlarged EU, all are likely to gain in some way from inward investment.

But Prague, Budapest and, to a lesser extent, Warsaw look set to be the biggest winners from the redrawing of the European political map. And although it is not easy to get information about property in the rural hinterlands of the Czech Republic, Hungary, Poland and Slovakia – nor of their eastern neighbour Romania (tipped for EU entry in 2007, along with Bulgaria), there are plenty of beautiful homes in areas of outstanding natural beauty throughout the region, and it is surely only a matter of time before they become more available to Western bargain hunters.

Czech Republic

The Czech Republic is, as a whole, hilly and picturesque, with historic castles, romantic valleys and lakes, and excellent facilities to 'take the waters' at one of the famous spas or to ski and hike in the mountains. Among the most beautiful areas are the river valleys of the Vltava (Moldau) and Labe (Elbe), the spa towns of Karlovy Vary and Mariánské Lázne, and the very beautiful region of south Bohemia.

Known as 'The City of One Hundred Towers and Spires', the Czech capital, Prague, has the kind of rich architectural heritage that is matched by few cities in the world. The centre, a UNESCO World Heritage Site, is a heady mix of Gothic churches, Functionalism, Art Deco, Art Nouveau, and modern architecture.

It is also a testament to its centuries-old ability to escape the worst ravages of war, although there is still work to be done to bring much of Prague back to its former glory. The Czechs, despite their economy having been reined back severely by Soviet Communism, are renowned for their independent spirit – something which should serve them well as they find their feet in the newly enlarged EU.

It is possible to buy properties in the Czech Republic, but only through a company. This can be a UK company which opens a Czech branch and buys the property through that, or a Czech company; there are pros and cons with each approach and it is essential to take advice on what works best in your particular circumstances. Czech mortgages are available for up to 85 per cent of the purchase price, over a maximum of 15 years, but again these can only be taken by out by companies rather than individuals.

Getting to the Czech Republic Fly to: Prague.

Examples of property prices in the Czech Republic

- Two-bedroomed 1930s villa in Neratovice (near Prague); 80 square metres of living space, on a plot of more than 500 square metres: €66,000.
- One-bedroomed duplex apartment in central Prague; 66 square metres of living space, with fitted kitchen: €73,000.
- Three-bedroomed penthouse apartment on two stories in Prague; over 200 square metres of living space; balcony, spiral staircase, underfloor heating: €221,000.
- 1940s villa in Cersonice (outskirts of Prague); 220 square metres of living space, converted into three large apartments; shared garden of 2,000 square metres, swimming pool and garage: €240,000.

Hungary

Of all the former Communist countries, Hungary has always been the most Western in its thinking, even if its progress towards market economics since 1989 has been more gradual than in Poland or the Czech Republic. The key to Budapest, its stunning and cosmopolitan capital, lies in its position. Made up of the twin towns of Buda and Pest, strategically located on either side of the majestic Danube, the city has alternated between immense prosperity and devastating upheaval as generations have fought for control of central Europe's main waterway. Hilly Buda is situated in the west, with its narrow cobbled streets and a mixture of medieval and neo-classical buildings almost totally reconstructed after the Second World War; to the east lies Pest, with its wide boulevards and Art Deco styles. Turkish, Venetian, Empire and Art Nouveau clash together in this city, and somehow it works.

Outside the capital, Hungary has many rural treats to offer, including the Carpathian Basin and its three main historic towns, Szentendre, Visegrad and Esztergom; and the mighty Lake Balaton (also known as the Hungarian Sea) – the largest stretch of inland water in central Europe. With water mostly only waist-deep, the lake offers sailing, windsurfing and fishing. Elsewhere there are long stretches of agrarian plain, and hilly skiing areas to the north.

It is possible to buy property in Hungary as an individual, but this relies on being granted a government permit, which can take several months to come through, if it is granted at all. A quicker alternative is to set up a registered Hungarian company, which costs around €600 to arrange, and half that per year as an ongoing cost; but remember you will be able to offset expenses against any profits for tax purposes. Transfer taxes are lower, too. Typical fees include 2 per cent lawyers' fees, 4 per cent estate agent's commission and 2 per cent purchase tax.

Areas considered best for investment, which many expect to bring in as much as 25 per cent a year in capital appreciation, include Pest's much sought-after fifth district; the sixth, seventh and thirteenth districts, also in Pest; and the eleventh district in Buda. Agents claim that rental yields of 8 to 9 per cent a year are achievable for well appointed, well marketed apartments aimed at Western European tenants.

Getting to Hungary Fly to: Budapest.

Examples of property prices in Hungary

- Ground-floor studio apartment in thirteenth district of Budapest; 39 square metres of living space; needs minor repairs: £35,000 (sterling).
- Second-floor apartment in sixth district of Budapest; 100 square metres of living space, undergoing conversion: £81,000.
- Two-bedroomed top-floor apartment in fifth district of Budapest; 116 square metres of living space, newly refurbished to high standard with air-conditioning: £185,000.
- Refurbished top-floor apartment in fifth district; 180 square metres of living space: £273,000.

Poland

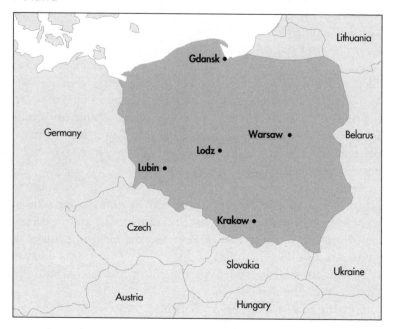

The largest economy in ex-Soviet Eastern Europe, Poland adopted a 'big bang' strategy of rapid transition to capitalism after the collapse of Communism. Price controls were removed at a stroke; production, distribution and trade were deregulated; large parts of the economy were privatised; the tax and fiscal systems were overhauled; and the national currency (the zloty) was made fully convertible. By the mid-1990s the economy was growing strongly and the country has received steady financial support from the International Monetary Fund (IMF) and the World Bank. Since the end of 1999 Poland's boom has come to an end, with unemployment shooting up to 17 per cent – but EU entry in May 2004 is expected to improve matters.

Poland has 22 national parks, some 1,200 nature reserves, more than 100 landscape parks and 400 protected areas. Large parts of Warsaw, the capital, were destroyed in the Second World War but have been lovingly rebuilt since then, and there has been an extensive building programme there – experts say this has kept a lid on house prices, but they should rise significantly over time.

As with many other countries in the region, foreigners must obtain permission from the minister of internal affairs in order to buy property, but setting up a company can get round many of the problems.

Getting to Poland Fly to: Warsaw.

Examples of property prices in Poland

- Flat in central Warsaw, with 70 square metres of living space plus terrace of 20 square metres; built in 2000, on two floors: £16,000 (sterling).
- Flat in central Warsaw, with 280 square metres of living space; built in 1995: £26,000.
- Five-bedroomed house on two floors in Warsaw; 190 square metres of living space: £41,000.
- Six-bedroomed house on four floors in Warsaw; built in 1945; 240 square metres of living space: £53,000.
- Luxury flats under construction in Krakow (Old Town); 85 to 102 square metres (larger ones have three bedrooms, two bathrooms, two balconies): €2,000 per square metre.
- Building land in three plots, with approval for up to six houses in Kryspinow (10 kilometres west of Krakow); 3,300 square metres: €85,000

Rest of the world

It is not just in European countries that buyers from the UK and other Western economies are spotting property potential. Potential buyers looking at property purely for investment purposes, rather than as a way of fulfilling their dream of owning a holiday or retirement home, are also looking further afield.

As with any other investment, it is vital to be realistic about the risks of such investments as well as the possible benefits. It is easy for developers to suggest one of their properties could be rented out for 40 weeks a year – especially when it is an area about which you know absolutely nothing – but is that really feasible? At the very least, visit the property you are considering buying to check not only its quality but how accessible it is. Be ruthless in your questioning, and request detailed evidence of all claims made in promotional literature. What proof exists of a demand for tourist accommodation in the area in question?

Talk to other buyers, and to locals, if you can, to get an idea of what they think of the development. Examine carefully what is happening with the economies and property markets of the region involved; look at worst-case scenarios as well as best-case ones.

Potential locations around the world

Some faraway areas tipped as property hotspots of the future include:

- **Brazil,** where £70,000 might buy you a brand new one-bedroomed flat in Rio, a two-bedroomed house with a pool outside São Paolo or a three-bedroomed villa in the up-and-coming north-eastern Aracuju region
- **Dubai,** where property ownership by foreigners was illegal until a couple of years ago, so expatriates working there were forced to rent; the law has since changed and a series of ultra-modern apartments and villas, aimed at the professional and holiday-home markets and costing from around £50,000, have hit the market
- **Egypt,** where a well-appointed two-bedroomed flat in Cairo would cost just £45,000, and where numerous developments are springing up around Red Sea resorts like Sharm El Sheikh and Hurghada, which are popular with divers, with entry-level apartments priced at around £20,000
- the Indian region of **Goa**, where a villa on a new development might cost you somewhere between £10,000 and £20,000
- the Kenyan resort of **Malindi**, where several actors and super-models already have homes and an acre of land could cost as little as £25,000
- **South Africa,** where a four-bedroomed bungalow with pool just outside Cape Town might cost you as little as £85,000.

Addresses and websites

General

Architects' Council of Europe
rue Paul Emile Janson, 29
B-1050, Brussels
Belgium
Tel: 00 32 2543 1140
Email: info@ace-cae.org
Website: www.ace-cae.org

Architecture and Surveying Institute
c/o Chartered Institute of Building
Englemere
Kings Ride
Ascot
Berks SL5 7TB
Tel: 01344 630700
Website: www.ciob.org.uk

Association of Building Engineers
Lutyens House
Billing Brook Road
Weston Favell
Northampton NN3 8NW
Tel: (01604) 404121
Email: building.engineers@abe.org.uk
Website: www.abe.org.uk

The British Council
10 Spring Gardens
London SW1A 2BN
Tel: 020-7930 8466
Website: www.britishcouncil.org.uk

Confédération Européenne d'Immobilier (CEI)
P/ Box 17330
2502 CH
The Hague
Netherlands
Tel: 00 31 70 345 8703
Email: vbo@vbo.nl
Website: http://web-cei.com

Conférence des Notariats de l'Union Européenne (CNUE)
Avenue de Cortenbergh 52-B-1000
Brussels
Belgium
Tel: 00 32 2513 9529
Email: info@cnue.be
Website: www.cnue.be

Department for Work and Pensions (DWP)
Correspondence Unit
Room 540
The Adelphi
1–11 John Adam Street
London WC2N 6HT
Tel: 020–7712 2171
Email: peo@dwp.gsi.gov.uk
Websites: www.dwp.gov.uk
www.thepensionservice.gov.uk

Department of Health (DoH)
Richmond House
79 Whitehall
London SW1A 2NS
Tel: 020–7210 4850
Email: dhmail@doh.gsi.gov.uk
Website: www.doh.gov.uk

Electoral Commission
Trevelyan House
Great Peter Street
London SW1P 2HW
Tel: 020–7271 0500
Email: info@electoralcommission.org.uk
Website: www.electoralcommission.org.uk

European Centre for the Development of Vocational Training (CEDEFOP)
PO Box 22427
Thessaloniki
GR-55102
Greece
Tel: 00 30 23 10 4901
Email: info@cedefop.eu.int
Website: www.cedefop.gr

European Council of International Schools (ECIS)
21B Lavant Street
Petersfield
Hampshire GU32 3EL
Tel: (01730) 268244
Email: ecis@ecis.org
Website: www.ecis.org

European Employment Services Network (EURES)
Tel: 00 800 4080 4080 (freephone)
Email: empl-eures@cec.eu.int
Website: www.europa.eu.int/eures

Federation of Overseas Property Developers, Agents and Consultants (FOPDAC)
Lacey House
St Clare Business Park
Holly Road
Hampton Hill
Middlesex TW12 1QQ
Tel: 020–8941 5588
Email: info@fopdac.com
Website: www.fopdac.com

Foreign and Commonwealth Office
Old Admiralty Building
London SW1A 2PA
Tel: 020–7008 1500 (*main switchboard*)
020–7008 0218 (services for Britons overseas)
Website: www.fco.gov.uk

Inland Revenue
Tel: (0845) 302 1455
0151 472 6192 (*centre for non-residents*)
Website: www.inlandrevenue.gov.uk

Law Society of England and Wales
Law Society Hall
113 Chancery Lane
London WC2A 1PL
Tel: 020–7242 1222
Email: info.services@lawsociety.org.uk
Website: www.lawsociety.org.uk

National Academic Recognition Information Centre (NARIC)
UK NARIC
Oriel House
Oriel Road
Cheltenham
Gloucestershire GL50 1XP
Tel: (0870) 990 4088
Email: info@naric.org.uk
Website: www.naric.org.uk

Office of Fair Trading
Fleetbank House
2–6 Salisbury Square
London EC4Y 8JX
Tel: 020–7211 8000
Email: enquiries@oft.gov.uk
Website: www.oft.gov.uk

Organisation for Timeshare in Europe (OTE)
78–80 rue Defacqz, 4th floor
B-1060 Brussels
Belgium
Email: info@ote-info.com
Website: www.ote-info.com

Retirement Pension Forecasting and Advice Unit (RPFA)
Department for Work and Pensions
Pensions and Overseas Benefits Directorate
Newcastle upon Tyne
NE98 1BA
Tel: (0845) 300 0168
Website: www.dwp.gov.uk

Royal Institute of British Architects (RIBA)
66 Portland Place
London W1B 1AD
Tel: 020–7307 3700
Website: www.architecture.com

*Royal Institution of Chartered
Surveyors (RICS)*
12 Great George Street
Parliament Square
London SW1P 3AD
Tel: 020–7222 7000
Email: contactrics@rics.org
Website: www.rics.org

Timeshare Consumers' Association
Hodsock
Worksop
Nottinghamshire S81 0TF
Tel: (01909) 591100
Email: info@timeshare.org.uk
Website: www.timeshare.org.uk

Embassies, consulates and chambers of commerce

Bulgaria

Embassy of the Republic of Bulgaria
186–188 Queen's Gate
London SW7 5HL
Tel: 020–7584 9433/9400
Email:
info@bulgarianembassy.org.uk

Cyprus

Cyprus High Commission
93 Park Street
London W1K 7ET
Tel: 020–7499 8272
Email: cyphclondon@dial.pipex.com

Cyprus Chamber of Commerce
(based in Cyprus)
Email: chamber@ccci.org.cui
Website: www.ccci.org.cui

Czech Republic

Embassy of the Czech Republic
26 Kensington Palace Gardens
London W8 4QY
Tel: 020–7243 1115
Email: london@embassy.mzv.cz

Estonia

Embassy of the Republic of Estonia
16 Hyde Park Gate
London SW7 5DG
Tel 020–7589 3428
Email:
Embassy.London@estonia.gov.uk
Website: www.estonia.gov.uk

Florida (USA)

The US Embassy
24 Grosvenor Square
London W1A 1AE
Tel: 020–7499 9000
Website: www.usembassy.org.uk

British Consulate, Miami, FL
1001 Brickell Bay Drive
Miami
FL 33131
USA
Tel: 00 1 305 374 1522
Website: www.britainusa.com

The Department of State
RA Gray Building
500 South Bronough Street
Tallahassee
FL 32399–0250
USA
Tel: 00 1 850 245 6500
Email: secretary@mail.dos.state.fl.us

Florida Chamber of Commerce
136 South Bronough Street
PO Box 11309, Tallahassee
FL 32302–3309
USA
Tel: 00 1 877 521 1200
Website: www.flchamber.com

France

*The French Embassy/Consulate
General*
21 Cromwell Road
London SW7 2EN
Tel: 020–7073 1200
Website: www.ambafrance-uk.org

Greece

The Greek Embassy
1A Holland Park
London W11 3TP
Tel: 020–7221 6467
Email: consulategeneral@
greekembassy.org.uk
Website: www.greekembassy.org.uk

Hungary

Embassy of the Republic of Hungary
35 Eaton Place
London SW1X 8BY
Tel: 020–7235 5218

Hungarian Chambers of Commerce and Industry (in Budapest)
Kossuth Lajos ter 6–8
H-1055
Hungary
Tel: 00 361 474 5100

Italy

The Embassy of Italy
14 Three Kings Yard
London W1K 4EH
Tel: 020–7312 2200
Email: emblondon@embitaly.org.uk

Latvia

Embassy of the Republic of Latvia
45 Nottingham Place
London W1U 5LY
Tel: 020–7312 0040
Email: embassy.uk@mfa.gov.lr

Lithuania

Embassy of the Republic of Lithuania
84 Gloucester Place
London W1U 5LY
Tel: 020–7486 6401
Email:
chancery@lithuanianembassy.co.uk

Malta

Malta High Commission
Malta House
36–38 Piccadilly
London W1J 0LE
Tel: 020 7292 4800
Website: www.magnet.mt

Poland

Embassy of the Republic of Poland
47 Portland Place
London W1B 1JH
Tel: 0870 774 2700
Email:
polishembassy@polishembassy.org.uk
Website: www.polishembassy.org.uk

Polish Consulate General
73 New Cavendish Street
London W1W 6LS
Tel: 0870 7742800
Email: kgrp.londyn@btclick.com

Portugal

The Portuguese Embassy
11 Belgrave Square
London SW1X 8PP
Tel: 020–7235 5331

Consulate General of Portugal
Silver City House
62 Brompton Road
London SW3 1BJ
Tel: 020–7581 8722

Romania

Embassy of Romania
Arundel House
Palace Green, no 4
London W8 4QD
Tel: 020–7937 9666
Email: roemb@copperstream.co.uk
Website: www.roemb.co.uk

British Romanian Chamber of Commerce
Website: www.brcc-ccbr.org

Slovakia

Embassy of the Slovak Republic
25 Kensington Palace Gardens
London W8 4QY
Tel: 020–7313 6470
Email: mail@slovakembassy.co.uk
Website: www.slovakembassy.co.uk

Slovak Chamber of Commerce
Website: www.scci.sk

Slovenia

Embassy of the Republic of Slovenia
10 Little College Street
London SW1P 3SH
Tel: 020–7222 5400
Email: vlo@mzz-dkp.gov.si

Spain

The Spanish Embassy
39 Chesham Place
London SW1X 8SB
Tel: 020–7235 555
Email: embespuk@mail.mae.es

British Chamber of Commerce (Spain)
Tel: 00 34 93 317 3220
Website:
www.britishchamberspain.com

Turkey

Turkish Embassy
43 Belgrave Square
London SW1X 8PA
Tel: 020–7393 0202
Email: turkish.emb@btclick.com

Airlines

Air Portugal (TAP)
Tel: 020–7932 3614
Website: www.tap.pt
American Airlines
Tel: 0845 778 9789
Website: www.aa.com

bmi
Tel: 0870 607 0555
Website: www.flybmi.com

bmibaby
Tel: 0870 264 2229
Website: www.bmibaby.com

British Airways
Tel: 0870 850 9850
Website: www.britishairways.com

easyJet
Tel: 0871 750 0100
Website: www.easyjet.com

Iberia
Tel: 020–8222 8900
Website: www.iberia.com

Monarch
Tel: 01582 400000
Website: www.monarch-airlines.com

Ryanair
Tel: 0871 246 0000
Website: www.ryanair.com

Virgin Atlantic
Tel: 0871 984 0840
Website: www.virgin-atlantic.com

Ferry, rail and coach links

Brittany Ferries
Tel: 08703 665 333
Website: www.brittany-ferries.com

Condor Ferries
Tel: 0845 345 2000
Website: www.condorferries.co.uk

Eurostar
Tel: 08705 186 186
Website: www.eurostar.com

Eurolines
Tel: 08705 808080
Website: www.eurolines

Eurotunnel
Tel: 08000 969 992
Website: www.eurotunnel.com

Hoverspeed
Tel: 0870 240 8070
Website: www.hoverspeed.com

P&O Ferries
Tel: 0870 600 0611
Website: www.posl.com

SeaFrance
Tel: 08705 711 711
Website: www.seafrance.com

National organisations

France

Caisse d'Assurance Maladie des Professions Libérales d'Ile de France
22 rue Vilet
75730 Paris
France
Tel: 00 33 1 45 78 32 00

Chambre des Experts Immobiliers (FNAIM)
129 rue de Faubourg Saint-Honoré
75008 Paris
France
Tel: 00 33 1 53 76 03 52
Email:
chambrenationale@expertfnaim.org
Website: www.experts-fnaim.org

Conseil National de l'Ordre des Architectes (CNOA)
9 rue Borromée
F-75015 Paris
France
Tel: 00 33 1 56 58 67 00
Email: internat@cnoa.com
Website: www.architectes.org

Fédération Nationale des Agents Immobiliers et Mandataires (FNIAM)
Website: www.fnaim.fr

Syndicat Nationals des Professionnels Immobilier (SNPI)
26 avenue Victor Hugo
75116 Paris
France
Tel: 00 33 1 53 64 91 91
Website: www.snpi.com

Spain and Portugal

Agents de la Propiedad Immobiliaria (API)
Consejo General de Colegios Oficiales de Agents de la Propiedad Inmobiliaria de España
Grand Via 66–2
28013 Madrid
Spain
Tel: 00 34 91 547 0741
Email: cgcoapi@consejocoapis.org
Website: www.consejocoapis.org

Associacion Profesional de Gestores Intermediarios en Promociones de Edificaciones (GIPE)
C/Salinas, 6–1⁰
29015 Malaga
Spain
Tel: 00 34 902 11 5295
Email: asociacion@gipe.es
Website:
www.web-cei.com/gipe.htm

Consejo Superior de los Colegios de Arquitectos de España (CSCAE)
12–4⁰ Paseo de la Castillana
28046 Madrid
Spain
Tel: 00 34 91 426 2167
Email:
consejo.internacional@arquinex.es
Website: www.arquinex.es

Fundacion Instituto de Propietarios Extranjeros (FIPE)
Apartado 418
03590 Altea (Alicante)
Spain
Tel: 00 34 96 584 2312
Email: info@fipe.org
Website: www.fipe.org

Ordem Dos Arquitectos
Travessa do Carvalho, 23
P-1249–003 Lisboa
Portugal
Tel: 00 35 1 21 324 11 00
Email: ri@ordemdosarquitectos.pt
Website: www.aap.pt

Italy

**Consiglio Nazionale degli Architetti
Pianificatori, Paesaggisti e Conservatori**
Via di S. Maria dell'Anima 10
00186 Roma
Italy
Tel: 00 39 06 688 9901
Email: esteri.cna@archiworld.it
Website: www.archiworld.it

**Federazione Italiana degli Agenti
Immobiliari Professionali (FIAIP)**
Piazzale Flaminio 9
00196 Roma
Italy
Tel: 00 39 06 321 9798
Email: fiaip@fiaip.it

USA

**American Society of Home Inspectors
(ASHI)**
932 Lee Street (Suite 101)
Des Plaines
Illionois 60016
USA
Tel: 001 800 743 2744
Website: www.ashi.com

**Florida Association of Mortgage Brokers
(FAMB)**
P O Box 6477
Tallahassee
FL 32314–6477
USA
Email: famb@supernet.net
Website: www.famb.org

Florida Association of Realtors (FAR)
Website: www.far.org

Florida Real Estate Commission
Website: www.state.fl.us
**National Association of Realtors
(NAR)**
30700 Russell Ranch Road
Westlake Village
CA 91362
USA
Tel: 001 805 557 2300
Website: www.realtor.com

Index